THE ROAD TO WEMBLEY 1966
from the archives of...

Charles Buchan's
FOOTBALL MONTHLY

Edited and written by: Andrew S. Dolloway

MMP

Max Media Publishing Ltd

Alf Ramsey

TOTTENHAM HOTSPUR AND ENGLAND

Copyright 2016 Max Media Publishing Ltd
First published in Great Britain by: Max Media Publishing Ltd 2016

ISBN 978-0-9954783-0-5

www.maxmediapublishing.com

Max Media Publishing Limited
49-51 Bancroft Lane, Mansfield, Notts. NG18 5LG

Edited and written by **Andrew Dolloway**
All images copyright SoccerAttic Ltd

Charles Buchan's Football Monthly content reproduced with permission from
Andrew Zienkiewicz & Simon Hollingworth at SoccerAttic Ltd. www.soccerattic.com

Associate Design by **Simon Meakin at In House Design**, Mansfield, Notts.
Printed by Zrinski, Croatia

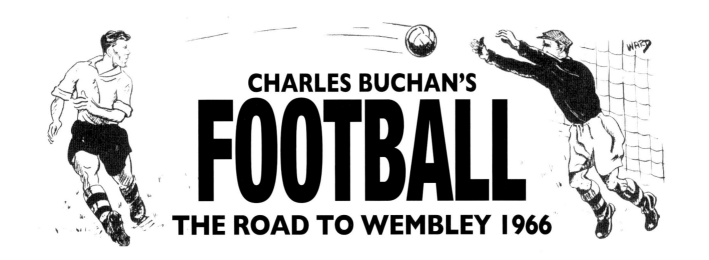

CHARLES BUCHAN'S
FOOTBALL
THE ROAD TO WEMBLEY 1966

WARD

Contents:

CHARLES BUCHAN'S
FOOTBALL
THE ROAD TO WEMBLEY 1966

Meet the
Charles
Buchan's
Football
Monthly Team

PETER COLLINS

PETER MORRIS

JOHN THOMPSON

ROLAND ALLEN

JOHN MACADAM

NORMAN ACKLAND

CHARLES BUCHAN

BBC

MMP
Max Media Publishing Ltd

Introduction

July 30th 1966, is still the most momentous and iconic day in the history of English football. A packed Wembley Stadium witnessed an epic encounter between England and West Germany to determine who could claim the title 'Champions of the World' and readers of the legendary magazine 'Charles Buchan's Football Monthly' had been on that journey with them through the previous three World Cup tournaments.

Let me give you a little background about what made Football Monthly so important and unique. It was back in September 1951 when the first issue hit the newsstands. The magazine was the brainchild of Charles Buchan, John Thompson and Joe Maxwell Sarl and was aimed at the growing number of football fans who were disenchanted with the quality and variety of football coverage that was on offer at that time. There were various periodicals such as 'The Sporting World' and the 'Weekly Sporting Review' that featured football, but they were padded out with other sports and the post war obsession on how to win the Football Pools. Of course every town and city had it's 'Pink Un' or 'Green Un' reporting on the local scene, but football fans were crying out, not only for their own magazine but also for some colour after the greyness of the war years and with paper shortages and working restrictions easing, this was the right time.

Charles Buchan was no mere figurehead, an esteemed and highly respected player for Sunderland, Arsenal and England until he retired in the mid 1920's. He then moved effortlessly into journalism for the News Chronicle, before also becoming a national figure on the BBC Light service, commenting on football matters.

Charles Buchan was also widely travelled, having not only served in the First World War but also having been on numerous tours with the England football team as a reporter. Although not a controversial figure, he held strong views on football, he particularly wanted to increase the status of the national team and was always open to new ideas. Charlie, as he was affectionately known, hated discrimination wherever he encountered it and the magazine often sponsored under privileged youngsters from around the world.

His partners in this venture were John Thompson and Joe Maxwell Sarl. John who was the de facto editor of the magazine, also worked as a reporter for the Daily Mirror and Joe, who was not a big football fan, was presumed to be the business brains behind the scenes. The first offices were a pokey affair on the Strand in London and as John Thompson recalled, "Money was tight, we were hard up for furniture, in fact to begin with we only had one chair and that was usually reserved for guests. There was a crack in the window and the sound of buses trundling up and down the road added to the noise. In winter that office was freezing, it was a usual sight to see us working in our coats and scarves".

The first issue was priced at 1/6d, expensive for the time, so it was not aimed at the lower end of the market, (this price would also ensure that readers cherished the magazine and it instantly became very collectable). The original cover featured Stan Matthews in colour and to provide content, various favours were called in from friends, for the first issue. Raich Carter discussed his new role as a manager and there was even an article by the Marquess of Londonderry on his recent conversion to football and how he had become a director at Arsenal (it was after finding himself seated next to the Arsenal chairman at a dinner he attended at Buckingham Palace). The highbrow tone continued with a short story from J.B. Priestley, this was clearly no ordinary magazine.

After a tentative beginning, Football Monthly quickly found its own voice. There were lots of interesting stories about clubs and players often flavoured by war anecdotes and also many rags to riches tales along the lines of 'pithead to football hero' reflecting that era. The writing and design always aspired to quality and innovation, this was reflected in the introduction of colour images, although these often had a surreal feel with the colour being airbrushed on to black and white pictures to create the desired effect.

Alongside all the usual club stories, from the early days the magazine contained lots of comment and photographs on the international game. England's summer tour to South America in 1952 was extensively covered, Charles Buchan himself had accompanied the team and the other journalists leant on his contacts and experience when abroad. Charlie knew the best restaurants and was often

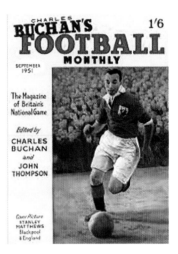

pictured with a local celebrity or dignitary.

As a proud Englishman, Charlie felt the pain more than most, as England's unbeaten home record against continental opposition fell to Hungary in 1953. He saw the writing was on the wall and that the English game had to modernize or risk being left behind. Writing in Football Monthly after the game he said, "Everything about the Hungarians looked modern compared to England, their preparation and tactics showed how far we had slipped, the pupils were now teaching the master". However John Thompson commenting on the 6-3 defeat said, "To mourn the death of English football was morbidly sensational".

The first World Cup that Football Monthly covered was Switzerland in 1954. Hopes that had been so high only two years previously were now in tatters, the England team arrived at the tournament on the back of another 7-1 mauling by Hungary. The magazine reported the tournament with a host of photographs and match reports, culminating in the surprising German victory. The magazine's

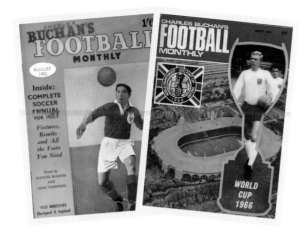

post cup analysis on the reasons for England's failure, found room for both sides of the argument; embrace the new ideas and tactics from the continent on one hand, or the British values of hard work and speed will come good in the end on the other.

The Football Monthly magazine meanwhile, was going from strength to strength, readership figures were increasing with each issue and the quality of print and design was also evolving. The success of the magazine also encouraged the team to produce a special annual, the first one came out for Christmas 1953 and was an immediate success. In fact the publishing of annuals carried on even after the magazine itself had ceased publication in the mid 1970's.

New regular journalists were joining the team as different sections were added to the magazine, these contained a wide range of characters. Leslie Yates, of Hungarian extraction who was eventually to become the magazine's longest serving contributor, had his regular feature, 'Soccer Sideshow', serving up an endless array of interesting football trivia. Whilst seventeen year old Brian Glanville began his contributions in 1952, with an extensive who's who of British players, containing the details of over 1,300 footballers that ran over six issues.

Then there was Norman Ackland who wrote about the amateur game, he was a rogue, thrown out of Trinity College,

Dublin for acting as a bookies runner and later seeing action on the beaches of Dunkirk. Added to this was John Macadam, he of the grand moustache, who kept dubious company around the world, particularly in New York and Chicago whilst following the boxing game. Also there was Clifford Webb, a larger than life viveur, editor of the Sporting Record who knew the journalistic industry inside out.

Wherever possible the magazine was always positive, everything was 'grand' and the reporters made for a fine team. Never condescending, they aspired to write intelligent and interesting articles, whilst always outward looking, you could always rely on the magazine periodically to point out the strange behaviour of those they termed the 'Continentals'. Often they had unpronounceable names and unsavoury habits, resorting to all sorts of shenanigans to beat the England team. Every year there would be photographs of rioting from South America or the referee being chased in Athens, tear gas and armed police. Even if we weren't winning on the pitch, at least we could take solace that this sort of thing could never happen here.

Football Monthly occasionally also had to deal with tragedy when it arose. The air disaster at Munich that not only decimated Manchester United but also ruined England's chances at the World Cup was handled sensitively, there was more to life

than football.

In light of this, England's early exit from the Swedish World Cup of 1958 was not unexpected. It was no disgrace to go out to the eventual champions Brazil, Charles Buchan was fulsome in his praise for this fine team and the precocious talent of a young Pele. A further redesign of the magazine with added features such as 'The Game Abroad', meant that by the end of the 1950's the circulation had reached 107,000, at which point the team finally felt confident enough to move to new offices on Fleet Street. It was here that the Charles Buchan's group increased the number of its publications, there were special one off football titles and also magazines covering a variety of other topics as varied as cycling and gardening.

With the economics of the country improving, there was a noticeable increase in advertising revenue and also a distinct improvement in the calibre of those advertising in the magazine. The strange sight of seeing Stan Matthews and Eddy Bailey promoting cigarettes in the mid 1950's had been replaced by adverts for companies such as Guiness and Umbro. The small adverts also provide a ready supply of unintentional humour from our present day position. "Do you want to grow five inches in only four weeks?", or "dramatically improve your eyesight?", well just send your five bob postal order and the

secret will be yours.

There was bad news in June 1960, after it was announced that Charles Buchan had passed away suddenly while on holiday in France. Tributes poured in and hundreds attended the memorial service at the church of St Bride's, including an array of football's greats and journalists from a variety of newspapers. Charlie was not just respected but loved by many.

Missed as he undoubtedly was, the magazine continued to thrive under the new stewardship of Pat Collins, more colour pages were added and the Boys Club membership topped 100,000 with the programme swop and fixtures wanted sections becoming popular features. Football manager Barry Fry when just a youngster, asked for help with autographs in 1958, TV presenter Jim Rosenthal asked for fixtures for his junior club Wolvercote Wanderers in 1963 and even author Sebastian Faulks had a letter published in 1967, the Charles Buchan's family crossed all ages and social backgrounds.

The number of countries now applying for entry to the 1962 World Cup in Chile reached an all-time high indicating the widening appeal of football and this tournament in particular. Prospects for England again appeared good, because as Football Monthly reported, England had looked in imperious form building up to the tournament in Chile, "We

can bring the Cup back", they proudly proclaimed, but form and confidence seemed to disappear as quickly as it had arrived, coinciding with Jimmy Greaves and Gerry Hitchens moving for big money, to Italy.

In the final months leading up to the tournament, the magazine had more features previewing the competition than ever before, what were the conditions likely to be and how were our rivals faring? There was a special colour send off for the team and a message of good luck from Billy Wright, but there was to be disappointment all round as England once more returned home early from an open looking tournament that was not only short of quality but was also stained by rough play and bad sportsmanship. With the next competition being held here, there was a real concern expressed in many quarters that we could embarrass ourselves. Pat Collins writing in the August 1962 issue said, "Don't the clubs realise the benefits of international football? There must be an occasion to put country before club".

The World Cup in Chile would prove to be manager Walter Winterbottom's last as he handed in his resignation. So the search began for the new man. Football Monthly recognized the changing role of the national team manager and the pressure he would be under. "The new England boss (whoever he may be) has my sympathy", wrote Pat Collins.

After his appointment Alf Ramsey was warmly welcomed. Alf had been a regular in the magazine pages since the very beginning, both as a player and manager. Throughout the years leading up to 1900 the criticism the manager was receiving in the national press was also reflected in the pages of Football Monthly. Although not quite so strident as the daily papers calling for the manager's head, there was severe criticism about the direction the team was taking and at one point there was an open letter to the manager questioning his tactics less than a year before the World Cup finals.

As the 1966 World Cup approached, real concern was raised in the magazine about how prepared for the tournament we were. Where were the new facilities? Contrast clubs such as Manchester United and Sheffield Wednesday with the inertia shown by others. This looked like an opportunity missed. The lack of Government involvement was noted, they had contributed virtually nothing and didn't seem to even understand the popularity of the sport.

Football Monthly produced a separate magazine to preview the tournament and readers were treated to more articles about the competing nations and lots of pictures of the stars who would be coming. With the tournament about to begin, Football Monthly asked a variety of personalities including Bill Shankly, what England's chances were, not good it seemed, but Pat Collins could be relied upon to be upbeat. "We can do it" he declared.

Despite the worries, in the usual British way, everything came good in the end. The tournament was a great success for its organization and enthusiasm, if not for some of the cynical and defensive football on show, but for a short while England forgot about its economic worries and London began to epitomize the

NAT LOFTHOUSE
'The Lion of Vienna'...

'Swinging Sixties'. If only Charlie Buchan had still been around to witness it.

After 1966, the magazine began a steady decline, the publication saw a gradual fall in sales as youngsters turned to other interests such as pop music. The magazine's proprietors failed to adjust to changing fashions, meaning that the layout began to look tired and Charles Buchan's dominant position as the leading football magazine was threatened by shiny brash new upstarts such as Shoot and Goal. The magazine continued through until 1973 when it was no longer economically viable to publish, a victim of the changing times, but for twenty years it led the way in football coverage and held a special place in the hearts of Soccer followers everywhere.

Even now, forty years on from the magazine's demise, no-one with a love of the game can fail to be charmed whenever they see a copy of Charles Buchan's Football Monthly.

In this book we have tried to capture the spirit and ethos of that timeless magical publication and provide a unique insight into England's quest for World Cup Victory, I hope we have succeeded.

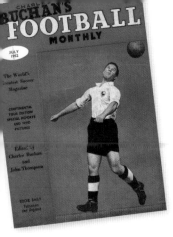

BILLY WRIGHT exchanges gifts with the
Austrian captain Gernhardt in 1951

By the time Football Monthly launched in September 1951, the disastrous Brazilian World Cup campaign including a defeat to the USA was twelve months past and already consigned to the history books as 'just one of those things', and the magazine was full of optimism. An article in the first issue expressing confidence in the future, overlooked the obvious decline in the standard of League football compared with pre-war. There seemed to be a lack of new talent and new ideas, club chairman, with their coffers filled once more, were more averse to change than ever. Only Spurs with their 'push and run' game seemed to offer any alternative to 'commando' style football.

The interests of the national team took second place to club fortunes, football fans have always been very parochial but it is still hard to believe now, that many England home games were often poorly attended and watched in lacklustre silence. Even in Football Monthly for the first half a dozen issues, there was barely a mention of England and virtually none of the world football scene.

As now, after every poor England result the media followed a very predictable pattern. Everything foreign was great and should be implemented totally, whilst a good result provided the exact opposite, often from the same reporters. "Why the moans?" asked Roland Allen, "Why are we still talking about coaching? Good players will always be good."

The victory over France in October was the first in a run of twelve undefeated matches for Walter Winterbottom's team, giving ammunition to those who thought there was little wrong with the British game. This period between World Cup cycles would always seem to coincide with the national team's best form as they always peaked before the tournament and for whatever reason were in decline by the opening ceremony.

November 1951 saw a visit to Wembley by Austria. Acknowledged as the best outfit in Europe, they would provide a stern test. A capacity crowd witnessed a thrilling 2-2 draw, made all the more exciting by a clash of styles and philosophies. England were full of pace, 'helter-skelter' against the more considered possession based football of the Austrians. Those who were interested in tactics saw the visitor's number five Ernst Ocwirk play a roving role behind his forwards but this went over the heads of most spectators.

The English season followed a traditional pattern, no internationals were allowed between the new year and spring so as not to interfere with the league programme. Therefore just as they might have reached some continuity, the national team was put into hibernation for five months until the traditional April international against Scotland, by which time the team on this occasion showed four changes from the side that had performed so creditably in the previous fixture. Even with only eight international games per season, club chairmen thought that this was too many. The situation was even worse for the other home countries, English clubs were forced to release English players but were under no obligation to do the same for Scottish, Welsh or Irish players for any game. This situation was exacerbated by the fact that international games were usually played on Saturdays clashing with League fixtures. The absolute low point for this scenario came when Scotland qualified for the 1954 tournament in Switzerland and even Scottish club Rangers refused to let any of their players travel as they were wanted for a club tour.

However, England's pride and standing in football was certainly raised after the summer tour of 1952. A low key draw away to Italy in Florence was followed seven days later by the return game with Austria in Vienna, which many observers called the greatest game that they had ever seen. After having his squad together for ten days, Winterbottom's team showed what they were capable of.

Tactically he got it spot on, deciding to sit back, give up possession and hit on the counter attack. Nat Lofthouse was the star, earning the soubriquet 'The Lion of Vienna', as England grabbed a 3-2 victory, made all the sweeter, as Football Monthly reported, by the presence of hundreds of squaddies who rushed on to the pitch at the final whistle to carry the players off shoulder high. The tour was rounded off in grand style with a 3-0 win over Switzerland.

After the highs of 1952, the following year would prove to be a watershed in the history of the English national game as the illusion of superiority would most emphatically be washed away by a Magyar tide.

In the meantime another summer tour had been planned, this time a lot more ambitious, as a four game trip to South America was scheduled. However by February Charles Buchan was calling for the tour to be called off after riots and bad behaviour by players and fans in Buenos Aires meant that that he feared for the player's safety. The tour only went ahead after the Argentinian President Juan Peron intervened to personally guarantee that there would be no incidents.

After what was supposed to be a warm up match against an Argentina XI (in fact a full strength Argentina team that beat an under prepared England 3-1). The 'full' international played several days later, had to be abandoned after only twenty five minutes due to a waterlogged pitch. There was no time to re-schedule the game, so the England team travelled onto Chile, where a 2-1 victory was gained. Seven days later in Montevideo, England fell to defeat by Uruguay, a team that was described by Charles Buchan as the best he had ever seen. This was a close game despite many of the England team suffering from 'dickie' tummy. The experience that the players gained from this tour cannot be overstated along with the extra time that Walter Winterbottom had to work with the players.

The tour ended on a high note as England had the satisfaction of thrashing the USA under floodlights in New York gaining some revenge for the defeat suffered three years previously in the World Cup.

The England team now seemed to be making good progress and at this point there was no reason to believe that a hurricane was about to hit English football. A regulation 4-1 victory over Wales came before the Football Association celebratory 90th anniversary game against the Rest of the World, a misnomer perhaps as the Rest of the World team were a scratch outfit made up entirely of players from Europe. This was not to detract from a hugely enjoyable occasion as both teams played out an entertaining 4-4 draw. A last minute penalty from Alf Ramsey saved England's unbeaten home record against foreign opposition, although this record was to last for only one more month.

A young Brian Glanville in his preview piece for Football Monthly gave the fans a taste of what they might expect for the upcoming game against Hungary in December. "Whatever the result, you will be deeply impressed by the Hungarians, for along with their ball control, artistic forward movements and clever positional play, they have now added more power in their finishing". They were to live up to all his predictions.

The Hungarians, already Olympic Champions were different. From the minute they came out to warm up they dazzled the watching spectators, amongst them future managers such as Malcolm Allison and Ron Greenwood, who from this day on saw that there was an alternative way to play. The almost casual way that Puskas and the other players flicked the ball between themselves in a pre-match display, showed a control and arrogance that was to be even more in evidence as soon as the game started. Immediately, Hungary were right at England with quick short passes followed by incisive long balls. The tactics and skills appeared to be on a different level and the score could have been far higher. The moment that perhaps lived on longest in the memories of those present was when Puskas put the England skipper Billy Wright on his back-side before slamming home.

It would not be an exaggeration to say that English football was shell shocked, some of the praise may have been a little over the top, but one thing was for certain, this was a brand of football that had never been seen in this country before. Only Stan

Cullis, Manager of Wolves was a dissenting voice. In an article about that game, he compared the Hungarian tactics to those he employed at his club and this was borne out subsequently with their results against Honved and Dynamo.

In what turned out to be his last international game as a player, Alf Ramsey had now found himself centre stage for the two most humiliating occasions in English football and he himself said that when he became England manager these memories had a direct effect on the way he approached the job.

To rational people, any thoughts that England could still win the World Cup in Switzerland were out of the question, but unbelievably by the time the re-match with Hungary took place in 1954, only weeks before the opening ceremony of the tournament, some journalists were predicting England could actually beat them. Tom Finney who had missed the Wembley game, was under no illusions, as were his team mates and the humiliating 7-1 defeat that followed was the worst sort of preparation possible for the competition. As John

Thompson pointed out in Football Monthly, "It's only sport, to mourn the death of English football is morbidly sensational".

So, it was a chastened England team that turned up in Basle for their first World Cup game against Belgium, a match they were expected to win, but with the Hungary beating undoubtedly still weighing heavily on their minds, they contrived to throw away a two goal lead and draw 4-4. A subsequent victory over Switzerland meant that they progressed through to the next round, but by dropping a point in their first game, they went into Pool Two and now had a far more difficult encounter against cup holders Uruguay than they should have had.

In typical English fashion, they saved their best performance for last, although it saw them eliminated, they lost 4-2, but at least they went out with dignity unlike the Uruguayans who alienated the crowd with their play acting and gamesmanship.

Once more the England team had come up short when it mattered, but there was hope that future changes in the structure to the national game might mean that they put up a better show next time.

Rugilo tips over the bar for Argentina in May 1951

WHY THE MOANS? OUR RECORD STANDS ALONE

By
Roland Allen

When people tell me, that football is nothing like as good as it used to be, I am tempted to use the ancient retort that it never has been. When we look back to Grandad's days we are liable to get it a bit out of perspective.

There is not much profit in looking backwards, anyhow. It is more intriguing to speculate about where we are going, than get worked up about where we have been. My view is that we have no more cause to worry about the future of the game in England, than we have to be ashamed of the past.

What real basis is there for the assertion that English football is being, or ever has been, humiliated by the foreigners, or that the masters should now become the pupils? A foreigner at the F.A. Cup Final assured me that the Argentinians were so fast that if they followed the England team through a revolving door they would come out first. I tried to stop him. I had heard that one.

He went on to insist that, with their five forwards in a line, moving at the speed of sound, these South Americans would just paralyze us at the Wembley Stadium.

Well, did they? Then came the Portuguese, who, we were warned after Wales had beaten them at Cardiff, were as likely as not to sweep us out of Goodison Park and through Mersey tunnel.

Well, that did not happen either. Am I to accept the shaking-up they admittedly gave us, both of them, as part of the process of humiliation? Not on your life.

This is football's Spring, when our thoughts, which never have been far from this fantastic and fascinating game, lead to the conclusion that there is not a lot wrong with the game as the English play it, and to a feeling of relief that the Armenians and Greeks are not also in the football fantasia.

If they were, there would be two more countries, which, in the season now upon us, we would be urged to imitate to prevent our Soccer from slipping over the precipice, to the edge of which, by all accounts, it clings precariously by the ends of the finger nails.

I have seen all the foreign sides, as they have followed each other for more than twenty years with the common ambition, to rub our noses in our own mud. One after another they failed to do so.

And let there be no doubt about this. The standard of English football at the moment is well below its peak. Yet we can show these records against foreign countries since the war, and during what we called a slump period: Matches at home: Played 10, Won 8, Drawn 2, Lost 0; Goals for: 36; Goals against 11. Matches away, including the World Cup: Played 16, Won 9, Drawn 1, Lost 5; Goals for: 42; Goals against: 17.

If I had briefed as Counsel for Defense of English Football I should be a bit cunning and let my case rest there.

No other country can challenge the home record. The mathematics are extremely complicated, but has any other country in the world achieved a higher proportion of victories abroad, in out of season matches, as the English?

We cannot and do not wish to take evasive action about the unfortunate happening in and around Rio last summer. We can take steps to see that it never happens again. It need not.

Remember the Americans beat us. I was talking about this to our old friend George Kay whose Liverpool team has toured in the United States, "The Americans have not bent to football yet," he said. "When they do, look out." Perhaps they now have. We must watch them. Some time later, Liverpool went out of the F.A. Cup competition, at Norwich. Once upon a time Arsenal were beaten at Walsall. That often happens when everything is staked on a single match. It does not prove, not at least to me, that Third Division football is better than that played in the First.

Nor do I reckon England would be asking for anything except trouble by imitating the methods of approach, of training and preparation, or, above all, the strategy and tactics of the Americans, or any of the others – even the few who had beaten us. That does not mean we can afford to be conceited or complacent about it.

Britain taught the rest of the world, then forgot some of the lessons. We still have something the foreigner have not, and that included some rather glaring faults and muddled ideas.

But our football retains an adaptability and a capacity for improvisation which so far have pulled us out of trouble, when teams from abroad have got us into it.

There is some significance in the fact that we have a fright in some of our home games, and have won them only after long periods of suspended anxiety. It has taken us a long time, in these games, to get back to the basic and fundamental principles of the game.

There has been a certain amount of tinkering and messing about with them. Teams like Spurs, Manchester United, Newcastle United, Preston North End and a few others achieved success last season largely through going back to them.

That is what this so-called new football comes down to. That is the lead for England.

It could be that our international teams have had some of their mediocrity thrust upon them through a confusion of ideas. Too many cooks. Too many selectors. Too many changes.

Technical committees are a grand idea, but dangerous. They can do no more than pool their ideas, so that the best can be taken from them.

There should be more players, past and present, on these committees. They are the people who do the job. Among the very important people in football, and those who think they are, the professors matter most.

They cannot be built into a successful team if they are regarded as mechanics, carrying through a job to a set formula, from a pile of plans.

They are, or should be, creative artists, to be blended not drilled. They are people with ideas and ideals. With a few exceptions, who should never be considered for international sides anyhow, they have a decent and deeply-rooted sense of duty to their clubs and their countries.

They will give all they have to their game I say their game because very few of them, and especially those who climb to the stars, are in football for what they can get out of it. If they were they would not work for the wages of an American baseball player's valet. Of all the artists in the sports circus they are the most meagerly rewarded.

They travel third-class. One of them had to stand in a train corridor on a four hour journey from Glasgow to his home. I saw two of them provided with sleepers on a night train to London through the kindness of a passenger who admired their football.

Late one night I met two international players at Paddington. They had stood all the way from Cardiff. They had been unable to get a place at any of the sittings in the dining car. It was crowded out with officials, managers, scouts and commentators.

This is no way to give players confidence in themselves, to make them think they are somebody, that they matter, that they are not merely people

who must be there to provide an excuse for the good time had by all on these occasions.

But if I seem to have been concentrating on what is wrong with English football, let it be said that I believe there is much more that is right with it. That is the objective of criticism. We have the right to discuss these things, and to argue about them among ourselves. We all want to keep our football where it started and where, I reckon, it stands still, at the top of the world. We shall do that if we face up to the fact that the rest of the world is

catching up on us, and concentrate on preventing them from passing us.

We can do that if we stick to our own ideas, do things our way, and not kid ourselves that imitation of the ways of the people we taught would be any more than rather insincere flattery of them. Our football, in this new season, and those which follow will be what we make of it, we have everything it takes. Yet the fact remains, and there is no point in overlooking it, that one of the troubles in this strange game is that the football people still seem afraid to give the players their freedom because they do not trust each other.

That is why the archaic system under which footballers are engaged, shackled,

bought and sold still persists as the biggest single blot on the industry. "If we allowed them to play where they liked we should lose all our best players" said a distinguished official recently. That, surely, is an extraordinary admission to make. And, to be logical, it could not happen to all the clubs, all the time, anyhow. The best players would go to the best clubs as they do now. The arguments for and against this system have been written round in circles and out to places of decimals. We will not go into all that again. I think the system should be swept away. It subsidized disloyalty. It encourages under-the-table and other illegal payments. Indeed it is the only thing which makes them possible. Most of all, as Mr. Tom Whittaker of the Arsenal said, when we were talking about the debut of one of his numerous new boys last season: "I could have brought an established player for a fantastic sum. Now I have got one for nothing, and there is a new player in first-class football." The transfer system does not make players. It simply moves them from one place to another, and often cramps their style as they are expected to live up to the absurd amounts paid for them. It is not much fun for a player to have a huge price tag round his neck. Ask any of them who have cost fortunes. So let us be fair to the footballers. Because, as has been said, they are the important people.

ENGLAND'S soccer team gave a convincing answer to the query: "Are these summer tours really necessary?" by drawing with Italy in Florence and defeating Austria in Vienna and Switzerland in Zurich—all within the short space of eleven days.

They established England's right to be No. 1 in the Continental soccer world. Their wonderful performance did more good to our prestige than many important conferences could do.

Field-Marshal Viscount Montgomery saw the match with Switzerland in Zurich. After it he said: "These games do much for peace. I wish there were many more of them."

Before the clash with the Austrians in Vienna, I went to the barracks and spoke to the men of the Dorsetshire Regiment. They hoped, but hardly dared expect, a victory over the Austrians, who had been rammed down their throats as the best team in Europe.

The enthusiasm of these soldiers

Tour Summary

May 18, 1952. *At Florence (attendance* 93,000).
  Italy 1 (Amadei), England 1 (Broadis).
May 25, 1952. *At Vienna (attendance* 65,000).
  Austria 2 (Huber, pen., Dienst), England 3 (Lofthouse 2, Sewell).
May 28, 1952. *At Zurich (attendance* 33,000).
  Switzerland 0, England 3 (Lofthouse 2, Sewell).
Goal Average of Tour : England 7 (Lofthouse 4, Sewell 2, Broadis 1).
  Against, 3.

---

after the victory was one of the highlights of the tour. They rushed on the field and carried the England players shoulder-high, a stirring sight on a Continental ground.

Englishmen resident in Vienna and Zurich also told me of the great good that had been done by our successes. To folk at home, they are just games.

To those abroad, they are a means of upholding the British reputation.

First and foremost I want to pay tribute to the grand qualities of the England team. They set out with a job to do and they did not slacken until it had been done—magnificently.

They played as a team, displaying such spirit, team-work and fiery tackling as had never previously been seen in matches abroad. The Continentals called them the "fighting machine."

It was like watching a League team challenging for the First Division championship.

They fought, too, like real sportsmen. They proved the wisdom of the F.A. policy of insisting that their men should uphold the British reputation for fair play.

For future tours like this one, players must always be brought together a few days before they set out for preparatory training. It was team-work that counted.

And only the best England players must be sent abroad. Country must come before club, and I am strongly of the opinion that touring teams should come under the ruling for home internationals. That is, players chosen must play unless injured.

There were many thrills that made one glad to be with this great England side. I left them with these main impressions:

1. Our methods in Britain are sounder and more reliable than those on the Continent. The Austrians and the Swiss tried strange formations

Jackie Sewell receives treatment from trainer Jimmy Trotter during the match in Vienna. Ivor Broadis, with his hands on Sewell's shoulders, and Stan Pearson, in white jersey, look on.

But in each case their defences were nothing like as solid as the English.

2. The ball distribution and quick positioning of the Austrian and Swiss forwards—delightful to watch—were not as enterprising as our own. They sent the ball accurately from man to man and rarely wasted a pass.

Our forwards could follow this example to a certain extent without cutting out the rapid thrust for goal.

3. Dienst, Austrian centre-forward, and Ballaman, Swiss outside-right, often showed how defences can be split wide-open by quick, first-time movements. England's forwards must learn to be as accurate with their passes and as quick thinking as these two are. English players wasted many opportunities by faulty passes made at the vital moment in front of goal.

4. England has at last discovered a half-back line worthy to rank with the giants of the past. Billy Wright, Jack Froggatt and Jimmy Dickinson were fiery but fair in their tackling and rarely allowed themselves to be drawn out of place by the intricate passing of some of the opposition. I have not seen such a good middle line against Continental teams since Crayston, Barker and Copping.

5. Gil Merrick, Birmingham goalkeeper, established himself as England's No. 1 goalkeeper. He surpassed even the acrobatic foreigners in handling the ball and in clearing his goal-mouth.

He was so superb that unlucky Bert Williams (Wolves), who was on the tour, never had the chance of a game. Merrick inspired the defence with complete confidence.

6. The coolness, clever positioning and neat distribution of right-back Alf Ramsey started many attacks and was a considerable help to all departments. Swiss people called him "The General."

7. Nat Lofthouse, Bolton centre-forward, drew the admiration of all the onlookers. They came to see "The Tank," as they had nicknamed him after reading of his dashing play.

They went away impressed by his skill and courage and the clever way he took his opportunities. Lofthouse scored four of England's seven goals in three games. He has never played better.

8. All the Continental teams feared Tom Finney as much as they ever feared Stanley Matthews. Yet, despite the close attention paid to him, Finney often left them bewildered by his footwork and quick acceleration in pace.

The opposition were always worried when he had the ball, never knowing what to expect. He is the type of player who must always be picked for this type of tour. We must breed or cultivate more like Tom Finney.

9. The new boys, Billy Elliott, of Burnley, and Ron Allen, of West Bromwich Albion, did very well in their first internationals. But they lacked the experience to overcome the body-checking tactics so favoured by Continentals.

I think it would be much better if budding young internationals like these two were blooded first in England "B" internationals. A few games against "B" teams from the Continent would show them what to expect.

10. In games abroad an injured player is not allowed to be treated by the trainers on the field. He must get outside the touchlines at once. We did not follow this practice and the crowd showed their displeasure by whistling and shouting.

I think the Continental custom should be introduced in our League games. Unless a player is badly injured, he should be made to go off so that the game can be continued at once.

Yes, these Continental tours are worth while. They show our style of play, and above all, our sportsmanship to the world.

We are still held in great esteem as footballers abroad and we must go on spreading the gospel. Even the Austrians, who are grand players, learned a great deal from us.

Walter Nausch, a former international left-half, now manager of the team, said: "We are very impressed by your retreating defensive style. It is so interesting that we shall probably try something like it."

To wind up : my congratulations to those English gentlemen who kept the unbeaten record in internationals that has lasted for more than a year. They were all heroes.

ENGLAND'S DRAW WITH ITALY

England's goal, scored by Ivor Broadis — standing over the fallen Italian goalkeeper.

Tom Finney, cutting in with an Italian in hot pursuit.

The Italian goalkeeper, Moro, leaps high to snatch the ball from Lofthouse.

VICTORY OVER AUSTRIA

Red-shirted Jackie Sewell, brilliant inside-right from Sheffield Wednesday, scored the second goal in England's 3-2 win Against Austria. In the picture above he is spurting between Musil, the Austrian goalkeeper, and right-back Roeckl.

In the picture below Bill Eckersley, dour little left-back from Blackburn, crouches alertly as goalkeeper Gilbert Merrick dives, but the ball has already gone wide.

Eddie Baily, another England player who looks unfamiliar in a red shirt instead of the white usually worn, whisks the ball away from the test of Schjeger, the Austrian right-half.

Huber, Austria's inside-left, places the ball perfectly to score with a penalty kick. Merrick moves to the right in a vain attempt to save.

THE DEFEAT OF SWITZERLAND

Three to one as English players guard their goal. They are (left to right) : Jack Froggatt, Jim Dickinson, the brilliant Portsmouth pair, and Alf Ramsey of Tottenham. The Swiss player (in red shirt) is inside-left Pasteur.

ENGLAND wound up a successful tour with a comfortable 3—0 victory over Switzerland at Zurich, but the game was rather an anti-climax after the stirring events in Vienna.

The Swiss, clever in control of the ball, played in slow-motion time. The result was that the England players were able to play at half-pace without ever getting really into their stride.

The Swiss methods were amazing. They had one full-back, four half-backs stretched right across the field, a roaming centre-forward often found in his own penalty area and four forwards.

I rated the Swiss four or five goals behind the Austrians. I believe if England had gone all out they could have won more easily.

But for once wing-halves Billy Wright and Jim Dickinson refrained from tackling quickly or with zest. Their passes, too, were nothing like as accurate as in previous games.

Stars of an England team which did its job efficiently and assuredly were the two Spurs, Alf Ramsey and Eddie Baily. Ramsey gave a copy-book display of clever positioning and precise kicking, while Baily engineered practically every attacking movement.

Dashing Nat Lofthouse was always too good for the Swiss defence. His goals were well-taken, and his leadership excellent. Ron Allen gave a promising display in his first international.

Jack Froggatt and Gil Merrick further emphasised their claims as England's No. 1 centre-half and goalkeeper.

Jackie Sewell, a great worker, scored first for England with a clever lob over a ruck of players in the Swiss goal. Lofthouse scored the second soon after half-time, and the third with the last kick.

Switzerland : Preiss ; Kernen, Bocquet ; Neukom, Eggimann, Schmidhauser ; Ballaman, Hugi, Bader, Pasteur, Fatton.

England : Merrick (Birmingham) ; Ramsey (Spurs), Eckersley (Blackburn) ; Wright (Wolves), Froggatt (Portsmouth), Dickinson (Portsmouth) ; Allen (West Bromwich), Sewell (Sheffield Wednesday), Lofthouse (Bolton), Baily (Spurs), Finney (Preston).

CHARLES BUCHAN.

Billy Wright, captain of England in all three matches of the Continental tour, shakes hands before the match in Zurich with the captain of Switzerland, centre-half Olivier Eggimann.

BACKS MUST BE SAFE AND TWO-FOOTED

By ALF RAMSEY
Spurs and England

MISTAKES made by full-backs can turn victory into defeat. Except for the goalkeeper, they are the last line of defence and should mould their style accordingly. Safety-first must be the slogan.

The whole secret is correct positional play. A back, for instance, must know exactly what his goalkeeper, his partner, the half-back in front of him, and, in fact, all the side, are doing.

Let me deal with each one separately. First, the goalkeeper. When he advances to meet a cross from the right-wing, it is the right-back's job to cover him by taking up position on the goal-line.

If the goalkeeper shouts for the ball, let him have it. But move into a position where you can deal with any other threat to the goal.

Then you must have an understanding with your partner. When he goes upfield, I, as a right-back, make a point of covering both him and the centre-half. I must not be caught square, or one well-timed through pass will find the goal uncovered.

And I always get into position to receive a ball from him. It may not come, but at least I know I am in position to help.

Now to the man in front of me. With the Spurs, it's Bill Nicholson, of course. Well, he takes the inside-forward so that I can concentrate on the wing-forward.

My main object is to keep in such close contact with Nicholson that I can cut off any pass intended for the wing-forward. It means a close study of your colleague's style.

There are times when the wing-forward gets the ball before I can get near enough to intercept it. Then it is my job to see that the winger does as little damage as possible.

So I keep him out on the touch-line whenever possible. Not only is there no danger to the goal there, but it gives time for my defensive colleagues to take up position.

One thing a full-back must not do in these circumstances is to rush in for a quick tackle. He will be easily beaten if the opponent has the ball under control.

Always, if possible, try to form a second line of defence with the centre-half. Cover him whenever possible.

Above all, if beaten, get back to goal as quickly as possible. Quick recovery is the hall-mark of a full-back.

You must be able to use both feet equally well. In fact, a right-back should be stronger with the left foot.

When clearing, the ball must be placed to a colleague. Low, whenever possible, so that defence can be turned into attack with one well-placed kick.

You cannot be too expert at kicking, heading, trapping the ball and the other finer points.

Practise until you are well-nigh perfect. And practise at close quarters, just as if an opponent were rushing down on you.

ALF RAMSEY.

Programme Exchange Corner will appear again in "Football Monthly" next month—on sale June 18. Make sure of your copy by placing an order with your newsagent NOW.

JACKIE SEWELL
Sheffield Wednesday
and England

BILLY ELLIOTT
Sunderland and England

IVOR BROADIS
Newcastle United
and England

GILBERT MERRICK
Birmingham City

SPOTLIGHT ON

ENGLAND!

Redfern Froggatt shoots. But Shortt has blocked the ball and Daniel is ready in case it spins away.

A leap by England goalkeeper Merrick against Wales

Froggatt's flying header makes it 3-1 for England. Daniel, extreme right, watches helplessly.

England's conquering heroes. Players are: back row (left to right) : Lofthouse, Ramsey, Merrick, Smith, Dickinson, Froggatt (J.) : Front row : Finney, Froggatt (R.), Wright, Bentley, Elliott.

FOOTBALL ASSOCIATION INTERNATIONAL

ENGLAND v WALES

EMPIRE STADIUM

WEMBLEY

OFFICIAL PROGRAMME · ONE SHILLING

We must have a "full-time" National team

DURING the next two years England's international eleven will meet the best countries in the world. Next summer there is the South American tour and, in 1954, the World Cup competition in Switzerland.

There is no doubt that the opposition will be trained specially for the events. The England players, comprising more or less a scratch eleven, will be up against National teams that have played together in many hectic struggles.

What preparations are the F.A. going to make for these tournaments? Are they going to take them as normal events and follow the procedure they adopt for home internationals?

If they do, then they are asking for trouble. The Continental games last May proved that the England team had nothing to spare against opposition which was inferior to what it is certain to meet in South America and Switzerland.

The experience of the Amateur team in the Olympic Games emphasised the point. A few weeks' training together is not enough when a team has to face the world's best.

Nor can our professionals be expected to produce their best form at the end of a strenuous League and Cup season. It is unfair to ask them to keep in training, and in peak condition, all the year round, without a break.

IN MY OPINION, THE ONLY WAY TO TACKLE THE SITUATION IS TO HAVE A NATIONAL TEAM, RUN ON THE LINES OF A LEAGUE CLUB, WITH ITS OWN MANAGEMENT, TRAINER, PLAYERS, AND, OF COURSE, A GROUND.

The management would present no problem. With F.A. members acting as directors, any manager like Matt Busby, Arthur Rowe, Tom Whittaker and Frank Buckley would be proud to take charge of the outfit.

The F.A. have the resources to pay such a man a salary of £5,000 a year.

Players are there, too. The England team which beat Austria would provide the nucleus. Gil Merrick, Alf Ramsey,

Billy Wright, Jack Froggatt, Jim Dickinson, Tom Finney, Nat Lofthouse or Jackie Milburn and Eddie Baily would be a strong foundation for any national side.

They could be augmented by blooded internationals like Bert Williams, Tom Garrett, Bill Eckersley, Bill Nicholson, Jackie Sewell, Les Medley and Ron Allen and promising young players like Harry Clarke, Bill Holden (Burnley), Peter Broadbent (Wolves) and Arthur Milton (Arsenal) to bring the complement up to the 20 or 22 players who would be required for the job.

The F.A. would have to compensate the clubs for releasing these star players for the National side. That should not inconvenience such a rich body.

The clubs would not like it, I know, but they should help in the National interests.

There would be no trouble about a ground. Wembley is ideal for such a team. I have no doubt that arrangements could easily be made to house the team there.

There would not be any difficulty either in fixing up a comprehensive list of matches for the team. Besides the usual series of internationals, games could be arranged with Continental countries and with the pick of the League teams.

These games could be played in midweek during the early and late parts of the season and under floodlight during the winter evenings.

A team of this sort would, I am sure, draw tremendous gates wherever it played. There would be no financial problems as far as it was concerned.

The management, too, should be allowed to sign on any young players who promised to develop into international stars. They should have the pick of the market for replacements and future building.

This team would then meet the opposition on fairer terms than it does now. I have no hesitation in saying it would put England on top of the world.

Is it too much to hope that the F.A. will plan along these lines for the 1954 World Cup? But some planning is essential if we wish to uphold our prestige abroad.

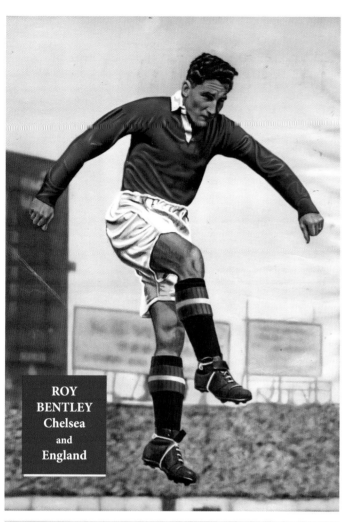

ROY
BENTLEY
Chelsea
and
England

WILF MANNION
Middlesbrough and England

BILLY WRIGHT
Wolverhampton Wanderers
and England

JACK MILBURN
Newcastle United
and England

THE FIVE ELMS "GENERAL"

A Profile of the Subject of our Cover Picture

ALF RAMSEY

—By—
JOHN THOMPSON

THE team was called Five Elms because that was the name of the street in which most of the boys lived. It was just one of the countless tiny clubs no one ever hears about, the clubs which are more important than anything in football because they are the heart of the game and it would die without them.

Among the eager youths of Five Elms was the dark-haired Dagenham grocer's assistant named Alf Ramsey, who was to become one of the greatest full-backs ever to wear the shirt of Tottenham Hotspur and England . . .

"In those days I never dreamt of ending up in League soccer, let alone being capped," Ramsey has said. But I am told that even then there were hints of the quality which has made him the perfect craftsman—his infinite capacity for self-instruction.

Watch Ramsey in any match and you will see a footballer who, having reached the top of his trade, still regards himself as a pupil of it.

It is Ramsey's diligence, his profiting from trial and error, which have made his style immaculate in appearance and profitable in effect.

During the war, as a sergeant in the Duke of Cornwall's Light Infantry, he was playing so well that he was recommended to Southampton by his commanding officer. Ramsey was then a centre-half, the position occupied at The Dell by Bill Dodgin.

Mr. Dodgin recalls: "It seems odd now to think that I used to move to full back to make way for Alf at centre-half!"

Later Mr. Dodgin, now Fulham's manager, became manager of Southampton. For a time, Ramsey was a subject for experiment. He was even tried as a centre-forward. He proved that he could score goals!

It was early in 1947 that his play began to earn more than local notice. As so often happens in football, the opportunity was caused by another player's misfortune.

Bill Ellerington had been taken ill after an F.A. Cup-tie at Newcastle, and it was during Ellerington's long absence from the team that Ramsey fully revealed his tremendous promise.

About that time, I remember Mr. Dodgin remarking that Ramsey, apart from his skill on the field, was also one of the most intelligent soccer "talkers" he had ever come across.

"Any man who talks football and thinks football every moment of his day, as he does, can't fail to make good," he added.

That was, of course, an early example of the single-mindedness which has been Ramsey's recipe for success.

His transfer to Tottenham Hotspur —in exchange, Southampton received Ernie Jones and a cheque—was finally negotiated by cable because, at the time of the transfer, the Southampton manager was on holiday in Brazil.

At White Hart Lane, Ramsey soon settled comfortably into the Tottenham set-up, still intently studying the game, still insistent that football must be played with careful precision.

His personal view is obvious to all who watch him. To Ramsey the field of play is what a map is to a general. And the map shows the whole picture—not the flanks alone.

For Ramsey the picture is equally broad. He sees the game not only as it affects his own local duties, but as a complete design in which defence and attack and right and left are fluid and must flow together.

The impression that he always has time to spare testifies to his coolness and his imaginative positional play.

His passing is calculated and firm and his refusal to waste the ball, however perplexing the pressure on him, was one clear example for the team-mates with whom he took part in Tottenham's championship triumph.

He owes much to the guidance he has received from manager Arthur Rowe and is grateful for it.

Ramsey, above all, is a conscientious and modest footballer, filled with the conviction—shared by all successful men—that there is always more to learn. . . .

Five Elms and all the other little unknown clubs in which stars are born can be very proud of such a graduate.

Alf Ramsey, Tottenham Hotspur and England full-back, goes up for a high ball during training. Although at the top of the tree, Ramsey still thinks he has a lot to learn—and trains and thinks, hard.

" He's from our nursery . . . ! "

ALF RAMSEY
Tottenham Hotspur and England

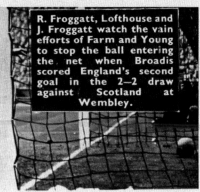

R. Froggatt, Lofthouse and J. Froggatt watch the vain efforts of Farm and Young to stop the ball entering the net when Broadis scored England's second goal in the 2—2 draw against Scotland at Wembley.

IN MY OPINION
This England side lacked a plan

By CHARLES BUCHAN

THE value of team-work was never better illustrated than in the international between England and Scotland at Wembley Stadium.

England came very near to losing the international championship because, though they played extremely well as individuals, they were not a well-balanced and co-operative side like the Scots.

Scotland played to a plan. Full-back Sammy Cox, until he was injured twenty minutes before the end, almost put Tom Finney out of the game by his close marking, and even after Cox's departure on a stretcher, left-half Doug Cowie carried on the good work.

And the wingers, Billy Liddell and Tommy Wright, played their parts by coming into the game and doing their share of harassing the opposition. While full-backs George Young and Cox covered big Frank Brennan, the centre-half, as if they had been club-mates for years.

On the other hand, there was no connecting link between the England defenders. Malcolm Barrass, centre-half, was a great stopper, but with full-backs Alf Ramsey and Lionel Smith formed a thin straight line that was too easily broken by the mobile Scottish forwards, splendidly led by Laurie Reilly, who scored their two goals.

Our wing-forwards, too, did not enter the picture like those of the Scots. Finney and Jack Froggatt were content to stay out on the wings, waiting for the ball to come their way.

But I must say, Finney showed what an artist he is. Though given little room by Cox, he made three openings, two of which were turned into goals by Ivor Broadis, his partner, and the third missed by Finney himself when he had only goalkeeper George Farm to beat.

It seemed to me that England were playing to a design, not of their own making, but set out for them. How else can one explain the occasions when the ball was sent hurtling across the Scottish goal with not an England player within reach?

And the quick, along-the-ground passing movements that broke down because the players had not time to get into position to receive the ball. They were moves out of the text-book that ought never to have been attempted.

A team of internationals should draw up their own tactical scheme around the table on the eve of the match, each player expressing his own ideas with a guiding brain, like team-manager Walter Winterbottom, blending them into a working pattern.

That is how Arsenal became the great combination they were during the 1930s. The players discussed the moves and pooled their brains to discover the best way of carrying them out.

With eleven great players like those of England talking things over, there should be forthcoming a decisive plan of campaign that would be effective

{Continued on page 25}

With Merrick out of goal it is left to Barrass to head clear from the goalmouth, watched by Dickinson and Ramsey.

Barrass, supported by Lionel Smith, again clears the England lines from the eager Scottish forwards.

OPINION
(Continued from page 24)

against any country in the world.

Still, England started out as joint international champions for the South American tour. A 2—2 draw with Scotland was not exactly a " wizard " performance but one in keeping with previous performances at Wembley where England has not beaten Scotland since 1934.

One of the outstanding England successes was Broadis, whose quick bursts through the Scottish lines always carried danger. He deserved a hat-trick to round off his fine display.

One could sympathise with Jack Froggatt on his return to the outside-left berth after two years as a centre-half and up against the massive right-back Young, the best in Great Britain. Jack did his best in the circumstances, but I thought it unfair to him to pitch-fork him into this position at such short notice. Teams :

England.—Merrick (Birmingham) ; Ramsey (Spurs), Smith (Arsenal) ; Wright (Wolves), Barrass (Bolton), Dickinson (Portsmouth) ; Finney (Preston), Broadis (Manchester City), Lofthouse (Bolton), Froggatt (R.) (Sheffield W.), Froggatt (J.) (Portsmouth).

Scotland.—Farm (Blackpool) ; Young (Rangers), Cox (Rangers) ; Docherty (Preston), Brennan (New-castle), Cowie (Dundee) ; Wright (T.) (Sunderland), Johnstone (Hibernian), Reilly (Hibernian), Steel (Dundee), Liddell (Liverpool).

Referee.—T. J. Mitchell (Ireland).

Goal-scorers.—England : Broadis 2. Scotland : Reilly 2.

Attendance.— 100,000. Receipts £49,700 (a British record).

Merrick goes down to save, with Wright and Barrass in the background. The Scottish outside-left, Liddell, follows up from the wing.

The water-logged state of the pitch in the abandoned game against Argentine is shown here as England centre-half, Johnston, sinks in the mud as he goes to tackle the Argentinian forward Cecconato.

England would have won this game

Argentine 0, England 0.
(Abandoned after 22 minutes)

THERE was no chance of this match being completed. Heavy rain made the ground of the River Plate Stadium like a miniature lake, and though referee Arthur Ellis gallantly carried on for twenty-two minutes, his task was hopeless.

The teams tried their best but could not propel the ball through the water more than three or four yards. Often three players were trying to move the ball at the same time with the result there were one or two incidents outside the rule book.

When a player fell, he slid yards through the water and came up covered in mud.

From what I saw, England were much the better side in the conditions. Lofthouse and Taylor were much faster than the Argentine defenders, while the tackling of Wright, Dickinson and Eckersley was so strong that the opposing forwards were fast becoming rattled.

The England team were right on their toes, out to avenge the defeat of the scratch eleven three days previously. I am convinced they would have won handsomely.

Taylor, twenty-one-year-old inside-forward, and Eckersley, last minute selection at full-back, were outstanding successes.

ENGLAND : Merrick (Birmingham City), Ramsey (Tottenham Hotspur), Eckersley (Blackburn Rovers) ; Wright (Wolverhampton Wanderers) (capt.), Johnston (Blackpool), Dickinson (Portsmouth) ; Finney (Preston North End), Broadis (Manchester City), Lofthouse (Bolton Wanderers), Taylor (Manchester United), Berry (Manchester United).

ARGENTINA : Musimessi ; Delacha, Garcia Perez ; Lombardo, Mourino, Gutierrez ; Michelli, Cecconato, Lacasia, Grillo, Cruz.

Referee : A. Ellis (England). Linesmen : A. Bradley and J. Lynch (England).

CHARLES BUCHAN.

LEN WARD

"Somebody said they needed punch in the attack ! "

Charles Buchan (right) in Santiago before the match with Chile. With him are John Graydon, of Kemsley Newspapers (centre) and the Chilean General of Police.

A WELL-DESERVED ENGLAND TRIUMPH

Chile 1, England 2.

ENGLAND gained her first victory and first-ever win in Chile after an exciting game at the National Stadium, Santiago, on Sunday, May 24. It was a battling triumph over adversity.

Dramatic and breath-taking ceremonies before the game, including chorus and calypso singing, and a display by the Chilean President's soldierly bodyguard kept the players waiting twenty minutes before the start.

There was also an interval of twenty-five minutes because two Chilean players refused to return until one of them had had an injection for an injury received just before half-time.

Though it was not a classic by any means, the game had its thrilling phases, most of them in England's favour. There were times when they displayed form worthy of the great Stadium, a huge Hampden-like bowl nestling at the foot of the snow-capped Andes mountains.

It was a setting much more spectacular than even the world-famous Stadium at Rio de Janeiro.

The 80,000 crowd, too, behaved splendidly. Except that they whistled instead of shouting or booing, they were just like an English crowd. They were not slow to appreciate the finer points of the play.

There was only one bad incident when, near the end, oranges were thrown on the field when Eckersley brought off one of his first-time tackles against the Chilean outside-right.

Though the Chileans were clever ball players, almost as clever as the Argentinians, they were goal-shy. Instead of taking a chance shot they persisted in passing and repassing in the penalty area, with the result that Merrick had not more than six shots to worry him.

Their defensive formation was three full-backs and two roving half-backs. It proved very sound, because of the close marking tactics and obstructionist methods adopted.

The Chileans knew all the Continental ways of body-checking and putting an opponent off balance. England thoroughly deserved the victory, though the forwards made hard

A moment of relief for Gil Merrick as the ball bounces off the upright. Harry Johnston seems transfixed by suspense !

work of it. All too often the inside-forwards dropped back to assist the defence when there was no need to do so. It was quite capable of holding the pirouetting Chilean attack.

When they discovered the right way to deal with the frustrating opposition there was no holding the England front rank. The right way was to play four of the forwards in line and by quick, through passes and fast positional play, carve holes in the strange formation.

Broadis and Taylor did this in the second half, when there was no doubting England would get goals. They would have scored more than two if wing-forwards Finney and Berry, well as they played, had not held on to the ball too long.

Some of the moves were beautifully carried out, and proved to the crowd that England's tactics and skill were superior.

This lesson must be drilled home to every future team that goes abroad. The foreigners do not know how to deal with the first-time passing move—like Spurs' " push-and-run " methods—and are easily beaten when they are persisted with. It is useless trying to beat

them with the ball. They will never allow it, by hook or by crook.

Outstanding men in the England defence, which tackled quickly and fairly, were wing-halves Dickinson and Wright and full-backs Ramsey and Eckersley.

They put up such a bold show that Chile were lucky to score the one goal seven minutes from the end, when a shot struck outside-left Diaz and was diverted past the helpless Merrick.

Though not at his best, young Taylor showed that he will quickly establish a claim for a permanent place in England's front line. True, he lacked experience against such opposition, but he was speedy, plucky, and ever-ready for a crack at goal.

He scored England's first goal three minutes after half-time with a lob from the edge of the penalty area that looked to me like a centre intended for Lofthouse.

But the winning goal had the hall-mark of class. The ball went from Wright to Finney, on to Broadis who cut through and passed back for Lofthouse to crash it into the net.

Taylor's goal was scored when Chile's centre-half Rojas was returning to the field. He walked on without the referee's permission while play was in progress. Luckily for England, Arthur Ellis did not stop play for this infringement.

Ellis, though making some mistakes, did a very good job of work. So, too, did the Chilean linesmen. They were quite impartial.

CHILE : Livingstone ; Fariaz, Nunez ; Alvarez, Rojas, Cortes ; Carrasco, Cremaschi, Melendez, Munoz, Diaz.

ENGLAND : Merrick (Birmingham) ; Ramsey (Spurs), Eckersley (Blackburn) ; Wright (Wolves), Johnston (Blackpool), Dickinson (Portsmouth) ; Finney (Preston), Broadis (Manchester City), Lofthouse (Bolton), Taylor (Manchester United), Berry (Manchester United).

Heads up in the Chilean goalmouth ! That's Broadis on the left—with Lofthouse on the extreme right.

CHARLES BUCHAN.

BEATEN-BUT BY THE BEST

says CHARLES BUCHAN

Uruguay 2, England 1

THOUGH England put up a magnificent struggle against the World Champions, they were beaten by a better all-round side.

But England were not at their best. The effects of the influenza and stomach troubles that swept through the camp while in Santiago were plainly apparent. The players were a yard slower in movement and a fraction slower in thinking.

That, however, does not detract from the merits of the Uruguayan victory. They are the best international side I have ever seen during twenty-seven years of watching National teams in various parts of the world.

Like the Argentinians, they were wonderfully clever in possession of the ball and in moving into position for the next pass. They had one invaluable asset ; they invariably found their man with the ball.

This is the lesson our players must learn. Too many of the England passes were intercepted, and what promised to be dangerous movements broke down. Inside-forwards Broadis and Taylor all too often delayed their passes until the opposition had time to cover.

We must also learn that the long, sweeping passes so often employed in England are useless against the Continental and South American system of close marking. We must go back to the old Corinthian methods

of close passing with every man slipping into position for the next move.

In this game, this applied particularly to the forwards. Once they had lost possession of the ball, they rarely moved back into position to relieve a hard-pressed defence.

In most cases, the half-backs and full-backs, when they did get the ball, had no one in position to take a pass.

Ramsey, Johnston and Eckersley, a gallant last line in defence, worked heroically but because the forwards were heavy-footed, did not reap the reward of their hard labours.

Frankly, the only forward to cause real trouble to the Uruguayan defenders was Finney. The outside-right brought off several grand individual efforts but had no real assistance in the vital penalty area.

This Uruguayan team really dictated the policy throughout. England played as well as they were allowed to in the circumstances. It was not good enough this time, but I had the feeling that if we met them again, we should turn the tables.

I understand Uruguay may play in London during our season, probably this November.

They have been invited to visit us and, if they accept, Londoners are in for a real football treat, better than anything seen from Argentina, Austria and the other Continentals who have tried to beat us in England.

The Uruguayans play text-book football, carried out at great speed and with perfect control. They have outstanding players in centre-half Carballo, centre-forward Miguez and in-

side-left Perez. The inside-forward covered a tremendous amount of ground, an example that should have been copied by Broadis and Taylor.

But the main point that struck me forcibly was their wonderful ball control. They were always the masters whether the ball came through the air or along the ground. Some of their trickery had to be seen to be believed.

It is a tribute to our defenders, especially to Dickinson, who played the game of his life, that they scored only twice.

The first goal in the twenty-sixth minute was a brilliant effort by outside-right Abbadie, a coloured winger, who beat Eckersley and Johnston before shooting past Merrick with his left foot.

The second, early in the second half, was headed by centre-forward Miguez from a Cabrera centre.

England were certainly unlucky on two occasions. Ten minutes after the start, a Lofthouse shot struck the right post, slipped across the goal, hit the other post and bounced out.

Then in the second half, a Broadis effort hit the right post and curled outside the goal when an equaliser would have been a wonderful tonic. England deserved the consolation goal scored by Taylor two minutes from the end.

Teams :—
URUGUAY : Maspoli ; Gonsalez, Martinez ; Andrade, Carballo, Cruz ; Abbadie, Schiaffino, Miguez, Perez, Cabrera.
ENGLAND : Merrick (Birmingham) ; Ramsey (Spurs), Eckersley (Blackburn) ; Wright (Wolves), Johnston (Blackpool), Dickinson (Portsmouth) ; Finney (Preston), Broadis (Manchester City), Lofthouse (Bolton), Taylor (Manchester United), Berry (Manchester United).

The ball flashes past Ramsey—with Wright running up to give his support—as the Uruguayan outside-left, Cabrera, shoots. But Merrick was on the spot to make the save.

England are on the attack but Maspoli, the Uruguay goalkeeper, has the ball covered as Berry (No. 11) puts in a powerful shot.

Maspoli saves once again and pushes the ball round the post for a corner. Taylor (No. 10) and Finney (No. 7) are England players in the picture.

Here is the first Uruguay goal. Outside-right Abbadie puts the ball past Merrick with a strong left-foot shot.

ENGLAND GAINS REVENGE AGAINST U.S.

England 6, U.S. 3

ENGLAND gained her revenge for defeat in the World Cup by beating the United States side at the Yankee Stadium, New York.

But it was not the completely convincing victory which I had expected. Although there was never any doubt about the eventual result, the English players showed natural signs of weariness.

The 10,000 spectators, smallest crowd ever to watch an England team in action, did not see the visitors scintillate as brightly as they hoped.

There were indeed times in the first half when the Americans came into the game quite prominently. Once they almost took the lead with Atheneos hooking the ball inches over the cross-bar at very close range.

England were inclined to fade away in spasms until they had the " reviver " of a goal by Ivor Broadis two minutes before half-time.

Then came a remarkable second half—and a hectic spell which produced 5 goals. I could not help admiring the fighting spirit of these unfancied Americans as they hit back against hopeless odds.

Tom Finney (49 minutes) and Nat Loft-house (55 minutes) seemed to have made the match safe when Otto Dekker, who had appeared on the scene as a first-half substitute, scored twice (59 and 67 minutes).

In the 66th minute, Atheneos scored from a penalty, while Lofthouse (60 minutes) and Finney (71 minutes), added goals for England.

Redfern Froggatt concluded the scoring to make it 6—3 for England.

England.—Ditchburn ; Ramsey, Eckersley ; Wright Johnston, Dickinson ; Finney, Broadis, Lofthouse, R. Froggatt, J. Froggatt.

United States.—Moore ; Milne, Keough ; Springthorpe, Dekker, Bahr ; Schultz, Connolly, Atheneos, McLaughlin, Chachurian.

CHARLES
BUCHAN'S
FOOTBALL
MONTHLY

1'6

JANUARY
1953

The World's
Greatest
Soccer
Magazine

PETER HARRIS
*Portsmouth and
England*

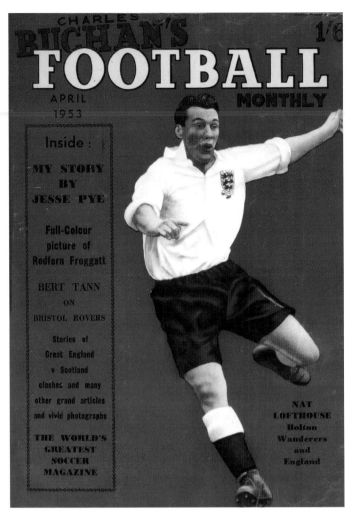

CHARLES
BUCHAN'S
FOOTBALL
MONTHLY

1'6

APRIL
1953

Inside :

**MY STORY
BY
JESSE PYE**

Full-Colour
picture of
Redfern Froggatt

BERT TANN
ON
BRISTOL ROVERS

Stories of
Great England
v Scotland
clashes and many
other grand articles
and vivid photographs

**THE WORLD'S
GREATEST
SOCCER
MAGAZINE**

NAT
LOFTHOUSE
Bolton
Wanderers
and
England

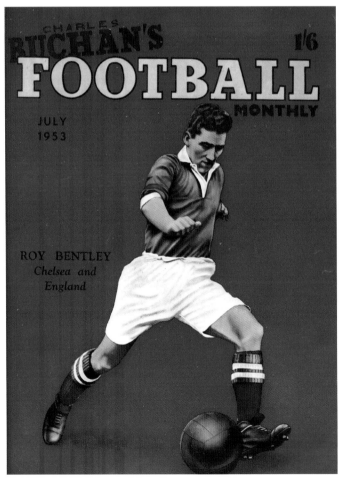

CHARLES
BUCHAN'S
FOOTBALL
MONTHLY

1'6

JULY
1953

ROY BENTLEY
*Chelsea and
England*

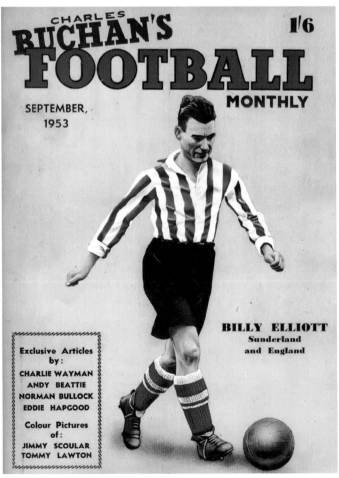

CHARLES
BUCHAN'S
FOOTBALL
MONTHLY

1'6

SEPTEMBER,
1953

BILLY ELLIOTT
**Sunderland
and England**

Exclusive Articles
by :
CHARLIE WAYMAN
ANDY BEATTIE
NORMAN BULLOCK
EDDIE HAPGOOD
Colour Pictures
of :
JIMMY SCOULAR
TOMMY LAWTON

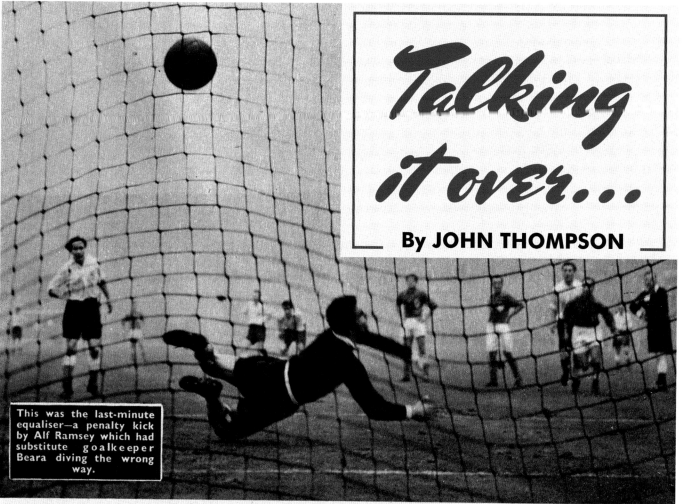

Talking it over...

By JOHN THOMPSON

This was the last-minute equaliser—a penalty kick by Alf Ramsey which had substitute goalkeeper Beara diving the wrong way.

ENGLAND drew with the Rest of Europe in a match at Wembley Stadium on October 21, 1953. Each team scored four goals. It was the ninetieth birthday of the Football Association.

And, as the music of the massed bands of the Grenadier and Scots Guards echoed across the mighty arena, and the occasion became one of unforgettable pomp and pageantry, I thought of the group of young men with now half-forgotten names, who met in a London tavern on an October evening long ago.

They had a wild dream . . . the birth of a football association which would bind together a game rent with varying rules and differences of opinion.

Perhaps some of those delegates from eleven obscure clubs visualised the future. It is unlikely. They were idealists, yet they were also men of modesty and patience. They tackled their task carefully and with a simplicity of purpose that conquered all their problems.

And, from those hopeful, humble, dreams came the great amalgamation of rich and powerful clubs and struggling little village sides which the Football Association embraces to-day.

They traced a pattern which the whole world imitated with diligent pride. They formed an association which has kept the game decent and free from evil.

And on this, their birthday, delegates from many nations had come to do honour to them. . . .

The bands march away. Here come the teams to line-up for the kick-off. . . . The familiar faces of our Englishmen, and, facing them in vivid blue shirts, the stars of Sweden and Yugoslavia, Austria and Spain, Italy and Germany.

There are 97,000 spectators here to see England defend her cherished record of having been unbeaten by any Continental invader on these shores.

The first cheer is for Stanley Matthews. Recalled by his country at the age of 38, Matthews soon shows that he has not lost the old arts and graces.

But already gaps are showing in the English defence. Too much is left to Gilbert Merrick.

This fine goalkeeper is to give one of his most splendid displays.

After five minutes, Vukas, brilliant inside-left from Yugoslavia, darts through. In a last despairing bid to stop him, Bill Eckersley brings him down. The referee awards a penalty. He has no other choice.

There is a hush as Spain's **Kubala** takes a leisurely run at the ball and pushes it wide of the diving Merrick. England are a goal down to this strange assortment from Europe, this Tower of Babel team that had admitted it had no chance.

NO TIME TO LOSE !

ONLY a very limited supply of back numbers of Football Monthly is now available. If you wish to complete your set of the world's greatest Soccer magazine you should lose no time.

Thousands of readers have told us they will always treasure this grand library of articles and pictures. If some of your copies are missing, apply without delay.

We can supply any issue or issues you need, except September, 1951, and August, 1952.

All you need do is to drop a line to Charles Buchan, 408, Strand, London, W.C.2, enclosing a postal order for 1s. 6d. for each copy you require.

State the month and the year of the issues you want. They will then be sent to you post free.

Cover players on available editions have been Billy Wright (October, 1951), Jack Milburn (November), Jack Vernon (December), Alf Ramsey (January, 1952), Jack Froggatt (February), Peter Doherty (March), Walley Barnes (April), Wilf Mannion (May), Tom Finney (June), Eddie Baily (July), Tommy Lawton (September), Derek Dooley (October), Billy Liddell (November), Trevor Ford (December), Peter Harris (January, 1953), Frank Brennan (February), Matthews and Daniel (March), Nat Lofthouse (April), Eddie Shimwell (May), Ted Ditchburn (June), Roy Bentley (July), Jackie Stewart (August), Billy Elliott (September), Vic Metcalfe (October) and Peter Farrell (November).

England v. Wales at Ninian Park, Cardiff. In last season's International England were lucky to beat Wales by the substantial margin of 4 goals to 1. Here Albert Quixall of Sheffield Wednesday and England is closely shadowed by Alf Sherwood, the Welsh full-back, and Ron Burgess, the Welsh captain

A near miss by England inside-forward Stan Mortensen. Rest of the World goalkeeper Zeman watches with relief as Mortensen's flying header goes over the bar.

BILL ECKERSLEY
Blackburn Rovers
and England

England celebrate the 90th anniversary of the Football Association with a ...

4-4 DRAW

The first goal—a penalty, taken by Kubala, for the Rest of the World.

Boniperti (Italy) scores the Rest of the World's second goal.

Matthews and Mortensen

Nat Lofthouse charges Beara, the Rest of the World goalkeeper

FOOTBALL ASSOCIATION 90th ANNIVERSARY
ENGLAND
v
REST OF THE WORLD

WEDNESDAY, OCTOBER 21st, 1953
KICK-OFF 2.30 pm
EMPIRE STADIUM
WEMBLEY

Talking it over...

By JOHN THOMPSON

Although the ball seems to be entering the net acrobatic Hungarian goal-keeper Grosics has actually turned it aside for a corner.

HUNGARY'S calm conquest of England at Wembley Stadium did not surprise me. It was as inevitable as sunset that a country which does not take the game seriously should eventually be routed by one that does.

In England the national team is regarded as an irrelevant appendage to the serious business of League and Cup competitions. There is no sense of urgency in the preparation of the chosen players. There is a smug refusal to learn from the methods adopted by foreigners.

The outlook is dark. There is at present no reason for hoping that England will soon regain her post-war supremacy.

The fiasco of the last World Cup apparently taught us nothing and it is probably too late now to do anything to improve our chances in the next World tournament in Switzerland in June.

Yet the fault does not lie entirely with those at the top. It stretches throughout a game which is suffering from complacency.

In the first issue of this magazine Football League president Arthur Drewry described the manner in which South American and Continental clubs make their grounds into social and sporting centres for local youth.

He added : " In my estimation those far-sighted enough to embark on such schemes would reap a rich reward."

There is no doubt at all of the truth of this. To-day thousands of boys lose interest in football when they leave school.

But how magnificently that enthusiasm would be maintained if more of our great League clubs took a more active interest in the care and happiness of boys who live in the neighbourhood of their grounds.

Lack of accommodation is a poor excuse. With imagination it can be overcome— even if it meant hiring a hall once a week

Mr. Drewry's wise words were published in " Football Monthly " in September, 1951. Yet few clubs have done anything about it. Too few have had the sense to see that by such schemes they would not only increase the number of potential stars but also add to their revenue in future gates.

I charge them with lack of ambition and of lethargy in carrying on in the same old way.

I charge them with being self-satisfied, with failing in their duty to young players in their neighbourhood.

I condemn them for spending ridiculous sums on transfers instead of spending it on the talent that exists on their own doorsteps.

Do not blame those outclassed English

players for the Wembley defeat. For them there was no disgrace in being dazzled by such brilliance.

And let us not take away any credit from the Hungarians. They proved, each one of them, that they were masters of their craft in all its skills.

They proved, too, that in team-spirit and in sportsmanship they had learned well from us—both in technique and in spirit.

England's bid to hold them was made gallantly and with courage. Yet it was as pathetic to watch as Canute must have been when he tried to stay the tide.

The English players too often made wild passes. The Hungarians found their man nine times out of ten. The English made two moves to bring the ball under control to every one made by their opponents.

Yet out of the gloom spectators could grasp the memory of ten flaming minutes of English glory.

The spell preceding the interval was inspiring to all of us because of English skill and perseverance. For those few moments there were dreams of what-might-have-been, visions of a wonder that never materialised.

Once again the English were fighting against impossible odds. Once again they were refusing to acknowledge hopelessness.

But with the fading light so did our hopes fade. After the interval was over the Hungarians hit back, ruthless in their mastery, calm and superbly confident.

Perhaps England's most glaring fault was the team's lack of understanding. When Hungarian players passed the ball they seemed to know instinctively where to put it.

The English in contrast were doubtful

of their colleagues' whereabouts and wasted precious seconds looking around them.

It was only natural that this should be so. The Hungarians had played together repeatedly and the English players had met each other only a few days before the game.

The players I most admired in the English team were Stanley Matthews, who kept three Hungarians busy for long periods, Stanley Mortensen, who proved again the size of his invincible heart, and Harry Johnston, who towered splendidly above the other English defenders.

But for Johnston the Hungarian score might have reached double figures.

Our wing-halves, Billy Wright and Jimmy Dickinson, can rarely have been so severely tested as they were by the incalculable Hungarian inside-forwards, Kocsis and Puskas. Both took a delight in doing the unexpected.

Player I felt most sympathy for in the English attack was George Robb. He rarely received the type of quick through-pass suited to his style and was often kept in idleness.

Jackie Sewell and Ernie Taylor were far below their normal form and compared unfavourably with their counterparts in the Hungarian side.

Star of the Hungarian forward line was centre-forward Hidegkuti whose hat-trick demonstrated that shooting ability is no longer a lost art on the Continent.

Hungary's other goals were scored by Puskas who back-flicked one into the net and hit the other by diverting a free-kick. The incomparable right-half, Bozsik, scored the sixth.

Sewell, Mortensen and Ramsey (from a penalty-kick) scored for England.

Afterwards there could be a wry kind of pride in the thought that England had first taught Hungary how our game should be played.

There could be a determination that. in humility, we should begin all over again,

And there could be the hope that, with English pluck, the faded glory might one day shine again. . . .

As the Hungarian players left the field the spectators applauded them. Smiling, they waved at the crowd. Then they ran down the tunnel leading to the dressing-rooms, into sporting history. . . .

A beautiful shot by Sewell gave England their first goal against Hungary at Wembley. Despite an acrobatic dive by the "Black Flash" Gyula Grosics, the ball entered the corner of the net

Alf Ramsey scores for England with a penalty kick, awarded for a foul on Mortensen.

The English team which met Hungary at Wembley. (Back row): Ramsey, Wright, Merrick, Johnston, Dickinson, Eckersley. (Front row): Matthews, Taylor, Mortensen, Sewell, Robb.

RON ALLEN
West Bromwich
Albion and
England

BILLY FOULKES
Manchester United
and England

JIMMY MULLEN
Wolves and England

JOHNNY NICHOLLS
West Bromwich Albion
and England

England's defence up against it, but centre-half Owen, pictured during a Hungarian raid, was always in the thick of it.

WITH ENGLAND IN HUNGARY

By CHARLES BUCHAN

Hungary 7, England 1

(At Budapest, Sunday, May 23, 1954).

ENGLAND were hopelessly beaten in all departments by a brilliant team. It was the worst defeat ever for a National team—and the worst humiliation.

There were never any prospects that England would make a fight. After the opening goal, scored from a free-kick in the 14th minute, we were outplayed, outwitted and generally forced to play second fiddle.

For one brief spell in the second half, when the England players began to move the ball quickly and accurately, there were slight hopes that we could make the score look flattering. But it lasted only a quarter of an hour.

Hungary then rattled on three goals in a wonderful three-minutes spell and proceeded to show England, in former years the masters, the way the game should be played.

Hungary are the best international team I have seen. I rank them even better than South American teams like Uruguay and Brazil, because they finish off superb midfield work by powerful and accurate shooting.

The speed of their forwards was amazing. They could give England's defenders a few yards start in a straight run and were infinitely faster on the ball and in taking up position. Prompted by inside-forwards Puskas and Kocsis, the wing-forwards, Czibor and Toth (playing his first international), were always dangerously aggressive, with Hidegkuti a skilful leader. I have rarely seen such high-speed classic forward play.

They were much too good for England's defence, the same as had given a great show against Yugoslavia the previous week. Apart from Sid Owen, our defenders were lured out of position and left standing by quick-silver opponents.

Billy Wright and Jimmy Dickinson were over-run and though Ron Staniforth and Roger Byrne kicked and tackled well, they had not the speed in recovery.

After a spell of even play, Hungary were awarded a free-kick just outside the England penalty-area. Puskas placed the ball, but it was left back Lantos who came up and crashed the ball past Merrick for the first goal. Twelve minutes later Puskas added a second after Staniforth had back-heeled the ball from the goal-line. In the 30th minute, Kocsis made the total three.

In the second half, Kocsis, Toth and Hidegkuti rattled on three more goals between the 14th and 17th minutes. Broadis from a free-kick by Dickinson, got some consolation for fine work by scoring England's goal in the 69th minute, but only three minutes later Puskas put on the seventh goal for Hungary.

That ended England's worst-ever performance. And made the F.A. selectors realise that our present tactical methods are outdated. If the defeat is the forerunner of a complete change of plans both in attack and defence, it will lessen the severity of the blow. Teams :

HUNGARY : Grosics ; Buzanszky, Lantos ; Bozsik, Lorant, Zakarias ; Toth, Kocsis, Hidegkuti, Puskas, Czibor.

ENGLAND : Merrick (Birmingham) ; Staniforth (Huddersfield), Byrne (Manchester United) ; Wright (Wolves), Owen (Luton), Dickinson (Portsmouth) ; Harris (Portsmouth), Sewell (Sheffield Wednesday), Jezzard (Fulham), Broadis (Newcastle), Finney (Preston). Referee : Signor Bernardi (Italy).

Yugoslavia 1, England 0

(At Belgrade, Sunday, May 16, 1954).

A FREAK goal three minutes from the end of a tough game brought England's defeat. It was a bad omen for the game with Hungary a week later.

Referee Steiner, of Austria, gave a free-kick for what I thought a perfectly fair tackle by Roger Byrne on the Yugoslav outside-right. Right back Stankovic, playing in his 50th international, and captain for the day, took the kick about 25 yards from goal.

His hard, fast shot struck a defender's outstretched leg, was diverted on to Sid Owen's back and fell at the feet of inside-right Mitic, who promptly crashed the ball past Gil Merrick.

It was a lucky goal, but it brought the Yugoslavs the victory they deserved. They were the more skilful side, better balanced and much faster in action.

Yet, in one way, England were unfortunate. They ran up against all sorts of sharp practices, obstruction, handling the ball and jostling. Their tempers must have been sorely tried by one of the worst exhibitions ever given by any referee anywhere.

One of Mr. Steiner's decisions certainly led to England's defeat. With no score and 23 minutes to play, Johnny Nicholls had the ball at his feet only four yards from the Yugoslav goal. His legs were swept from under him just he was about to put the ball in the net. Even the 60,000 crowd laughed when the referee waved play on.

It was an amazing decision at a critical time. A goal, even a penalty goal, would have been the tonic our forwards badly needed.

Except for Ivor Broadis they had seldom been in the game before then. I am certain they would have been inspired by taking the lead.

Wing forwards Tom Finney and Jimmy Mullen never got clear of close-marking opposition, while Nicholls and Ron Allen had not the experience required against strong, stop-at-any-price defenders. Only about half-a-dozen times did they combine like a first-class attack.

In contrast the defenders were in brilliant form. Owen gave a great display and the other defenders rallied round him, covering and positioning splendidly.

Billy Wright and Jimmy Dickinson tackled strongly and used the ball well. Behind them, Ron Staniforth and Roger Byrne had a complete understanding with goalkeeper Merrick, forming an effective barrier close to goal.

Staniforth had two problems to face. The Yugoslavs brought on a substitute outside-left, Zebec, in the 43rd minute. The Hudders-

—AND YUGOSLAVIA

Grim moment in the Yugoslavia goalmouth as Beara punches clear in a mid-air duel with England's Ivor Broadis.

field right-back, mastered him just as he had outplayed Dvornic, the original outside-left, in the first half.

There was tremendous excitement when Mitic scored the winning goal. Hundreds of people rushed on the field and held up the game for a few minutes.

England has never yet beaten Yugoslavia in an international. Here we lost a great chance of opening the account. Teams :

YUGOSLAVIA : Beara ; Stankovic, Crnkovic ; Cajkovski, Milovanov, Boskov ; Milutinovic, Mitic, Vukas, Bobek, Dvornic. (Substitute outside-left Zebec.)

ENGLAND : Merrick (Birmingham) ; Staniforth (Huddersfield), Byrne (Manchester United) ; Wright (Wolves), Owen (Luton), Dickinson (Portsmouth) ; Finney (Preston), Broadis (Newcastle), Allen (West Bromwich), Nicholls (West Bromwich), Mullen (Wolves).

ENGLAND'S FAILURE IN BELGRADE

No second chance for the wily Rajko Mitic, thanks to England centre-half Owen, who cleverly covers goalkeeper Merrick, as the Yugoslavia inside-right makes a last-minute bid to score.

England's Merrick dashes out and falls to his knees in a successful attempt to prevent goal-hungry Mitic from outwitting the entire England defence.

There was no stopping this one, as Mitic, Yugoslavia's inside-right, slashed the ball home for the match-winner at Belgrade and Merrick fell back helplessly. Watching, and unable to do a thing about it, are England backs, Byrne and Staniforth.

Charles Buchan's
SWITZERLAND
WORLD CUP REVIEW

V championnat
du monde
de football
15 juin
4 juillet

SUISSE '54

basel
berne
geneve
lausanne
lugano
zürich

GER

WEST GERMANY 3 *Morlock 11min, Rah 18, 84min*
Turek, Posipal, Liebrich, Kohlmeyer, Echel, Mai,
Morlock, F.Walter, Rahn, O.Walter, Schafer

HUNGARY 2 *Puskas 6min, Czibor 9min*
Grosics, Buzanszky, Lorant, Lantos, Bozsik,
Zakarias, Czibor, Hidegkuti, Toth, Kocsis, Puskas

Sunday July 4th 1954
Attendance 60,000
Venue: Wankdorf Stadium Berne

Matthews' magic not enough

England 4, Belgium 4.
(At Basle, Thursday, June 17, 1954.)

ENGLAND paid the penalty for easing up in the second half against Belgium in their first World Cup game.

After establishing a two-goals lead, and apparently running the Belgians off their feet, England began to play exhibition football, allowed the opposition to get right back into the game and force extra time.

Belgium, mainly through the efforts of centre-forward Coppens, who generally had the beating of Owen, made a fiery start. In the sixth minute inside-right Anoul gave them the lead.

Taylor made a penalty spot chance for England which Finney sent over the bar; but before the interval England were in front.

Broadis equalised, then Lofthouse made it 2—1 with a great goal—a swallow-dive header from a Finney centre.

England were completely on top when, after 57 minutes, a shot from Broadis struck the Belgian right-back, Dries, and cannoned into the net for 3—1.

Unfortunately, the England players then began to take things easily, with the result that Anoul and Coppens scored further goals for Belgium.

In the second minute of extra time Lofthouse again put England ahead, but three minutes later Dickinson had the misfortune to head through his own goal—and there the scoring ended.

Staniforth, Wright and Dickinson did their best to fill the gaps and took a lot out of themselves. Of the forwards Matthews was the star, giving a great exhibition of wing play. At times he had the Belgian defenders bewildered.

England: Merrick (Birmingham); Staniforth (Huddersfield), Byrne (Manchester United); Wright (Wolves), Owen (Luton), Dickinson (Portsmouth); Matthews (Blackpool), Broadis (Newcastle), Lofthouse (Bolton), Taylor (Manchester United), Finney (Preston).

Belgium: L. Gernaey; M. Dries, A. Van Brandt; C. Huysmans, L. Carre, V. Mees; J. Mermans, L. Anoul, H. Coppens, D. Houf, H. van den Bosch.

Referee: Emil Schmetzer (Germany). Attendance 20,000.

Wolves wing did great job

England 2, Switzerland 0.
(At Berne, Sunday, June 20, 1954.)

ENGLAND had a shock when it was found just before the game that Stanley Matthews and Nat Lofthouse were unable to play. But the remodelled team did a magnificent job.

The inclusion of the Wolves left wing, Wilshaw and Mullen, added punch and liveliness to the attack. Though Taylor, in his club position of centre-forward, made many mistakes, the line moved much more smoothly than against the Belgians.

It was not until the 43rd minute that England scored. Then a pass by Wilshaw was flicked forward by Taylor to Mullen who coolly rounded the Swiss goalkeeper and pushed the ball into the net.

The second goal came in the 24th minute of the second half. Staniforth sent the ball through to Wilshaw who cleverly beat two opponents before shooting past Parlier, the great Swiss goalkeeper.

England: Merrick (Birmingham); Staniforth (Huddersfield) Byrne (Manchester Inited); McGarry (Huddersfield), Wright (Wolves), Dickinson (Portsmouth); Finney (Preston), Broadis (Newcastle), Taylor (Manchester United), Wilshaw (Wolves), Mullen (Wolves).

Switzerland: E. Parlier; A. Neury, R. Bocquet; W. Kernen, O. Eggimann, H. Bigler; C. Antenen, R. Vonlanthen, E. Meier, R. Ballamann, J. Fatton.

Referee: I. Zsolt (Hungary). Attendance 30,000.

England 2, Uruguay 4.
At Basle, Saturday, June 26, 1954.

ENGLAND were knocked out of the World Championship by Uruguay, but they were magnificent in defeat. With the run of the ball in their favour they would have at least drawn with their mighty opponents; mighty both in skill and in physique.

It was poor goalkeeping by Merrick that largely brought about our downfall. When England were only a goal down thirteen minutes from the end and hemming the tiring Uruguayans in their own quarters, he allowed a simple shot from Ambrois, their inside-right, to pass into the net.

But for this unfortunate lapse, England would, I am sure, have drawn level and gone on to victory in extra time over a side that was content in the end to waste time in every possible way.

The Uruguayans were a big, strong team with an amazingly clever attack. But the England defenders tackled them like terriers.

The match was played in heavy rain Puskas, started in the Hungarian team although clearly unfit. But he opened the scoring after six minutes. Hungary went two goals up through Czibor. However Germany with two quick goals equalised within ten minutes. Morlock and Rahn scoring. The winning goal came with only six minutes of the game remaining. A powerful shot from Helmut Rahn beating Grosics from the edge of the box. Despite heavy pressure and Puskas having a goal disallowed for offside, Germany hung on for a famous 3 - 2 victory.

DUNCAN EDWARDS who was to
die tragically young

The years between 1954 and 1958 finally saw the Football Association recognize that changes were needed. The realization that they were falling behind had been incontrovertibly hammered home in the defeats by Hungary. Walter Winterbottom had long recognized this, but only now was he able to begin introducing the changes he knew were necessary to help the national team. The international committee under the influence of Winterbottom, introduced an imaginative four year plan that was to have the emphasis on youth. Under 23 international matches were to bridge the gap between club football and full international fixtures. These were to take place more often, thirteen such games were played before 1958 and promising youngsters like Ron Clayton and Duncan Edwards were to come through this system. Lancaster Gate, home of the F.A. was to house a database of all the promising footballers in the country.

Another change was to be the reduction in the size of the selection committee from eight to three. It would now comprise of the chairman, (at this moment H.S. Shentall), AN Other and manager Walter Winterbottom who would have the final say. It was hoped that this would end the constant changing of line ups, often based on transient form, or selectors pushing the claims of their favourites. Finally they would try to schedule get-togethers for the players where possible during the season.

According to Tom Finney, club chairmen were still afraid that players would return from international duty with their heads full of 'fancy dan' ideas and not stick to the 'up and at 'em' football that the fans wanted.

Post World Cup, England began with a parochial encounter against Wales before following this up with the visit from world champions West Germany, Wembley was full to capacity to welcome them in December 1954 and the crowd paid record receipts of £51,716 for the privilege.

The highlight of the encounter was the return of Stan Matthews, who even at the age of thirty nine was to lead the Germans a merry dance and inspire England to a famous 3-1 victory. On this occasion the perennial problem of accommodating Matthews and Finney in the same team was solved by simply moving Finney to outside left. The uncomplaining Tom would do this for the team, to the detriment of his own game and on this occasion it worked to perfection. Len Shackleton, on what turned out to be his last appearance, also starred. (One too many disagreements with the selectors finally did for him.)

As was usual, another six months past before the next international. It turned out to be well worth the wait. A 7-2 crushing of Scotland with Dennis Wilshaw of Wolves scoring four goals. Even more significant was that this game saw the debut of Duncan Edwards, who despite his youth, was already recognized as a formidable talent.

Almost overnight the England team was beginning to take on a more youthful look. Where several years before the cupboard seemed to be bare, suddenly a crop of talented youngsters, many under the guidance of Matt Busby at Manchester United were emerging. Alongside Edwards at United were Roger Byrne and Tommy Taylor, plus there was also Ron Flowers of Wolves and Ronnie Clayton at Blackburn.

Winterbottom was clearly using this period to try out as many players as possible, during 1955 thirty two different players were used with a further twenty nine players used the following year. Results and performances obviously varied, but it was felt that with the Sweden World Cup in mind, things were moving in the right direction.

Around this time, with the advent of floodlights, it became fashionable to invite 'star' foreign teams over to England for challenge matches. Wolverhampton

Wanderers were at the forefront of this movement and they helped restore a lot of pride and confidence back into the English game with an enthralling series of matches at Molineux. Indeed after success over Dynamo Spartak and Honved, there were some calls for Wolves to represent England. It was proved that at club level at least, we could compete with the best. Charles Buchan said, "We may be inferior on ball control, distribution and positioning but an all action approach can work". Cliff Bastin, ex Arsenal star, when asked for his opinion, was more forthright, "Don't kid yourselves, we have fallen behind".

Football Monthly's foreign correspondent, Bill Croft, reporting from the game between Racing Club Paris and Sunderland, noted a conversation between French supporters that he had overheard, "I hope we cease to invite clubs like this, who can teach us nothing and entertain us so little". Still, even if our football wasn't as good, we could always congratulate ourselves on British behaviour both on and off the pitch. In Football Monthly's edition of February 1956, alongside pictures of rioting fans was the headline, 'We might be rubbish at football but you will never see scenes like this'.

One of the greatest problems in world football at this time was the different interpretation of rules. The British game was out of step with the rest of the world, particularly 'shoulder barging' and rough treatment of goalkeepers. Our game was still very physical and this approach never went down well abroad, whilst our players were upset by the continental way of sly shirt pulling and obstruction. Many games between the home countries and continental opposition degenerated into free for all's. It was clear that we needed to change our approach as we were in the minority.

In May 1956 the Wembley crowd were treated to the best and worst of international football as Brazil paid their first ever visit. The Brazilians were visiting Europe as part of their meticulous preparation for the 1958 World Cup. Determined to leave nothing to chance, they travelled with not only a twenty strong squad of players but a backroom staff that the England team could only dream of. Alongside coaches, were physical trainers, doctors, chefs and even a psychiatrist.

The game itself was pure theatre, after bursting into a two goal lead, England were pushed back as the Brazilians showed what they were capable of, but it was in the second half after they had equalized that the South Americans revealed their quirky

side. After a Brazilian player inexplicably handled to give away a penalty, they refused to hand the ball over and at one point looked as if they would leave the field. Finally they were persuaded to carry on, the penalty and another subsequent one that was awarded, were both missed, before England eventually ran out 4-2 winners as the opposition lost their discipline and self-control.

England themselves were now to set off on their own summer tour, beginning in Sweden before ending up in Berlin for the return game with West Germany at the Olympic Stadium. Amazingly by now, seven players in the team that played that afternoon were twenty three or under. They put on an amazing show, a 3-1 victory including a majestic goal from Duncan Edwards, as he surged past three defenders and crashed in a long range effort. At last it seemed that England could look forward with optimism to the World Cup Finals if they were able to qualify.

Unlike previous qualifying campaigns where the Home Championships were used by Fifa, now England were placed in a three way competition with Denmark and the Republic of Ireland, home and away ties with only the winners of the group going through to the finals.

On paper this seemed a straight forward task, even more so when England started by beating Denmark 5-2 in December 1956. Qualification was assured within the space of eleven days the following May when they followed up this result by beating Ireland 5-1 at home, Denmark 4-1 away and ended with a hard fought draw in Dublin.

A surprising home defeat to Northern Ireland, only the second time in sixty five years they had lost to the Irish, was played out before only 42,000 apathetic fans. This was the only blip in a highly successful year and the final game of 1957 saw a return to form as France were hammered 4-0. Little did everyone know but disaster was soon to strike England's World Cup ambitions.

The events of February 1958 were not only catastrophic for Manchester United, but they also ripped the heart out of the England team. The deaths of Duncan Edwards, Roger Byrne and Tommy Taylor, plus the psychological effects on Bobby Charlton, left Walter Winterbottom with an impossible task, you couldn't replace genius. The cover of the March issue of Football Monthly poignantly featured Duncan Edwards.

Walter Winterbottom was now left with only four games to reorganize his line-up. Jim Langley, Bert Slater and Derek Kevan were drafted in as replacements for the first three of these internationals but the manager wasn't convinced, making further changes and giving debuts to three more players in the last warm up game. This was an historic first encounter in Moscow against the USSR, who would by coincidence also be England's first opponents in Sweden only three weeks later. Colin McDonald replaced Eddie Hopkinson in goal after he conceded five in Yugoslavia, Tommy Banks came in at full back and also Eddie Clamp took Ronnie Clayton's position after he had lost form and confidence.

England's preparation for the tournament was again terrible. After the game in Moscow the players were allowed to return home, not meeting up with their team mates again until shortly before they were to leave for Sweden. In fact they were the last team to arrive in Scandinavia. Their hotel was situated right in the centre of Gothenburg and they were constantly visited by well-wishers disturbing their preparation.

England's twenty man squad for the tournament was considered unbalanced by most judges, it contained ten forwards and only three wing halves. By choosing Derek Kevan over Brian Clough it seemed that there was more emphasis being placed on work rate rather than skill.

Before the opening group match against the USSR, football found itself on the front pages as well as the back. To the dismay of England captain Billy Wright, a Sunday paper was to run a story about his romance with Joy

WALTER WINTERBOTTOM enjoys a light hearted moment with his players

TOMMY TAYLOR in action against West Germany in Berlin

Beverley, one of the famous singing sisters. This was not the whole issue, the fact that she was still married was what caused moral outrage amongst some sections of society. The England team did not appreciate this disruption to their preparation before a major tournament.

The game against the USSR could not have begun in a worse fashion. The team were sluggish and outplayed all over the pitch and they found themselves two goals behind after an hour of play. However, suddenly from out of nowhere, England began to find their form. A disallowed England goal seemed to unsettle the Russians who retreated into a defensive formation and inspired England to launch a series of attacks that culminated in Derek Kevan pulling a goal back when he scored from close range. Tom Finney who had already been the subject of some harsh tackling, now seemed to be singled out for the 'treatment' by the Russians. As time began to run out, Bobby Robson had a goal unluckily disallowed, before five minutes from the end the referee awarded England a penalty and with a distinct lack of volunteers, Tom Finney stepped up to score the equalizer. You wouldn't have guessed it, but Tom later said that was the most nervous that he had ever been on a football pitch. This was a good draw in the circumstances but you could not overlook the fact that for the majority of the game, England had been second best.

England's second game was against the favourites Brazil in the same Gothenburg stadium. This match was to divide opinions. Winterbottom knew that if the team tried to beat Brazil at their own game, they would lose. So the manager devised tactics to sit deeper and frustrate the opposition whilst relying on quick counter attacks. There was

a blow before the game when Finney was ruled out, Alan A'Court taking his place. The game ended 0-0, but it was an exciting clash of styles. The journalists and spectators thoroughly enjoyed it, but the public back home watching on television thought it was poor performance. Des Hackett of the Daily Express said, "The English played like tigers," whilst Peter Lorenzo of the Daily Herald said, "It was wonder football at a wonder pace".

Now England knew that they had to beat Austria in the final game to progress further in the tournament, whilst hoping that Brazil could beat Russia in the other game. Once more their first half performance was poor, lacking any sort of cohesion they fell behind and in truth were lucky not to go in two down, but it was a different story after the break. There was an equalizer from Haynes and constant attacking before they fell to a sucker punch, but this only made England more determined and Kevan again equalized, but despite almost constant pressure they couldn't force a winner, meaning England shared second spot with the USSR.

The rules of the competition at this time said that if teams were level on points, there would be a play off and this took place only two days later. Two debutants, Peter Brabrook and Peter Broadbent performed well as England produced a solid performance, but despite disallowed goals and Brabrook twice hitting the post, they fell to a one goal defeat.

The team had performed creditably and as Billy Wright put it, "luck should not be essential, but you cannot achieve much without it". It was a different opinion back home amongst supporters and the team returned home to calls for sackings and a massive overhaul for the system.

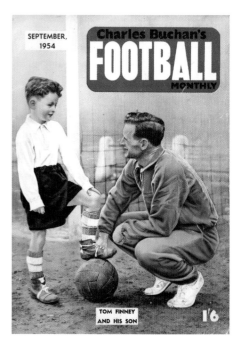

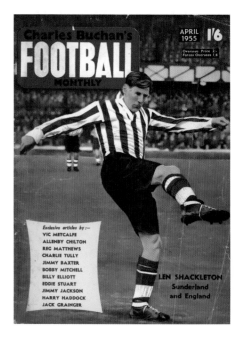

LET US KEEP IT BRITISH

The word "fighting" has slipped into the vocabulary of English football. It is a dangerous word. Soccer must remain a game of skill, says

ROLAND ALLEN

IT is our proud boast that the British do not kick a man when he is down. It used to be, indeed, only under great provocation, and then with some reluctance and the suggestion of an apology, that they would even knock him down.

I have come to the conclusion that the efforts of a lot of foolish people to tamper with, or even to change, this admirable national characteristic have had as much to do with England's Soccer decline as any other factor.

If that is true—and I saw a tremendous amount of evidence to support it during last season—it will be a long time before we win the World Cup. And, if ever we do, the price might prove to have been greater than the prize.

A dangerous delusion is spreading through football that there is a short cut to the top by way of brute force.

It is, of course, a long time since we won the various lawn-tennis championships at Wimbledon or, until last summer, the cricket "Ashes," or showed the faintest signs of sweeping the board at an Olympic Games.

We do not breed world boxing champions. The Rugby Union, very wisely I think, keep out of world competition, although their scope is more restricted than that of the Soccer people.

These things are mentioned because they show that Soccer is merely going the way of all the other games at which the British used to be masters of the world.

They prove that the Soccer decline is not a problem in itself, but only a small part of a much bigger and wider one.

The news that Sir Stanley Rous had been elected to membership of the M.C.C. started the thought that better results might be achieved if the problem were tackled in its broader aspect, rather than in bits and pieces by the various governing bodies of the sports concerned.

It might be argued that there is no connection between through passes and leg breaks, the cannon-ball service, an uppercut, a Rugger scrum, or passing the baton in a relay.

There is not, of course, in the technical sense, except that they all demand the basics of balance and control. The connection and the similarity is in the British approach to these various skills.

I get the impression that the English—and you can include the Scots if you wish—have not the patience and the concentration necessary to master these various skills. That is not entirely through laziness.

When I was discussing the F.A. coaching plans with Sir Stanley Rous, he pointed out that their object was not to produce international footballers for England, but to make it possible for as many people as possible to reach a standard at which they would get pleasure, not only from playing the game, but from making themselves more efficient at it.

In that connection, and in comparison with the foreigners, I would say there are now more people in England who play football well enough to get real fun from it than there have ever been ; and, in proportion to the population, more than in any other country in the world.

The position in cricket is similar, and that is something for which we are entitled to feel thankful.

There is a standard below which no game can be really enjoyed. I am sure the University people, who have achieved near miracles in raising the efficiency of their football, get much more of a kick from it now than they used to do when it was just a rough and tumble.

They were not badgered and talked into it. They were not forced to undergo the coaching and devote time to the practice necessary for their remarkable improvement.

They did it voluntarily ; and they have, as I can testify, come to think it was well worth while.

Where is the manager or the coach who can persuade England's young professionals that making themselves masters of their trade should not be merely a duty, or a self-imposed penance, but something bringing a rich reward ?

I do not think we shall get far with our youngsters by telling them they are lazy and inefficient. We shall make even less progress by merely telling them, as so many people now are doing, that all they need do is to get tough and "get stuck in."

There is far more to it than that.

Nor do I believe that it is entirely fair to blame the players at all for the English failure to keep pace with the rest of the world.

Nor is it much good pointing out to them that people like Stanley Matthews, Billy Wright, Leonard Shackleton, Ivor Broadis, and the select few others whom we can call really great players, have achieved that status at the expense of much self-sacrifice and hard work.

Footballers have to be persuaded ; not kicked and driven into the belief that it is worth while to give all they have because there is a reward for doing so.

Not £50 a match, or even £150 and a sports car—which the Italians of 1934 were supposed to have been promised.

No, the reward would be a deep satisfaction in having accomplished something personal ; of having proved that an English footballer can do anything a foreigner can do—and then some.

He can, you know, if that point of view is brought home to him. The arguable question is : how can it be done ?

It will not be achieved by breeding a race of fighting footballers.

In other words, we cannot change the British character and outlook, even for football prestige. That, at least, is my firm opinion.

The word "fighting" has slipped into the vocabulary of English football. It is a dangerous word. Football is a game of skill and not fisticuffs or anything remotely resembling them.

Is brute force to become the decisive factor ?

The master footballer does not bash his way to the top. I have never seen Stanley Matthews, Tom Finney, Len Shackleton, Ronnie Allen and the others going in feet first, to get the ball at all costs.

Neither F.I.F.A. nor the Hungarians did it. Chelsea, my team of the season, did not do it. When the Spurs won the championship—and include Manchester United and Everton in this—they did not do it.

And, even if we never win the World Cup, I do not want to see a team in England jerseys kicking and bashing their way to winning matches.

My way would be harder, and would take longer ; but it is the only way.

I am not prepared to forecast the winners of the World Cup, but if it is one of the teams which go in for the rough, tough and fighting stuff, I shall be the most surprised person in my village.

" MARILYN MONROE !—WHERE ? "

THE GAME ABROAD
by BILL CROFT

I HEAR that three South American countries would be willing to form a team to meet a "Europe" side.

Best time for such a match, it is thought on the Continent, would be just after the World Cup tourney, to be played in Sweden in 1958.

Enough talent would be assembled then, and the game could be played in Stockholm, or some other European capital, without piling up the expenses.

The South Americans, however, are said to be ready and willing to play the match well before the next World Cup competition.

* * *

REFERRING to libel and slander actions that arose over football disputes in Italy, a leading official of the Federation said: "They had nothing to do with sport."

Noting this remark, the *Semaine Sportive*, published in Switzerland, stated: "The legal actions only emphasise what everyone knows—that many of Italy's professional clubs are controlled by rich incompetents, and that financial jiggery-pokery is going on.

"There are clubs that never publish balance-sheets, others that keep double accounts, and still others whose financial position is revealed only to the teams' backers.

"*Several clubs with big debts have found a soccer fan rich and vain enough to help them out for the mere honour of calling himself the chairman.*"

One Italian club is said to have paid over £300,000 in transfers in one season, including huge sums for foreign players with Italian blood in their veins—even if it has been diluted.

The biggest scandals, however, were the alleged paying of bribes to teams willing to lose.

* * *

SEPP HERBERGER, trainer of the German team for last year's World Cup win, says of the Russians:

"All foreign sides playing them should scheme, and make full use of, the counter-attack.

"Russian attackers are at their best when thrusting at retreating players. Their defenders can be caught on the wrong foot by retreating players flashing into the offensive."

Herberger also stresses the Russians' well-known physical fitness. "It is a point," he says, "which is well known everywhere, but which many non-Russian players, *because they would rather take things easier, don't like discussing.*"

Hungarian football boss Gustav Sebes also stresses the Russian players' stamina. "Just as noticeable," he adds, "is the reluctance of the Russians to take shooting chances." Fritz Walter, the German captain, said after Russia had beaten Germany in Moscow this season: "In the last 15 minutes we had everything the Russians had got — except stamina."

* * *

Jiggery-pokery in Italian Soccer

BULGARIA, England's opponents at Sofia on October 23 in a qualifying match for the next Olympic tourney, were beaten by Czechoslovakia and Rumania in qualifying games for last year's World Cup.

England have never played Bulgaria. Eire beat Bulgaria 1-0 in Paris in the Olympic tourney back in 1924.

Two of Bulgaria's finest feats were the draws (both 1-1) with Hungary in Budapest, in 1952, and in Sofia, the following year. Russia beat Bulgaria 2-1 in the Olympic tourney of 1952.

Bulgaria's football is run by the country's Physical Culture and Sports Supreme Committee. Clubs were abolished 11 years ago, and the game is now played by Soccer sections of general sports organisations.

The leading competitions are for the Republican Cup, and for a trophy given by the Soviet Army.

* * *

B. VUKAS

F. WALTER

J. SCHIAFFINO

A. KUBALA

B. ZEBEC

G. NORDAHL

W. LIEBRICH

TALKING IT OVER...

by John Thompson

THIS is Britain. This is the home of football, the land where the great game was born and where it flourishes more healthily than it does anywhere else in the world. And I am sick and tired of foreigners who sneer at us.

This is the country where Soccer is ruled with honesty of purpose, sometimes unwisely, sometimes well. But those who rule it are honest and true to themselves and to their beliefs.

This is a land and a game in which we can take pride. And I have no time for those who praise everything Continental and condemn all that is British.

They are as mistaken and as dangerous as the guilty men who refused to recognise the technical skills which foreigners have acquired.

Reforms in Britain? Of course there is need for them. But let us carry them out in our own way and not at the dictation of those who understand neither our temperament nor our native capacity to make triumphs out of retreats.

★

"Imitate foreigners in all they do," I am told. At a match in which Portsmouth's brilliance overwhelmed Chelsea, a friend explained pompously: "That's the Continental style."

Continental poppycock! Portsmouth had played the old British way, the way football was being played here **when foreigners were begging us for coaches so that they could be good pupils.**

"Imitate the foreigners," I am told. In Britain the only corkscrews are put to good use in club boardrooms. But in France they found that a leading club had been paying for points so that it could gain promotion. And not long ago there was talk of corruption in Italy.

In Britain, some folk may be stupid, but they are straight.

Imitate the foreigners? In South America, during Arsenal's tour of 1949, I saw Bryn Jones move to meet the ball after the opposing goalkeeper had made a save. "A player came at me from behind and squeezed my throat," he told me. Police charged on to the field, hitting out with truncheons. Other foreigners pull jerseys, use their elbows and artfully trip opponents.

In Britain the players may sometimes be a little slow, reluctant to adopt new ideas. But their vigour is disciplined and honest. With rare exceptions, they are worthy of British sportsmanship.

They have a tradition to maintain and they do it well. I am proud to have friends among them.

I am told by some critics that the Football League must be torn down and built anew and that a select little League would improve the English international side.

But would YOU wreck a structure that rules the game so fairly Saturday after Saturday; the organisation which is strict and impartial, free of corruption and scrupulous in all its dealings? Which clubs would you choose . . . and which would you omit? Current form means nothing . . . or would you judge teams by performances that are long past and half-forgotten?

And who can deny that small clubs are as important to their local communities as big clubs are to theirs?

Is there not the inherent British sympathy for the underdog ranged against this idea, the sympathy which makes us cheer Walsall when they beat Arsenal and York when they lick Tottenham?

Would you judge clubs on last Saturday's form, on gate receipts, or on the successes or failures which they might achieve in the future?

I would leave the League alone—apart from the introduction of the four-up and four-down idea, denial of which has long handicapped the underdogs.

★

I have never subscribed to the view that all the best football is seen in the First and Second Divisions. Many matches between more humbly-situated teams have provided as much skill as have encounters between their wealthier colleagues.

That great leveller, the F.A. Cup, proves this point season after season, for the small clubs which do well in it do not batter their way forward.

They meet class with class and succeed because, on the day, they play better football.

Remember giant-killers Millwall and Leyton Orient, Colchester and Port Vale? It was certainly not brute strength that allowed any of them to find Cup glory.

Small clubs fight on against overdrafts and rising expenses, against those who jeer at them and against drooping gates.

Through it all they continue to give pleasure and excitement to their loyal supporters.

I, for one, would do nothing to make their struggle more difficult than it is.

In the meantime, let us set to work in our own way to improve the entertainment that football provides, to increase its artistry and to provide better facilities for watching it.

But let us do it in our own way, not as imitators of foreigners.

We will get there in the end, blundering a little on the way, as we do in our wars, arguing among ourselves, shrugging aside dictators—and winning the last battle out of sheer cussedness. . . .

THAT BADGE!

HERE'S the badge that caused countless arguments. It is the one worn by Stanley Matthews, of Blackpool and England, in last month's coloured cover picture—the most controversial front page we have ever used!

All over Britain there were heated discussions in offices, factories and schools. Phone calls and letters to Charles Buchan demanded: "Since when has Stanley Matthews been an Irish international. Surely the inscription under the shield should read: 'England'?"

The answer is that the picture was quite correct. There was no mistake. Matthews DID in fact wear this shirt and this inscription on his shield. The word "Ireland" was there because the match in which he was playing was AGAINST the Irish and it is the custom for the badges to name the OPPOSING team.

But thanks a lot to all of you who took such a keen interest in our cover. It proves your enthusiasm for "Football Monthly" and your excellent eyesight!

JOHN ATYEO
Bristol City

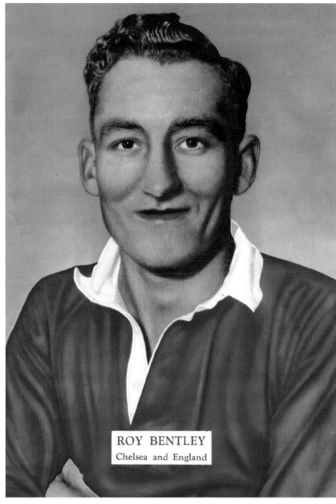

ROY BENTLEY
Chelsea and England

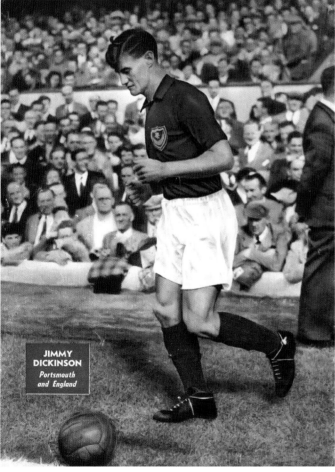

JIMMY
DICKINSON
Portsmouth
and England

ROGER BYRNE
Manchester United
and England

Billy Wright and West Germany's Posipal exchange pennants before the friendly at Wembley in December 1954

Roy Bentley has his effort disallowed against West Germany

Another scene from the match, Roger Byrne tackles Uwe Seeler

Len Shackleton chases a through ball in vain

FOOTBALL ASSOCIATION INTERNATIONAL
ENGLAND
v
GERMANY
WEDNESDAY, DECEMBER 1st, 1954   KICK-OFF 7.0 p.m.

EMPIRE STADIUM
WEMBLEY

OFFICIAL PROGRAMME   ONE SHILLING

Action fro

Ronnie Allen follows up to score England's second goal!

Matthews the hero of England victory

Roy Bentley turns away after scoring against West Germany

he BIG match!

THOUGH England should have beaten Germany by a bigger score than 3—1 at Wembley, a fair share of the honours of a patchy game went to the World champions.

With only three of the team that beat Hungary in the World Cup final in Switzerland last summer—full-backs Posipal and Kohlmeyer and centre-half Liebrich—they made England fight hard for more than an hour.

Unfortunately for them the forwards, all of whom were taking part in their first full international, had no experience of the big occasion.

They passed accurately, but usually squarely across the field, and moved into position quickly but had neither the craft nor guile to outwit the strong England defenders.

When they did break through, especially in the first half, they tried to walk the ball into the net instead of shooting. They were easily trapped, too, by England's full-backs. I counted three offside decisions against them in the first five minutes.

England's forwards, on the other hand, had the experience, and their ball control was brilliant. Matthews, Shackleton and Finney gave delightful exhibitions of ball wizardry. But only on occasions did we see sweeping movements in the pattern of the Hungarians or the Uruguayans.

Matthews, who first played against Germany twenty years ago, waltzed past left-back Kohlmeyer almost as he pleased. He sent across a stream of centres that should have brought goals.

Though goalkeeper Herkenrath brought off many fearless saves by throwing himself at the feet of oncoming forwards, Finney, Allen and Shackleton should have had at least half-a-dozen goals.

They also made the mistake of indulging in exhibition play after they had established a two-goal lead early in the second half. Only a jolt in the shape of a German goal, restored their balance.

England's defence was solid and reliable. The return of Williams in goal inspired his colleagues to their best display of the season.

Full-backs Staniforth and Byrne moved upfield confidently and cut off the German wing forwards before they could make openings.

The only fault I could find in the defence was the slowness of wing-halves Phillips and Slater in getting the ball through to their forwards. They lost chances of setting the attack in motion by holding on to the ball far too long.

England started off as though they would

OPINION
Continued from page 3

sweep the Germans off their feet. But it was not until the 28th minute that they set off on the road to victory.

Bentley scored the goal after Posipal had cleared a shot from Finney off the goal-line. Many opportunities, though, were missed by faulty shooting.

It looked after three minutes in the second half, when Allen increased the lead after Herkenrath had bravely saved an effort by Finney, that England would walk away with the game.

They would have done so, I thought, if they had not proceeded to indulge in fancy work which led nowhere against the strong-tackling Liebrich, and Posipal.

When in one of their rare breaks-away, outside-left Beck beat Williams with a low shot, the Germans threatened to make a great rally.

But this spurred the England forwards on and in three minutes, Shackleton put the issue beyond doubt by cleverly chipping the ball over the advancing Herkenrath for a third goal.

In the closing stages, England penned the Germans into their own quarters. They could not, however, break down the splendid resistance of the German defenders who, when the attack had faded out, pulled forth their finest efforts.

England won, and won comfortably, but it was not a performance that will live long in the memory.

ENGLAND : Williams (Wolves) ; Staniforth (Huddersfield), Byrne (Man. Utd.) ; Phillips (Portsmouth), Wright (Wolves) (captain), Slater (Wolves) ; Matthews (Blackpool), Bentley (Chelsea), Allen (W.B.A.), Shackleton (Sunderland), Finney (Preston).
GERMANY : Herkenrath ; Posipal (captain), Kohlmeyer ; Erhardt, Liebrich, Harpers ; Kaufhold, Pfeiffer, Seeler, Derwall, Beck.
Referee : V. Orlandini (Italy).
Attendance : 100,000. Receipts : £51,716 (a Wembley record).

LEN SHACKLETON
Sunderland and England

With Herkenrath, plucky German goalkeeper, lying helpless Len Shackleton dashes on towards an empty German net. But at the last moment Shackleton lost control of the ball and England just missed what looked a certain goal.

★ **Hungarians say oxygen may be harmful**

★ **Pools finance German Soccer Schools**

★ **Ten brothers in a Swedish team**

HUNGARY has just decided that, on present evidence, the giving of oxygen to footballers appears to have no advantages. A few doctors think there may be risk of it doing more harm than good.

Sports Vice-Minister Gustav Sebes—whom we know as Hungary's Soccer boss—asked the country's best-known sporting doctors, and a State laboratory, to investigate.

Experiments were carried out with players of Vasas, of Budapest. The investigators' report says :

"No increased stamina was noticeable in players who were given oxygen. The intervals that occur between periods of great physical strain on the field enable players to recuperate from the loss of oxygen. Normal breathing during a half-time interval of 10 or 15 minutes is sufficient to restore balance."

A professor at Hungary's Higher School of Physical Education is among those who think the giving of oxygen *may* do more harm than good. He gives the opinion cautiously, and says he needs more evidence before he can definitely make up his mind.

Inquiries into the oxygen problem continue in Hungary.

*   *   *

Spain was, I think, the first European country to give oxygen to footballers. The idea was introduced by the trainer of Espanol, of Barcelona, who was impressed by reports of its effects in South America.

Espanol had a fine run of successes after oxygen was introduced. It has since been said that this good playing period may have been a coincidence, or that the Espanol players benefited by auto-suggestion.

Pools in Western Germany contribute

THE GAME ABROAD—*by BILL CROFT*

::

Our correspondent on the Continent, who has followed foreign football for 30 years

10 per cent of their receipts to the promotion of sport. Football gets just over half of this, and uses most of its share to run five Soccer schools.

A friend of mine who recently visited the school at Barsinghausen, about 18 miles from Hanover, says it is " a sportsman's paradise."

Besides playing pitches and several acres of park-land, it has two swimming pools, lecture rooms, reading rooms, a cinema, a restaurant, and tea-rooms.

*   *   *

When my friend remarked to a German : "This looks like a miracle," the German said :

"You're wrong. This place results from the common-sense use of what we consider to be a just contribution by the pools to the game on which they are based."

At one time four of the eight Austrian professionals in France were out of the game with injuries, and there are complaints that Austrians signing for French clubs risk " rough treatment."

A report of " concerted moves by

French players to make things unpleasant for imported Austrian professionals " is nonsense.

A trainer of a club employing Austrians says that probably *a few* French players try to put Austrians out of action.

There may be something in that.

Arguing against this theory, a critic says :

" Austrian football is well known to be less vigorous than French. Probably the Austrians with French clubs are not hardened to our sort of tackling. Another important point is that seven of the eight Austrian professionals in France are 30 years old or more."

*   *   *

A playing " balance-sheet" of Rapid of Vienna, a well-known Austrian team, is interesting.

Up to the time I write, the club's "friendlies" since the war number 190, most of which were played abroad. Rapid have won 116 of the matches, drawn 25, lost 49.

*   *   *

Travels by Dynamo of Moscow have caused arguments in Paris as to when this team first played in the French capital.

The date was January 1, 1936, when Racing Club de Paris beat them 2—1.

Racing Club's inside-right was an Englishman named Kennedy, one of the relatively few players from the U.K. who have been successful in France.

The Racing Club's trainer in Kennedy's time was George Kimpton, an old Southampton player.

Here are two examples of how organisation abroad differs from ours.

The professional team at Vicence—an Italian town with a population of 80,000 —plays in Division II of the National League. But it is not called " Vicence."

Its name is "Lanerossi," in other words, " Rossi wool."

The team is financed by a great wool-making concern at Vicence, founded by Baron Rossi. The name helps to publicise a commodity.

Can you imagine one of our well-known teams having the name of a local product in place of the city or town?

My second example takes us to Brazil.

The famous professional club Fluminense, at Rio de Janeiro, is merely part of a general sports club which has 20,000 members.

For a subscription of £8 a year (less for women and children) the 20,000 can practise various sports on the club's vast grounds, and watch the professional football team's home games.

*   *   *

Ten brothers named Arvidsson, whose ages range from 17 to 38, play for a team in the little Swedish town of Skattkaer.

The eleventh player is a son of the oldest brother.

●

Bill Croft tells of experiments with oxygen treatment that have been made in Hungary. These two Hungarian stars—Puskas (left) and R. Hidas—don't look as though they need it !

BILL SLATER
Wolves and England

DON REVIE
Manchester City
and
England

FRANK
BLUNSTONE
of Chelsea
and
England

JACK MILBURN
Newcastle United
and England

Denise Wilshaw leaps high against Scotland

Williams beaten by Kopa from the penalty spot against France

Action against Spain in Madrid

OUR CAMERA CAPTURE

OPINION
by CHARLES BUCHAN

Albert Quixall in a vain scoring bid during the match against Spain.

NOW is the time for blunt words. The truth about our international failures has been lost in a mirage of excuses for too long.

The fact is that England's Continental tour in May provided yet another example of how our team utterly fails to rise to the occasion against Continental sides.

The defeats in Paris by France and in Oporto by Portugal should not have happened, and the draw in Madrid with Spain could easily have been turned into victory **by a team that played with understanding and with a definite purpose.**

Our trouble is due, in my opinion, to badly-planned tactics. We go on to the field expecting to be allowed to play football in our own way and according to our own ideas.

But whether we like it or not, obstruction and destructive methods are part-and-parcel of the Continental style of play. They interpret the laws in a different way from us. When we play abroad we *must* play according to their interpretations.

Not only that, we cannot hope to play "push and run" Soccer against Continental opposition. They will never allow a player to run on to the ball as we do.

We have, however, persevered with this style of play for several years without any great success. It is a style insisted upon by one man in charge of the team **and with players temperamentally unsuited to the job.**

Now is the time for a change. International players must be given a chance of expressing **their own ideas** of how the games should be played.

After all, it is the players who have

to do the job on the field. They should be allowed to develop their own plan, under the guidance of a manager, of course.

They should be the best players in England with minds of their own. It should not be difficult for them to sift out a workable plan of campaign.

I recall in South America an England player saying, "*I cannot play according to rigid instructions.*" No international should be asked to.

All successful League clubs of recent years have made the best use of their players' brains. **It seems strange that when playing for England, an international star has to sink his individuality.**

Scotland, beaten 7—2 by England at Wembley in April, did wonderfully well to draw with Yugoslavia in Belgrade and better still to beat Austria in Vienna. I am told they worked out their successful plan among themselves. *It brought dividends.*

Scotland went on to put up a great display against the Hungarians in Budapest. I am told that they created a splendid impression and might have won but for defensive errors and a missed penalty kick.

The main thing is that their skill and pluck certainly did not disgrace the old Scottish craft. The 100,000 spectators who crowded into the vast stadium gave them a tremendous ovation at the end of the game.

When Gordon Smith opened the scoring to give the Scots a 1—0 lead at half-time, it seemed that the unexpected might happen, that Hungary would be conquered. But seven minutes after the interval Hideguti equalised and Kocsis and

ENGLAND IN ACTION!!

Spanish goal-keeper Carmelo stops a dash by Lofthouse.

Finney is " grounded " but he has just scored England's third goal.

A great shot by Lofthouse is tipped over the crossbar.

Atyeo and Perry in a raid on the Spanish goal.

Perry's goal rockets into the net.

England 4, Spain 1
At Wembley Stadium, Wednesday, November 30, 1955

ALTHOUGH they did not always dominate this patchy encounter in the fog, England were worthy winners over a Spanish side which was weak and ill-disciplined in its defensive tactics.

At one period, when England had scored twice in the first twelve minutes, it looked as though the match would result in an even heavier win, but the Spaniards fought back well. For twenty minutes before the interval they were the more impressive combination.

The English goals were scored by John Atyeo (11 minutes), Bill Perry (12), Tom Finney (49), and Perry (62). Arieta replied for Spain in the eightieth minute.

Perhaps the most disappointing feature of the game was the fact that England failed to maintain the tremendous momentum with which they had started. Had they done so, this would have been one of Wembley's most memorable occasions.

Promising displays were given by the young English inside-forwards, Atyeo and Haynes, and the attack was dashingly led by Nat Lofthouse.

Tom Finney was the victim of a foul early in the game. He took the penalty kick himself, but it was saved by Sanchez Carmelo, the acrobatic Spanish goalkeeper.

As the fog thickened the match was finished under floodlights, the first time for a full international in England.

ENGLAND.—Baynham; Hall, Byrne; Clayton, Wright (captain), Dickinson; Finney, Atyeo, Lofthouse, Haynes, Perry.
SPAIN.—Carmelo; Segarra (captain), Campanal; Mauri, Garay, Magueregui; Gonzalez, Paya, Arieta, Domenech, Collar.
Referee: M. Guigue (France). Attendance 95,550. Receipts £45,100.

An exchange of gifts before the kick-off by the two captains, Juan Segarra and Billy Wright.

ENGLAND 4 - BRAZIL 2

Tommy Taylor of Manchster United scores England's first goal. A forward pass from Edwards to Matthews, square across to Haynes, a touch forward to Taylor and an unstoppable first timer found the net. (Below) Grainger, a new cap, scored two goals. Here he has just scored the fourth, a header from Matthews pass. That's Stanley in the far background.

This was one of England's best games

ENGLAND 4, BRAZIL 2
(at Wembley Stadium, Wednesday, May 9, 1956)

AFTER one of the most amazing internationals ever seen at Wembley, England gained a clear-cut victory over a collection of ball-juggling Brazilians who were without a team-plan of any kind.

The game had everything—penalty-kick failures by Atyeo and Byrne, a player walking away with the ball and refusing to give it up, and a wealth of clever ball play by both sides, especially Brazil.

A great start—Taylor scored in the second minute and Grainger in the fifth—inspired England to one of her best performances.

Though Paulinho scored a freak goal eight minutes after the interval and Didi equalised three minutes later, goals by Taylor and Grainger gave England the mastery earned by superior tactics.

Clayton, Wright and Edwards were the backbone of a fast, strong-tackling England. The forwards, well led by Taylor, marred their display by missing chances. Stanley Matthews again delighted with his wonderful footwork and had a part in three goals.

ENGLAND : R. **Matthews** (Coventry); **Hall** (Birmingham), **Byrne** (Manchester U.); **Clayton** (Blackburn), **Wright** (Wolves), **Edwards** (Manchester U.); **S. Matthews** (Blackpool), **Atyeo** (Bristol C.), **Taylor** (Manchester U.), **Haynes** (Fulham), **Grainger** (Sheffield U.).

BRAZIL : Gilmar; D. Santos, N. Santos, Zozimo, Pavao, Dequina; Paulinho, Alvaro, Gino, Didi, Chanoteiro.

Referee : Mr. M. Guigue (France). Attendance: 97,000. Receipts : £47,000.

Here it is - England's third goal, being scored by Tommy Taylor.

● ● ●

Not many get past England goalkeeper Reg Matthews and, he makes a nose-dive save at the feet of Gino.

Well, it's just one of those things! Billy Wright, captain of England, shrugs his shoulders as Brazilians walk off with the ball after a dispute during the England - Brazil match at Wembley in 1956

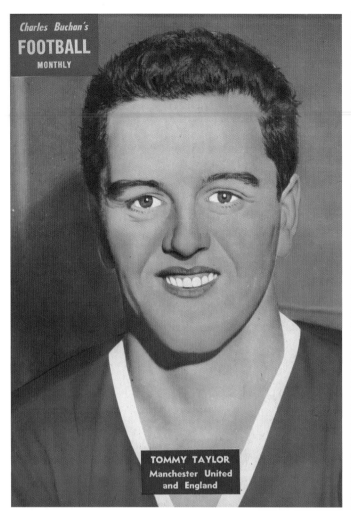

Charles Buchan's
FOOTBALL
MONTHLY

TOMMY TAYLOR
Manchester United
and England

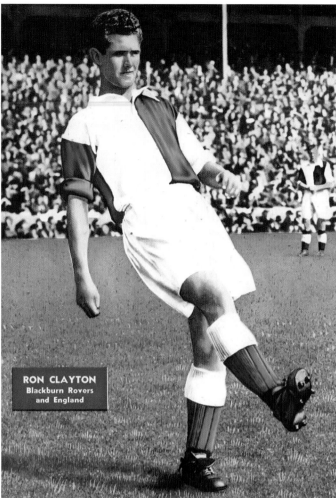

RON CLAYTON
Blackburn Rovers
and England

JACK FROGGATT
Leicester City and England

GEOFF BRADFORD
Bristol Rovers

THE GAME ABROAD
by BILL CROFT

They didn't enter for the Olympic Games because—

SOME Continental critics think a World Soccer League is probable by 1975, and a certainty by the year 2000.

They base their opinion on the stimulus given to international matches by improved air transport and the extension of floodlighting.

Artificial lighting is making the game possible at periods and hours which would be too hot for day matches.

Prophets of a World League—which would have to be played over a period of three or four years—point to the success of the World Cup competitions, the new European Club championship, and other international tourneys.

★

MUCH more interest is being taken abroad in plans for the World Cup tourney of 1958 than in this year's Olympic Games Soccer championship.

Millions of foreign fans will follow the Olympic clash only because it has attracted certain giants of the 1958 World Cup.

Olympic Games snow-white amateurs to play in the World all-comers tournament? All done by State-aid—job, flat, promotion, allowances, expenses and other privileges.

Says a Continental Soccer leader: "With us, the old idea of amateurism is dead. We didn't enter for the Olympic Games tourney *because our amateurs would rather pocket the money the trip would have cost.*"

★

GROUPINGS for the next World Cup eliminating games have produced no more than the expected amount of grousing abroad.

The entry—51 teams from the 82 countries affiliated to the International Federation—is easily a record.

The usual crop of sensational results is expected before the 16 survivors assemble for the final stages with Germany (holders) and Sweden (hosts), who get free passages to the first round proper.

★

THE three-team groupings, with one qualifier from each trio for the final stages, are hailed as an improvement on groups of four with two qualifiers.

A Swiss critic says: "England, bracketed with Eire and Denmark, looks a certainty for Stockholm. Scotland, grouped with Spain and Switzerland, has less than an even chance. Wales, with

Their amateurs preferred the money!

Czechoslovakia and East Germany as rivals, will find the road to "the last 16" very steep. Northern Ireland, bracketed with Italy and Portugal, will reach the first round proper only by a miracle.

★

WHEN all French professional clubs have floodlighting, League games may be played on Friday nights instead of Sunday afternoons, because of the effect of week-end motoring on match receipts. Twenty-five per cent of the higher-paying category of French Soccer fans are estimated to own cars, most of which, whatever the football attractions, are used for Sunday outings.

"Catch these people, and please others, too, by Friday night games," say the innovators. "*Give them a sports aperitive to their week-ends.*"

One enterprising manager thinks it almost certain that in two or three years time French League games in April, May, August and September will be played on Friday nights.

We are wondering if the last chapter of the story of Sedan, the workers' team I've told you about, has been written.

You may remember that, after doughty deeds as amateurs, Sedan turned professional for 1953-54 and, that season, finished fifth in Division II of the League and reached the Cup semi-finals.

In 1954-55 they won Division II and made a French record by playing 29 consecutive League games without defeat.

When last May, they reached the Cup semi-finals again, with practically the old one-time amateur side, a booklet about them, entitled "Once upon a time . . ." was published.

They went on to win the Cup, and a seventy-year-old Frenchman said "I again believe in fairy tales."

It is as though one of our amateur teams, say Crook Town or Hendon, turned professional and, with the same players, went on in three seasons to win a Wembley final.

★

INTERNATIONAL half-back Roger Gabet, Racing Club de Paris, said after a Paris v. Berlin match (1—1) in the French capital: "We ought not to play against German clubs. Like the British, they put too much vigour into friendlies."

Chile, given the World Cup tourney of 1962, will enlarge accommodation at her chief ground, at Santiago, to 150,000.

Argentina might have got the 1962 tourney if she had not been absent from world competitions since 1934.

"Had an easy afternoon — got sent off after five minutes!"

"Why don't you stop talking about the passes you make at football, and make some at me!"

ENGLAND'S TRIUMPH OVER GERMANY

A raid on the German goal by Colin Grainger (lying on the ground) and Tommy Taylor (just behind him).

A splendid save by Reg Matthews. He is watched by Roger Byrne (No. 3), Jeff Hall and Ron Clayton.

This was the scene of England's 3-1 triumph over the Germans, a great stadium packed with more than 90,000 spectators.

WE CAN WIN THE WORLD CUP IF...

Sweden vs England friendly match - 16th May 1956

IT seems a little premature to be thinking about the next World Cup competition which takes place in Stockholm in the summer months of 1958.

But it must be the thought uppermost in the minds of the F.A. selectors even now. Before many weeks are past, they have to select England's team to play Denmark in the first game of the qualifying competition at Wolverhampton on December 5.

England have been grouped with Denmark and Eire and each has to play the other twice, home and away.

Only one game—that against Denmark —will be played during this season. The other three games will be played next May and will take the place of the customary Continental tour.

I understand England will play Eire at Wembley on May 8, 1957—the day originally fixed for the visit of Russia's international side but unacceptable to them—the return with Denmark in Copenhagen on Sunday, May 12, though this day may be changed to mid-week, and the second game with Eire in Dublin on Sunday, May 19.

The December game with Denmark gives the selectors a wonderful opportunity for laying the foundations of a first-class side. It should not be a very difficult job.

Already young players like Reg Matthews (Coventry), Jeff Hall (Birmingham), Ron Clayton (Blackburn), Duncan Edwards and Tommy Taylor (Manchester United), Johnny Haynes (Fulham), and Colin Grainger (Sheffield United) have proved their worth in international games and are ripe for selection.

And there are other talented youngsters like Harry Hooper and Peter Broadbent (Wolves), Alan Finney and Albert Quixall (Sheffield Wednesday), Vic Groves (Arsenal), David Pegg (Manchester United), Trevor Smith (Birmingham) and Maurice Norman (Spurs), who only need the taste of international play to qualify for inclusion.

With the ripe judgment of Billy Wright (Wolves), Roger Byrne (Manchester United) and Nat Lofthouse (Bolton) to bring the best out of the younger element, the selectors have an abundance of material. It is up to them to find the right blend.

Of course, I have omitted those two outside-right wizards, Stanley Matthews and Tom Finney, because I think it too much to hope they will be able to hold their World Cup places in two years' time.

I expect the selectors will choose a party of about 18 players before the Denmark game. I hope they will call them together as often as possible.

I know that League clubs do not like their players to be away from training quarters for long periods, but I can see no reason why they should not congregate about five days before each international, Football League or representative game.

That would give them many chances of playing together and developing a keen understanding. An attacking plan could be thrashed out and, with judicious coaching, the side could become a devastating force before the qualifying games next May.

Then, with another 12 months to go before the visit to Stockholm, England could have a team capable of winning the World Cup.

Stan Matthews is foiled once more by Beara the Yugoslavian goalkeeper

Colin Grainger is thwarted by the upright against Wales

Billy Wright & Ivan Horvat, Yugoslavia's captain exchange souvenirs

Tommy Taylor opens the scoring against Denmark in the World Cup qualifier

★ ★ ★ ★ ★ ★ ★ ★ ★ ★ ★ ★ ★ ★ ★

COLIN GRAINGER
Sunderland
and England

REG MATTHEWS
Coventry City

JEFF HALL

BEDFORD
JEZZARD
Fulham
and England

Startling new tactical Soccer plan

OPINION by CHARLES BUCHAN

Former captain of England, Sunderland and Arsenal

STRATEGY plays an important part in football. Continental and South American teams place a lot of faith in systematic tactics.

Austria were the first to adopt the roving centre-half plan, with a great player, Ocwirk, taking over the role and making Austria the best Continental team for many years.

Then Hungary introduced the deep-lying centre-forward plan so ably exploited by Nandor Hidegkuti. There is no need to remind you they have ruled the Soccer roost for at least four years.

In contrast, British teams, with the exception of a few, like Manchester United, with their switching forwards tactics, Tottenham Hotspur with the "push and run" style, and Manchester City since they adopted the "Revie"

plan, have remained at a standstill ever since Arsenal transformed the game in 1925 by employing the "stopper" centre-half.

Now another Continental country—Spain—is branching out in another direction. It is "different" from that of any other country and is certainly amazing.

It has been sent to me by a friend in Barcelona. It is a plan devised by the football coaches of Catalonia, and, I think, will be discussed in Soccer centres all over the world.

In order to help you to understand the new theory, I have had two diagrams made—1 and 1A. I shall refer to them when explaining the changes in formation.

Briefly, the defensive set-up is nearly the same as that which brought Arsenal such supremacy in the 1930s—goalkeeper, three backs and a mid-field rover like Alex James to co-ordinate defence and attack.

The only difference is that the full-backs make their stand outside the penalty area. Arsenal's defenders usually retreated to the penalty line before they put up a resistance.

The change gives the goalkeeper full sway in the whole of the penalty area. He becomes more like a "fourth back."

So far, there is nothing complicated. But the rest of the scheme is not so easy.

Instead of an inside forward, like James, becoming the mid-field schemer, the job is given to a wing half-back. As another half-back, the centre-half, has dropped back to make the third full-back, there are two half-back vacancies.

These are taken by the inside forwards falling back into the half-back line. The positions vacated by the inside forwards are taken by the wing forwards, who move inwards and form a spearhead attack with the centre-forward.

This is fully set out in diagram 1. There you see the centre-half (No. 5) has dropped back into the third-back position. The right half-back (No. 4) takes over the midfield "roaming" job and the left half-back (No. 6) moves into the centre-half berth.

To fill the half-back vacancies, the inside forwards (Nos. 8 and 10) have fallen back on a level with the centre-half (No. 6).

The wing forwards (Nos. 7 and 11) converge towards the centre-forward (No. 9), making a three-pronged attack.

Of course, there can be variations in the deployment of the defence players. For example, diagram No. 1A shows how an inside forward (No. 10) can assume the centre-half role, leaving the left-half undisturbed. Similarly, the inside-right (No. 8) could be the No. 5.

(Continued on page 4)

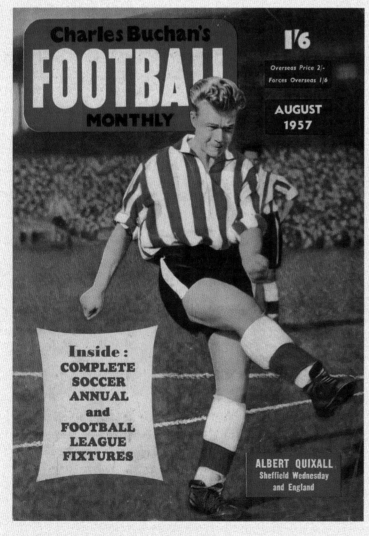

Charles Buchan's FOOTBALL MONTHLY

1'6
Overseas Price 2/-
Forces Overseas 1/6

AUGUST 1957

Inside:
COMPLETE SOCCER ANNUAL and FOOTBALL LEAGUE FIXTURES

ALBERT QUIXALL
Sheffield Wednesday and England

OPINION
(Continued from page 3)

There are, I believe, great possibilities about this novel style. There is a lot to be said for and against.

In my view, the advantages are:

1. *The wider radius of action given to the goalkeeper brings him more into the game. Not only can he deal with most of the high centres but he can start many attacks with quick throws-in to his colleagues.*

2. *The defensive line taken by the full-backs outside the penalty area reduces the chances of giving away a penalty kick to a minimum.*

3. *Defensive strength is concentrated in the centre, where it is most needed.*

4. *The midfield roamer can not only help in defence but support attacks made from any quarter of the field.*

5. *There would be increased fluidity in defensive movement with eight players taking part.*

6. *Wing forwards, instead of being out of action for a good part of the game, as they are now, would play a bigger part.*

7. *Reserves coming into the team would understand the system and the covering and understanding would not be weakened by the absence of star players.*

★

So much for some of the advantages. But I must say there are also points I do not like. They are:

1. *It is mainly a defensive plan. With as many as eight defenders, time will be wasted in developing attacks.*

2. *The style is too stereotyped. Each player must conform to pattern and must be skilful enough to do his job completely. One weak link would snap the defensive chain.*

3. *Variety of method would be cut down. The use of the long or cross-field pass would be very limited, and those dangerous raids by fast wing-forwards practically eliminated.*

4. *There would be no surprise breakaways. Nearly every attack would have to be started from well within the team's own half of the field, with the risk of a pass being intercepted with the players out of position. And the opposition would be given time to mark closely every man.*

5. *Opposing defenders would also concentrate on the approach to goal. Though there would be plenty of opportunities for wing half-backs to exploit the gaps on the flanks, the centre would still be guarded.*

6. *There is no allowance made for dealing with the unorthodox. Players like Stanley Matthews, Len Shackleton and Tom Finney could upset the machinery with their superb artistry.*

I have studied the plan very carefully. I have come to the conclusion that it cannot be carried out successfully by the majority of our League clubs or our minor clubs.

It is essentially a plan for experts. I have little doubt that a few British clubs, like Manchester United, Spurs, Wolves, Rangers and Celtic, could make a go of it, but I think it is too technical for the average team.

I should, however, be pleased if it were adopted by England's international team. Eleven top-class internationals could develop it into a World Cup-winning plan.

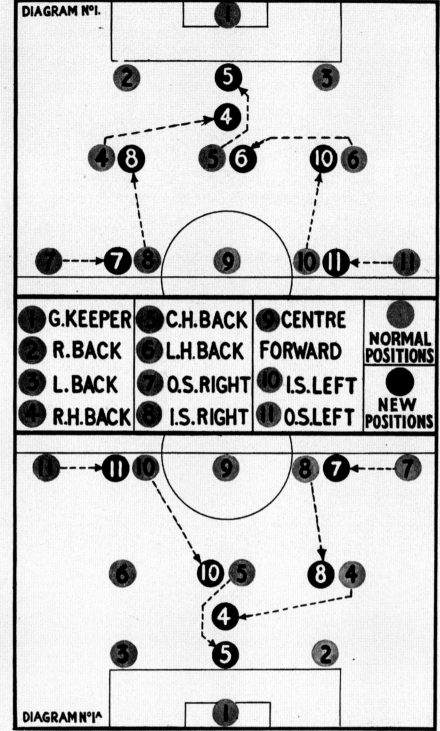

DIAGRAM Nº1.

① G.KEEPER	⑤ C.H.BACK	⑨ CENTRE FORWARD
② R.BACK	⑥ L.H.BACK	
③ L.BACK	⑦ O.S.RIGHT	⑩ I.S.LEFT
④ R.H.BACK	⑧ I.S.RIGHT	⑪ O.S.LEFT

NORMAL POSITIONS

NEW POSITIONS

DIAGRAM Nº1ᴬ

England's triumph over Denmark

ENGLAND 5, DENMARK 2
(At Wolverhampton, Wednesday, December 5, 1956)

A HAT-TRICK by centre-forward Taylor and two goals by inside-left Edwards crushed the amateurs from Denmark who put up a surprisingly good show in the World Cup preliminary tie.

Now England visit Copenhagen for the second leg next May with the commanding lead of three goals. They should make certain of a place in the final tournament in Sweden in 1958.

But there were many disappointments in England's side, especially among the younger element. Outstanding players were Finney, who outshone Matthews, Clayton, Wright and Ditchburn.

The Danes, all part-timers, were wonderfully fast, especially wing-forwards J. Hansen and P. Hansen. The superior stamina of England eventually wore them down.

Centre-forward Neilson scored their goals, the first two minutes after Taylor had got his second for England and the second midway in the second half.

ENGLAND : Ditchburn (Spurs); Hall (Birmingham), Byrne (Manchester Utd.); Clayton (Blackburn), Wright (captain) (Wolves), Dickinson (Portsmouth); Matthews (Blackpool), Brooks (Spurs), Taylor (Manchester Utd.), Edwards (Manchester Utd.), Finney (Preston).

DENMARK : Drengsgaard; Larsen, V. Nielsen; F. Nielsen, O. Hansen, Olesen; J. Hansen, Petersen, O. Nielsen, Jensen (capt.), P. Hansen.

Referee : M. Gigue (France). Attendance : 54,000.

SOCCER SIDESHOW

SIX months ago a panel of Continental critics gave first place in their "world ranking list of national teams" to Czechoslovakia, with Russia second, Uruguay third. Hungary fourth.

Making another list two months ago they put Hungary on top, followed by France, Czechoslovakia, Brazil.

Some privately apologised to Hungary for under-estimating her players in the earlier ranking. Others apologised publicly. Why did any of them bother?

The earlier reckoning was made on the basis of the poor results Hungary had obtained.

Now, in a Continental review of "leading Soccer feats of 1956," Hungary gets first place for what is called the "miracle" of the four away wins on her autumn tour (over Yugoslavia, Russia, France and Austria).

IMMEDIATELY after Hungary had beaten France 2—0 in Budapest last October, I asked a leading French critic what chance—in the light of that game—he gave France in her match with England at Wembley on November 27. He said:

"We're not so cheerful about Wembley as we would have been at this time in 1955 or 1956. Against Hungary our reshuffled attack was a fiasco.

"Our main hope is that England's football is still—if you'll excuse the term—a little old-fashioned, and that we can produce the sprightliness, and those sparks of genius, that have often served us so well.

"On their form against us, the Hungarians are making a come-back. The blend of old and young players worked well. It isn't the Hungarian wonder-team of a few years ago, but I would rank it among the world's present best three or four."

ONE of the great surprises of 1957," is how the victory of France in the World Military Tournament in Buenos Aires was described.

After eliminating games in various parts of the world, the Argentine, Brazil, France and Italy were left for the Buenos Aires proceedings, and France looked a 50-to-1 outsider.

Yet in the deciding match, after she had drawn with Italy and beaten Brazil (4-1), she skittled the Argentine 5-0 before a crowd of 60,000.

These Frenchman had for months been at the Joinville camp, near Paris, where prominent sportsmen doing military service are concentrated.

They get first-class training facilities and coaching, and chances to develop a grand team spirit.

When the winning team returned to France, they were given ten days leave. Their success did European Soccer a good turn, for South Americans have a tendency to under-rate the game on this Continent.

ONE of the arts of the game is passing the ball, and that's what we're doing," said a French Cabinet Minister when asked why the Government would not help build a successor to the out-of-date Colombes Stadium, near Paris.

The Government, the Municipal Council of Paris, and the County Council for the Colombes region have for years argued about financing the project.

French critics say the Colombes ground, France's biggest, built as an all-round stadium for the Olympic Games of 1924, is now "scandalously old-fashioned"; that Paris needs a ground to hold 120,000 instead of the 65,000 that can squeeze into Colombes; that many countries not so big as France have stadiums infinitely bigger and better than hers.

If France had pools, a small levy on stakes would provide the money. Another suggestion is that 100,000 fans should put down £20 each for the new stadium and eventually be repaid in tickets for glamorous matches.

WHILE I write, negotiations for the first inter-Continental match—Europe v. South America—are slowly but steadily progressing.

The International Federation has sanctioned two games (home and away), stipulating that profits would be equally divided between the European Union, the South American Confederation and itself.

There'll be talk about these two glamorous games when national leaders gather in Sweden for the World Cup next June.

Development of international play since the war, and now this inter-Continental project, are points for those who want fewer League fixtures.

An Austrian executive said recently: "International games, on club as well as national level, have, more than anything else, enabled Soccer to maintain popularity in the face of increasing counter-attractions."

THIS man deserves a title," claimed Swedish fans when they heard Italian praise of the "noble spirit" of their compatriot Gunnar Nordahl, centre-forward for Rome.

Nordahl, knowing his club wasn't well off, declined to accept bigger bonuses than his team-mates, though entitled to them by contract.

This so impressed the Rome directors that they wrote to the Swedish Foreign Minister thanking his country for producing such heroes.

"A man can honour his country in many ways," said the letter. "He can perform sensational exploits. But like Gunnar Nordahl he can also do credit to his race by exemplary conduct, professional conscientiousness, general integrity, and sportsmanship."

I've heard of no scramble to imitate Nordahl.

MANY foreign fans fear that force may count more than finesse in the impending World Cup games in Sweden. Such fears have been expressed to me within the past six months by critics of a dozen countries. Their views include:

An Argentinian: A certain type of football is called virile, vigorous, robust, fiery, hard, lusty, powerful, athletic, muscular or manly by people who at the bottom of their hearts know that the right word is 'rough', if not 'brutal'.

A German: The 'victory through force' tendency in Soccer has become commoner since the beginning of last year. It makes the replacement—with safeguards—of injured players the biggest problem in the game.

A Hungarian: I take the philosophical view that non-artistic players can't resist being too tough with the artistic.

An Italian: Every art-loving Soccer fan hopes Sweden will see a victory of brain over brawn.

A Spaniard: Football's greatest irony is that eleven 'thugs' can be allowed to finish a game against ten, or maybe nine, or even eight, gentlemen. My country won't be represented in Sweden, but my dream is that all the games there should be played throughout by 22 players.

There are other foreign critics who think the virility, roughness, brutality, or whatever you like to call it, is inevitably wrapped up with the increasing speed of all sports.

My own thoughts are for the World Cup referees. May abundant discernment and strength be theirs.

GIVE SUBBUTEO

If you – Your boy – Your Dad – Or the friend in your life is

FOOTBALL CRAZY

GIVE SUBBUTEO

THE INDOOR TABLE REPLICA OF ASSOCIATION FOOTBALL

SUBBUTEO Regd TABLE SOCCER

Handsomely boxed and complete with Goals and Balls, etc.

22 miniature figures dribble, tackle, crack in goals, dive and save them—and are always at your command to produce all the thrills of real League, Cup and International Football BY FINGER TIP CONTROL

PRICES 10/1d., 20/1d., 48/8d. Post Free or write for full details and order form to:

P. A. ADOLPH (DEPT 49)
LANGTON GREEN, TUNBRIDGE WELLS, KENT

Develop Self Confidence—Master

JU-JITSU

You can "get tough" and make any attacker helpless with lightning speed with the Morley Rapid Ju-Jitsu Course — or money back. Teaches you all the knock-out blows, holds, etc., shows you how to throw a stronger man to the ground in a moment. Develops your body and gives you self confidence in any encounter. You acquire this devastating weapon in a few weeks. For both sexes. Complete fighting system, 10/-. Details 2d. Sent under plain cover. **John J. Morley** (Ju-Jitsu).

A SWISS critic comments on the goal-posts decision for the 1958 World Cup games in Sweden:

"For the Swedish matches they'll be oval. For the World Cup of 1954, in Switzerland, they were square. Why does the International Federation allow either shape? Because oval posts favour scoring, and scoring is the salt of the game."

URUGUAY players apologised to the public for their poor show after being beaten by Paraguay in their eliminating round of the World Cup.

Then the President of the Uruguayan Football Association suggested a series of games between the two countries, with profits to go to Paraguay so her players could have extra comforts on their World Cup travels.

Other South American countries are expected to help. Paraguay will need it. Her biggest stadium holds 25,000, and strict economy is the rule.

1958 WORLD CUP — STOCKHOLM

AND

W.S.T.S. "ON THE BALL" AGAIN

We are pleased to offer complete arrangements for the World Cup Football Championships. Here is a wonderful opportunity to enjoy a first-class holiday and at the same time see the closing stages of the World Cup. Send for special leaflet outlining the following inclusive Tours:—

BY SEA	BY AIR (BEA/SAS)
13 days, £57 15 0.	Night Tourist, 7 days, £64 15 0.
	14 days, £85 10 0.
17 days, £68 10 0.	Day Tourist, 9 days, £85 5 0.
	13 days, £97 0 0.

PRICES INCLUDE

Sea or Air Travel from London and back to London; Meals en route; Hotel accommodation and demi-pension; Transfers in Stockholm; Best seats at the Solna Stadium for quarter-final, semi-final and final; Services of local representative in Stockholm.

To assist clients, an instalment plan of 12 monthly payments is available.

SPECIALISTS IN SPORTING TRAVEL AND ALWAYS FIRST IN THE FIELD

WORLD SPORT & TRAVEL SERVICE

(Prop.: Lairdways, Ltd.)

198-199 SLOANE STREET, LONDON, S.W.1
Telephone: SLOane 7242-7243

Join Buchan's Boys Club...

Fill in this Form NOW

Please enrol me as a member of the CHARLES BUCHAN'S BOYS CLUB, for which I enclose P.O. value 1s.

BLOCK CAPITALS

NAME ....

Address ....

....

Date of Birth...

Post this coupon with your P.O. for 1s. to Charles Buchan's Boys Club, FOOTBALL MONTHLY, 408 STRAND. LONDON, W.C.2.

and wear this grand badge!

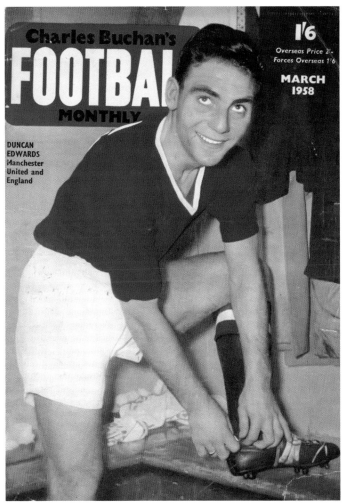

Charles Buchan's
FOOTBALL
MONTHLY

1'6
Overseas Price 2'-
Forces Overseas 1'6
MARCH
1958

DUNCAN
EDWARDS
Manchester
United and
England

Charles Buchan's
FOOTBALL
MONTHLY

1'6
Overseas Price 2'-
Forces Overseas 1'6
MAY, 1958

NAT
LOFTHOUSE
Bolton Wanderers
and England

Inside:
SPECIAL
CUP
FINAL
SOUVENIR

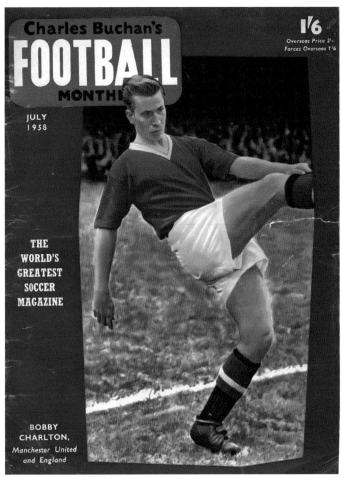

Charles Buchan's
FOOTBALL
MONTHLY

1'6
Overseas Price 2'-
Forces Overseas 1'6

JULY
1958

THE
WORLD'S
GREATEST
SOCCER
MAGAZINE

BOBBY
CHARLTON,
Manchester United
and England

Charles Buchan's
FOOTBALL
MONTHLY

1'6
Overseas Price 2'-
Forces Overseas 1'6

JUNE
1958

JOHNNY HAYNES
Fulham and England

F.A. SELECTORS are planning for the final stages of the World Cup which will take place in Stockholm, Sweden, next June.

I understand that the home representative matches will be used more or less as preliminary games with a view to finding the best England team for the difficult task ahead.

The selectors hope they can decide on the final eleven before the game with Ireland on November 6, and that they can keep the players together for the remaining internationals so that they can become a really blended eleven for the World Cup-ties.

After the Ireland game, there are six representative matches in which the team would have the opportunity of welding together.

There is the game with France at Wembley on November 27, the inter-League match with the Scottish League on March 26, the Scotland game at Hampden Park, a meeting with Uruguay or the Argentine or Spain on May 7 and a Europe tour embracing games with Jugoslavia and Russia, in May.

These exciting events should give the players the opportunities they need for getting accustomed to the style and peculiarities of their colleagues.

They will also have the chance to develop plans and tactics that must help in improving the team as a whole.

Providing the plans mature, they are a step in the right direction.

England would be able to field at Stockholm a side more representative of our football style than any international side called upon for many years.

There is only one criticism I have to make—the plans are twelve months late. They should have started before the first international a year ago.

Throughout last season there was so much chop and change—notably in the forward line—that the players never really got a chance to settle down.

If only the proposed plans had been in operation then, England's team would practically choose itself NOW.

I must admit, though, that despite the many changes in England's ranks during the last twelve months, the nucleus of a fine side is there. There seem to be automatic choices for at least six positions.

At full-back, **Roger Byrne** (Manchester United), with either **Geoff Hall** (Birmingham) or **Maurice Norman** (Spurs) as his partner, make an ideal combination.

And the half-back line, which served England so well last season, should again be a power.

Ron Clayton (Blackburn Rovers), **Billy Wright** (Wolves) and **Duncan Edwards** (Manchester United) should again prove the backbone of an international side which conceded an average of less than a goal per game in the 12 matches last season.

It is the forward line that has given the selectors the biggest problems.

The only near certainties one can name are **Johnny Haynes**, Fulham inside-left, and at wing-forward **Stanley Matthews** or **Tom Finney**.

But with the majority of places practically booked, the selectors should not have too difficult a task in carrying out their plans—especially when one views the wealth of talent at their command.

For example, there are goalkeepers **Reg Matthews** (Chelsea) and **Alan Hodgkinson** (Sheffield United). I feel that either is capable of emulating the mighty deeds of Frank Swift and Bert Williams.

At half-back, **Eddie Colman** (Manchester United), **Trevor Smith** and **Dick Neal** (Birmingham) are challenging for regular places. And all are so young that they must eventually make the grade.

In the front rank, **Tommy Taylor** and **David Pegg** (Manchester United), **Albert Quixall** (Sheffield Wednesday), **Peter Broadbent** (Wolves), **Brian Clough** (Middlesbrough), **Gordon Turner** (Luton), **John Atyeo** (Bristol City), **Bryan Douglas** (Blackburn Rovers) and **Jimmy Bloomfield** (Arsenal) will be knocking at England's door before November.

So you see, the selectors have the material. It is up to them to find the best blend in the quickest possible time.

Mel Hopkins, the Welsh left-back (extreme left) rushes in desperation after the ball which he has just passed into an empty goal. He is too late and Kevan jumps for joy as England are one up.

It is a good plan, but a year late...

ROGER BYRNE
Manchester United and England

Alan A' Court slides home the equaliser against N. Ireland

Bobby Robson scores England's second goal against France

The World Cup can come to Britain!

AFTER six and a half hours deliberation in Stockholm, the F.I.F.A. decided on the groupings for the World Cup preliminaries to be played in June.

I think they came to a wise conclusion when they divided the 16 competing countries into four areas—America, Great Britain, Eastern Europe and Western Europe—and placed one country from each area into each group.

This ensured that the four American countries—Argentina, Brazil, Mexico and Paraguay—and the four British countries —England, Ireland, Scotland and Wales —were not asked to knock one another out in the preliminary stages.

This is only fair. After all, if the American countries, or the British, were called upon to meet neighbouring countries in the first round, they could have done so in their own lands and before their own supporters.

There would have been no need for all of them to travel thousands of miles to do the same thing in Sweden. The top two teams in each group could have gone forward to the quarter finals.

As it is now, each country has been given a chance to make progress against opposition from other areas. It makes the competition much more world-wide.

There are of course four teams in each group who play three games on the League principle. The top two teams move forward to the quarter-finals.

In the event of a tie for second place, the two teams concerned play a deciding game.

The quarter-finals, semi-finals and final will be on the knock-out principle like our F.A. Cup. But in the event of a draw, extra time of 15 minutes each way will be played.

Here follows the one point I do not like about the competition. In the event of a draw after extra time, the teams will replay. Then, if still undecided after extra-time, the winner will be "determined by lot". In other words, by the toss of a coin or by drawing a ball out of a hat.

Action from the Scotland game

Derek Kevan scores an historic goal in Moscow

ARGENTINA, glad she avoided Brazil in the draw, expects a more difficult time than her neighbour Paraguay (which is bracketed with Scotland, France and Yugoslavia).

Argentinian players have been asked to damp down their optimism.

All South American fans expect Paraguay ("The world's most-improved team") to reach the quarter-finals. Said a Paraguayan trainer: "Technically we can match our opponents. In the matter of temperament, we should beat them."

The draw satisfied the French. Not that they under-estimate Scotland, Yugoslavia and Paraguay. They think they have a slightly-better-than-evens chance against all three.

From Yugoslavia's record in recent years you might have thought the draw would have come as a pleasant surprise. It didn't. She seems to magnify her opponents' qualities and triumphs, and minimise her own.

★ ★ ★

GERMANY was pleased with the draw. The following statement, surprising to most foreign critics, is credited to trainer Sepp Herberger: "We fear Czechoslovakia and Northern Ireland more than Argentina.

"The Czechs' excellent team-work, and the Irishmen's formidable energy, will bother us more than the 'ballet football' of the Argentinians."

Sepp Herberger is among those planning for a tactical change for each match.

The Czechs think they will reach the last eight. "Strong opposition," said a Federation executive when questioned about Germany, Northern Ireland and Argentina. "But that's probably their opinion about us."

SWEDEN, grouped with Wales, Hungary and Mexico, thinks the draw, could have been a good deal worse, and that she has an even chance of joining the last eight.

Mexico's recent improvement is a worry. So is Hungary, but Sweden thinks Wales can be beaten and had reckoned Mexico was in the bag. Now there'll be no easing up in the pre-quarter-finals struggle.

The Mexicans think they will give any team a worrying 90 minutes. "We know little about the Welsh, the Hungarians or the Swedes," they say, "but we do know our game is better now than it was in 1954, when we gave France a run for her money." France beat Mexico 3—2 in Switzerland in 1954.

We will remember them . . .

BENT   COLMAN

JONES   WHELAN

TAYLOR   PEGG

ROGER BYRNE

DUNCAN EDWARDS

DESPITE the many thousands of words that have been written about the terrible air disaster on February 6 that cut down so many Manchester United players and officials, I find it difficult to realise they will no longer delight us with their skill and courage.

United had become world-famous, even to a greater extent than Arsenal in their palmy years. They owed a great deal to the sportsmanship, the ability and the team spirit of great men like Roger Byrne, Geoffrey Bent, Eddie Colman, Mark Jones, Bill Whelan, Tommy Taylor, David Pegg, and Duncan Edwards.

To the relatives of these lovable young men who lost their lives I extend, on behalf of many "Football Monthly" readers who have asked me to do so, and my staff, our deepest sympathy. May time heal the deep wounds inflicted.

And to those United members severely injured, like Matt Busby and Johnny Berry, I sincerely hope they will soon be restored to complete health; and that before long they will be able to take up life's threads where they were broken.

To me personally, it has been a great shock. I had seen them, at Highbury the previous Saturday, give a wonderful exhibition of Soccer, one of the best for many years. I thought then, United, blossoming further with more experience, would become the finest Soccer machine of the century.

Adding to the shock was the loss of so many journalistic friends with whom I had travelled to many corners of the earth and spent so many happy hours.

They were able men who wrote about the game and players without fear or favour.

Since the war, Manchester United have been without rival in League, F.A. Cup and European Cup.

It was a team of experts playing for the good of the side as a whole. And now some of those experts have passed away, their parts in the victory plan will not be overlooked or forgotten.

England, too, will sorely miss the artistry and wholehearted work of Byrne, Edwards and Taylor.

I have been in the company of these outstanding players many times. Their modest, unassuming behaviour was a credit to their club and to their country.

Every day that passes, I receive messages of sympathy from all over the world. I pass them on to United officials with a sad heart. With the memorial words of former heroes: *"At the going down of the sun and in the morning, we will remember them."*

CHARLES BUCHAN.

VERY soon now the excitement and thrills of the F.A. Cup and League championships will be over. The players of the various League teams will go on their different ways and most of them will pass out of the limelight for another three months.

Which means that our soccer interest will be concentrated on the World Cup competition in Stockholm in June. And because England, Scotland, Ireland and Wales are taking part this interest will be general throughout the British Isles.

It is strange that in our tight little islands, there has been comparatively little preparation for what is regarded elsewhere as the World's finest competition. Our League and Cup commitments stand in the way of team building and team work training until a few weeks before the actual event.

South American and Continental rivals, of course, spend months finding the best collection of players for the job, as I know from experience. I have been in the training camps of many countries during the final stages of World Cup preparations.

Some years ago I watched the Swedes in training, just at the time when centre-forward A. Jeppson, the man who once saved Charlton Athletic from relegation, was bidding for fame.

So it was a great pleasure to receive recently a letter from George Raynor, that virile little Yorkshireman who will be Sweden's team manager in this year's World Cup tournament, giving me some details of what is being done by the host country.

Raynor, I have always felt, is one of those really top class Soccer coaches and tacticians whose true worth has never been fully appreciated in this country.

Formerly a player with Sheffield United, Bury and Aldershot, George became a successful coach in Sweden just after the war. He steered the Swedes to an Olympic Games amateur title in 1948 and was entirely responsible for their fine run in the World Cup tourney in Rio de Janeiro.

Then he had a spell in Italy, where he was associated with the Lazio club in Rome. He returned to England for a short while as trainer and then team manager to Third Division Coventry City.

George left his Coventry job. The Swedes welcomed him back with open arms!

His main task was to rebuild the Swedish national team which has been sadly depleted in recent years by the migration of many of their best players to Italian professional clubs.

The Swedes, naturally, are anxious to put up a good show in the first post-war World Cup series to be staged on their own soil.

George tells me that when he returned to Sweden just over a year ago, he travelled all over the country watching players with every club and re-establishing old contacts.

Now, he says: "I know every player, trainer and official like the back of my hand."

He has no vote on the Swedish selection committee which consists of Eric Persson (Malmo), C. E. Hallden (Norrkoping) and E. Jonasson (Boras), but sits in at meetings and gives technical advice.

The Swedes have had a trying time since 1956 when they forced a goal-less draw with England. K. Svensson (63

OPINION BY CHARLES BUCHAN

All eyes on the World Cup now

caps) decided to retire at the comparatively early age of 30, Julle Gustavsson, Kajan Sandell and Bengt Lindskog went into Italian football and the skipper Sven Ove Svensson was badly hurt.

In his letter, George Raynor recalls that he and his selection committee decided to base the Swedish side on Norrkoping, League champions in the 1956-57 season.

Goalkeeper R. Svensson was persuaded to make a come-back and the role of strategist was given to Gunnar Gren.

Sweden's first international against Austria in May, 1957, ended up 0—0 and the team's tactics were criticised as being too defensive.

"But," says George, "I was determined that we should not run into a series of defeats if we could help it. The morale of the 'builders' had to be kept up."

Against Hungary and Norway, Sweden did not concede a goal but it was still felt that the forwards must be more

In June, several combinations were tried and newcomers tested in "B" and Under-23 internationals.

Then came success with a 5—0 victory against Finland, a 2—1 away win over Denmark, followed by another five goal spree against Norway.

Last November the cream of Sweden's top players were assembled at Ystad for ten days' special training, coaching and exchange of ideas.

Sixteen of the party were chosen for the game with West Germany at Hamburg which the Germans won 1—0. "We deserved at least a draw and but for atrocious finishing by our forwards we would have won," declares George.

Following that narrow defeat it was realised that Sweden's priority need was an outside right and a goal-getting inside forward. The men wanted were in Italy, but Sweden got permission to use them in the World Cup this summer.

At the Ystad conference in November, elaborate plans were laid down for "off season" training based on the team tactics evolved for the game with West Germany.

This month the players again got together at Ystad with a view to building up a national team squad for the first of the new season's internationals against Switzerland early in May.

On May 18, the Swedes will take 20 players to a secret training camp a few miles from Stockholm and here selection of the Swedish players from Italy will be finalised.

"Obviously," says George, "if they are better than the homesters and can blend in, they will be chosen. Right winger Hamrin and inside-forward Lindskog are certainties."

Veteran Liedholm can be a "general" if he maintains his present form. There are doubts about Nacka Skoglund who although a top player on his day, is inconsistent.

The Swedes have a scout in Italy watching points, and Raynor himself expects to go there before the World Cup opening date.

In his most comprehensive letter, George Raynor suggests that soccer folk in Sweden are now wondering whether their side's chances will be affected because the tournament follows so quickly on a strenuous season.

But, as he points out, the same applies to the four British countries. He sums up by saying he believes Sweden have it in them to upset quite a few of the odds.

England, he thinks, still have a good chance despite the loss of players like Tommy Taylor, Duncan Edwards and Roger Byrne in the Manchester United disaster.

Scotland, he maintains will reach the quarter finals, for they are a hard side to beat. Wales are not a cohesive side in the best sense of the word, but with John Charles and Cliff Jones in their attack, they could win any match in 20 minutes.

Northern Ireland? They may provide the big surprise, thinks George, for they have a wonderful team spirit, allied to the outstanding skill of such stars as Danny Blanchflower and Jimmy McIlroy.

Danny, by the way, was my unhesitating choice as Footballer of the Year—and this choice was based on his consistently fine form for Spurs, coupled with his wonderful display for Ireland against England at Wembley, when he was the architect of a famous and historic victory.

Pele s

ENGLAND 2, RUSSIA 2.
(Gothenburg, June 8 — Group 4)

ALTHOUGH losing 2—0 after 58 minutes, England staged a fighting recovery. Derek Kevan put them back into a game they looked certain to lose when he headed in a Billy Wright free kick in the 65th minute. Five minutes from the end Finney equalised from a penalty.

Russia, without captain and left-half Netto, were the better side for much of the game but their robust spoiling tactics were unworthy of them.

At a time when England were showing up poorly, Russia went ahead through Simonian in the 14th minute. England's defence was again wide open when Alexander Ivanov scored a second goal in the 58th minute.

ENGLAND: McDonald (Burnley); Howe (West Bromwich), Banks (Bolton); Clamp (Wolves), Wright (Wolves) capt., Slater (Wolves); Douglas (Blackburn), Robson (West Bromwich), Kevan (West Bromwich), Haynes (Fulham), Finney (Preston).

RUSSIA: Yashin; Kessarev, Kuznetsov; Voinov, Krizhevsky, Tsarev; Alexander Ivanov, Valentin Ivanov, Simonian, Salnikov, Ilyin.

REFEREE I. Zsolt (Hungary). Attendance 59,000.

SWEDEN 2 *Liedholm 4min, Simonsson 80min*
Svensson, Bergmark, Axbom, Borjesson, Gustavsso
Parling, Gren, Liedholm, Hamrin, Simonsson,
Skoglund

BRAZIL 5 *Vava 9, 32min, Pele 55, 80min, Zagalo 68mi*
Gilmore, D. Santos, Bellini, Orlando, N. Santos, Dic
Zito, Garrincha, Varva, Pele, Zagalo

Sunday June 29th 1958

Attendance 49,737

Venue: Rasunda Stadium, Solna, Stockholm

Sverige'58
Världsmästerskapet i fotboll
8-29 juni 1958

ENGLAND 0, BRAZIL 0.
(Gothenburg, June 11 — Group 4)

ENGLAND'S performance in holding the powerful ball-playing Brazilians to a draw deserved praise. But they owed much to their defence in which goalkeeper Colin McDonald excelled with several superb saves while right-back Don Howe had probably his best international.

England's attack was disjointed and Kevan had another game in which little would go right. Bryan Douglas was again out of form and Alan A'Court who deputised on the left-wing for the injured Tom Finney was seen only in flashes in the second-half.

Robson and Haynes fell back to help out in defence whenever required, but could not match the shrewd ball-control of the brilliant Brazilian inside-pair, particularly Didi.

ENGLAND: McDonald (Burnley); Howe (West Bromwich), Banks (Bolton); Clamp (Wolves), Wright (Wolves) capt., Slater (Wolves); Douglas (Blackburn), Robson (West Bromwich), Kevan (West Bromwich), Haynes (Fulham), A'Court (Liverpool).

BRAZIL: Gylmar; Di Sordi, Nilton Santos; Dino Sani, Bellini, Orlando; Joel, Didi, Mazzola, Vava, Zagallo.

REFEREE: A. Dusch (West Germany). Attendance 50,000.

ENGLAND 2, AUSTRIA 2.
(Boraas, June 15 — Group 4)

AGAIN England saved their World Cup hopes with a fighting recovery after being twice behind in this vital Group 4 clash. Fortunately, Russia were beaten by Brazil and England earned a play-off.

In the 15th minute, Koller shot home from 25 yards through an unsighted England defence following a corner. Eighteen minutes from time Austria's second goal came when Korner's 30-yard drive bounced in off a post.

Haynes scored England's first 11 minutes after half-time when Szanwald failed to hold A'Court's shot. Haynes provided Kevan's equaliser with a typically shrewd pass. Wright, Kevan, McDonald and A'Court stood out for England but Robson was out of touch.

ENGLAND: McDonald (Burnley); Howe (West Bromwich), Banks (Bolton); Clamp (Wolves), Wright (Wolves), Slater (Wolves); Douglas (Blackburn), Robson (West Bromwich), Kevan (West Bromwich), Haynes (Fulham), A'Court (Liverpool).

AUSTRIA: Szanwald; Kollmann, Svoboda; Hanappi, Happel, Koller; Koslicek (E.), Koslicek (P.), Buzek, Koerner, Senekowitsch.

REFEREE: J. Blankhorst (Holland). Attendance: 20,000.

ENGLAND 0, RUSSIA 1.
(Gothenburg, June 17 — Group 4 play-off)

ENGLAND were really unlucky in this vital game for twice Peter Brabrook of Chelsea, making his England debut, hit a post with Yashin, the Russian goalkeeper, beaten, and once he got the ball into the net only for referee Dusch to disallow the goal for handling.

Ironically, Russia's match winner through left-winger Ilyin came off a shot which went in off an upright. Russia had the edge for the opening 20 minutes but England were on top for much of the second-half when the ball would not run for them in front of goal.

England with three changes, performed better than in their previous games but still lacked punch in attack although Brabrook was an aggressive winger in the second half and Broadbent showed flashes of skill earlier on. Defensively, England did well with Howe, Wright and McDonald outstanding. But the Russians were technically superior.

ENGLAND: McDonald (Burnley); Howe (West Bromwich), Banks (Bolton); Clayton (Blackburn), Wright (Wolves), Slater (Wolves); Brabrook (Chelsea), Broadbent (Wolves), Kevan (West Bromwich), Haynes (Fulham), A'Court (Liverpool).

RUSSIA: Yashin, Kessarev, Kuznetsov; Voinov, Krigevsky, Tsarev; Apoukhtine, Ivanov (V), Simoniane, Falaine, Ilyin.

REFEREE: A. Dusch (Germany). Attendance: 20,000.

Liedholm fired Sweden ahead after only five minutes. This was the first time Brazil had been behind in the tournament. The lead lasted only four minutes before Vava equalized, the same player added another shortly afterwards to give Brazil the lead. From then on the game was Pele's, he added Brazil's third goal after fifteen minutes and then helped Zagalo add a fourth before Pele himself finished off proceedings with a fifth to seal a 5-2 win.

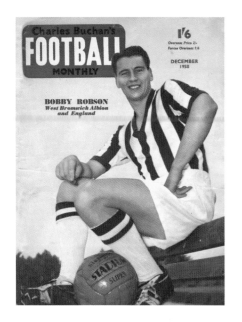

JIMMY GREAVES opens the
scoring against Spain

Once again England had left a World Cup early, not disgraced, in fact they could take great heart from the way they had gone 'toe to toe' with eventual champions Brazil. Tom Finney had watched the final back in Preston with friends, who had not been impressed by the Brazilian style of football. Brought up on 'blood and thunder' soccer they thought the South Americans played like 'fairies'. This was a typical belief of the British football fan, who would rather we didn't win the Cup if it meant altering the way we played and adopted 'foreign' ways.

In truth, although the preparation could have been better, the air disaster that took out three Manchester United players was a huge contributing factor to England not progressing along with the gruelling nine month slog that was League football back home.

Walter Winterbottom once more extracted further concessions from the F.A to help with the task of building a successful national team. Contrast our approach with the planning that had accompanied Brazil and it reflected badly on England, the world's premier football country. But now England would appoint their own physiotherapist and team doctor and would begin a campaign to monitor the fitness levels of the players. Eventually it seemed as if those in charge of the game had finally woken up to what was happening in the wider world of sport.

Four months after the play off defeat to the USSR, the Russians visited Wembley for their first visit. This time England made no mistake, trouncing the visitors 5-0, three goals from Johnny Haynes, who had been pushed further forward by Winterbottom in a tactical innovation, to make an extra

attacker. This game was also memorable because it saw the last appearance in an England shirt for Tom Finney and the final international goal for Nat Lofthouse, who called it a day himself after the next game against Wales.

The manager continued his policy of introducing younger players, they were definitely more open to new ideas, Bryan Douglas and Jimmy Greaves making their debuts over the next twelve months.

It was fitting that Billy Wright reached the milestone of 100 international appearances against Scotland at Wembley on the 11th April 1959. Billy had re-invented himself as a centre half in the mid 1950's to extend his career. A perceived lack of pace had threatened his wing half position, but he continued to serve his country both on and off the pitch with great distinction. He too announced his retirement on 105 caps, shortly after the USA game that concluded the summer tour to South America.

Wright, along with several other players had been badly shown up on this tour. Totally outclassed by Brazil and Peru, they were not even able to salvage any pride against a weak Mexico team, losing this game 2-1. The only bright spot was an 8-1 victory in America, but it would be clutching at straws to gain any satisfaction from that result.

The search was on for Billy Wright's replacement, Trevor Smith of Birmingham was given the first chance, followed by Bill Slater of Wolves and Ken Brown of West Ham, before the manager finally settled on Peter Swan of Sheffield Wednesday. The contrast between the two couldn't have been greater, Swan could play, but he was

best known for his uncompromising and physical attitude. Now England could mix it when necessary on the world stage, this represented a further change in philosophy.

In total, Walter Winterbottom had tried twenty six players during 1959 in an attempt to find a blend, but the final ignominy of the year came with a home defeat to Sweden in October, who in truth strolled through the game and deserved to win by a greater margin.

Any hope that there would be an upsurge in fortunes in 1960 did not materialize. Five further games without a win, ending with an October defeat in Hungary, seemingly left spirits at a low ebb before England began their next World Cup qualifying campaign with a game against Luxembourg.

Just as England had looked a team bereft of confidence and ability, out of nowhere they were reborn as a super scoring goal machine. A settled forward line now featuring Bobby Smith at centre forward suddenly clicked. 5,9,4,5,9 and 8 goals being amassed against Northern Ireland, Luxembourg, Spain, Wales, Scotland and Mexico. The undoubted highlight of this campaign being the 9-3 mauling of the Scots before a watching Queen Elizabeth, in a mesmerizing display of football. This meant that an incredible 40 goals were scored in only six games, the most devastating series of games in the history of the English national team.

The 4-2 victory over Spain was viewed at the time as almost as important as the defeat to Hungary had been eight years previously. On this occasion the crowd provided an electric atmosphere for the most anticipated international game for years. The reason for

BOBBY CHARLTON hurdles
the Mexican goalkeeper Mata

this was the presence of the all conquering Real Madrid players Di Stefano, Gento and Santamaria in the Spanish team. The English public had been thrilled by their exploits, particularly the 7-3 victory over Eintracht in the European Cup Final and only five months previously they had crushed England 3-0 in Madrid, but on this occasion the tables would well and truly be turned.

Any nerves England may have felt were eased by a first minute goal from Greaves, but in an enthralling game Spain fought back to equalize and looked to take over. It was at this point that England captain Jimmy Armfield who was to have one of his greatest games for the country, almost single handedly turned the tide as he tackled inside forward Luis Suarez out of the game. Without his influence, England took control once more and convincingly moved ahead and by the second half the crowd were treated to something they thought they would never see. In Madrid the Spanish players had humiliated the English with fancy flicks as the players lunged in. However, this time, after Bobby Smith had scored a twenty five yarder, it was our turn. Bobby Robson who had suffered in Spain collected the ball and beckoned the Spanish to tackle him and as they responded, he cheekily 'nut megged' the player and called his team mates to join in with a show of skill that had the crowd howling with laughter and appreciation. The significance wasn't lost on those in the press box who had been forced to endure England being humbled on some foreign field numerous times and patronizing after match speeches. At last the team had regained the respect of Europe and proven to themselves that they could compete with the best.

World Cup qualification continued with an away draw in Portugal, the other team in England's group, although the fact that Benfica were to play the European Cup Final only twelve days later might have contributed to their insipid performance. This was the most important game of the tour, so there was a slight feeling of anticlimax as England followed this up with a victory in Italy. There was personal satisfaction for Jimmy Greaves as he scored the winner only weeks before he moved to Milan.

Hopes for the future had been raised, but team selection was to be disrupted after Greaves and Hitchens moved abroad to continue their club careers in Italy. This meant they wouldn't always be available for selection and by the time the World Cup qualifiers resumed with the reverse fixtures, they had to be replaced in the line-up by debutants John Fantham of Sheffield Wednesday and Ray Pointer of Burnley. Qualification was assured after victories over Luxembourg and Portugal but the fluency of the previous season was missing. The goals had now dried up, they could only manage four goals against Luxembourg at a half empty Highbury, before two goals were enough to knockout the Portuguese.

The build up to Chile could now begin in earnest. Winterbottom began experimenting with his squad and tactics, debuts for Miller and Angus of Burnley, followed by first starts for Ray Crawford and Johnny Byrne, plying his trade with Third Division Crystal Palace and then a first sighting and a goal for Roger Hunt of Liverpool in a victory over Austria. The lack of support and interest in the national team was highlighted in that the biggest Wembley crowd for the last three internationals played at Wembley before the World Cup was only 45,000. The biggest

concern however was the lack of cutting edge, particularly when faced with the new trend of 'blanket defence', although many critics were convinced that when Greaves and Hitchens could be restored to the side, things would click once more.

Walter Winterbottom had already visited Chile to make sure that all arrangements were in place for the team's training base. England were to be the guests of the Braden Copper Company, based at their headquarters one and half hours away from the match venue. The company did England proud, laying out a perfect practice pitch and building a gymnasium. The site also contained a golf course and other leisure facilities including a snooker room. On this occasion, there could be no excuse on this score.

When the squad had been announced there were several surprises. Forwards Bobby Smith, Ray Pointer and Ray Crawford were left out and untried Middlesbrough player Alan Peacock was drafted in. Winterbottom also left behind Johnny Byrne, perhaps the closest in style to Hitchens who had been struggling for form after a hard year in Italy.

This time England set off early for Chile, taking in a warm up match in Lima against Peru, where Walter Winterbottom handed a surprise debut to Bobby Moore. Moore was considered 'one for the future' but because of illness to Peter Swan and lack of form in others, he was fast tracked into the team and was to star in the tournament. After a convincing win, hopes were high that England could put up a good show.

The choice of Chile as host for the World Cup was surprising, after Switzerland and Sweden, there was the thought that a more traditional soccer country should be chosen. Chile only really had four suitable stadiums. The one at Rancagua where England were to play all their group games only held 25,000 and was quite primitive. The European countries were also dismayed that it was decided to use the lighter Chilean ball, a

definite advantage to the South Americans, but as Brazil pointed out, they had used our ball in 1958.

As usual the tournament began with high hopes, but immediately degenerated into a free for all with defensive football and worse still, violence on the pitch marring the opening games. Four players were sent off and it was calculated that thirty four players had been injured just in the first round of matches. Injuries were even so serious that some players were forced to go home. Against this background England began their campaign with a disappointing 2-1 defeat. In front of only 8,000 spectators, the best that could be said was that at least this was a game played out in a competitive and sporting manner, in stark contrast to preceding games. Although England weren't at their best, it was an even game, but the result turned on two mistakes. Firstly Ron Springett was caught unawares by a long range effort, before an uncharacteristic slip by Flowers let in Albert for what turned out to be the winner. The Hungarians had clearly identified Haynes as the danger man and Markus spent the whole game shadowing him and as a result England's attack was blunted.

Winterbottom now had only two days to raise the spirits before the next game, a tough looking encounter with Argentina. The South Americans were once more deprived of many of their best players who had been 'stolen' by either Italy or Spain and relied on a smothering defence. However, on this occasion England produced a much more positive approach. The only change saw Alan Peacock given his debut in place of Hitchens. Peacock was to make an immediate impact, his goal bound header was handled and Ron Flowers, for the second successive game, slotted home the penalty. With Moore impressive in defence and Armfield supporting the attack from

right back, England took complete control and gained a three goal lead before the Argentinians were gifted a late consolation.

The England selectors were now faced with a selection problem. The deciding group game was against Bulgaria, considered the weakest team. By now exhaustion was taking its toll and really with hindsight, fresh legs were needed, but in the end the selectors decided on an unchanged team.

The match that subsequently took place was described as the worst international they had ever seen by the watching journalists. Bulgaria pulled everyone behind the ball and England had neither the wit nor energy to create anything. The players received such criticism, much of it based on a perceived lack of effort. Some went so far as to say they weren't bothered about representing their country now that they were on big money playing for their clubs. (The maximum wage had been removed eighteen months previously.)

The only saving grace was that with results going in their favour, England went through to the next round, although by again finishing second in their group, they had to face Brazil in the quarter finals and there were not many who gave them any hope of progressing.

In the event once more, England went out of a competition with their best performance. Along with Brazil they produced the game of the tournament so far. Although the selectors had once more named an unchanged line up, there was a surprise however when the teams came out. England had been forced into a late change, illness to Peacock meant that Hitchens regained his place.

The match started at a furious pace, England giving as good as they got. There was a respite from the action when

Jimmy Greaves captured a stray dog that had wandered onto the pitch. England's resistance was finally broken in the thirty second minute when Garrincha headed powerfully home. This spurred England on to further action and they gained their reward only six minutes later when Hitchens headed home after a Greaves effort had hit the post.

The second half was even more frantic than the first, Brazil laying siege and finally breaking England's spirit with two goals and as hard as England tried they were unable to get back into the game.

Once more England were praised for their tenacity and fair play, but again they had come up short and with the country hosting the tournament in four years time, there was real concern that England may embarrass themselves in front of a watching world.

Now was the time for decisive action.

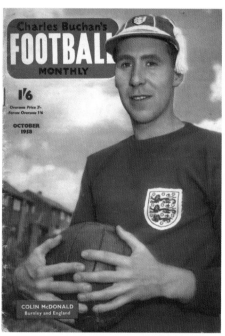

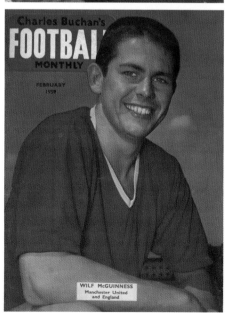

ALAN A'COURT
Liverpool
and England

ALAN HODGKINSON
Sheffield Town
and England

DEREK KEVAN
West Bromich Albion
and England

EDDIE CLAMP
Wolves
and England

DON'T WE CARE ABOUT ENGLAND?

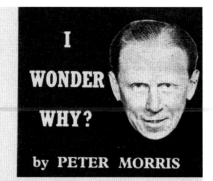

I WONDER WHY?

by PETER MORRIS

DID you shed a few tears, go off your food and lose sleep when you heard of England's soccer eclipses in South America? Or did you tell yourself that if more players from your club had been in our national team we should have done better?

Perhaps you thought that if Wolves, or Manchester United, or Arsenal, had gone out there as club teams to represent England, the Brazilians, the Peruvians and the Mexicans wouldn't have had it so easy.

Maybe you would have been right. But the point I'm trying to make is that the average fan in England is far more interested in his own League team than he is in our national team.

At least, that's the impression I get from letters received in this office over the past few weeks.

Wolves supporters were convinced that the League champions, as a team, would have done us proud. And don't forget they had four men in the England party, anyway!

From Manchester, those red-hot United worshippers chipped in with their claim that the whole of the Old Trafford attack should have been fielded by England.

United were represented by Bobby Charlton, Wilf McGuinness and Warren Bradley. "But," say our Manchester readers, "Bobby Charlton and Bradley would have been three times as effective if they'd had Viollet, Quixall and Scanlon around them."

See what I mean? Club before country every time.

What a difference in Scotland, Wales and Ireland, where pride and fervour is so intense . . . where the performance of the national team ranks above all else.

In Scotland, when England visit Hampden Park, the League programme is suspended. Nothing, in the eyes of the patriotic Scots, can overshadow the big game.

Irish and Welsh hearts beat as one when it's international day, and the players of those two gallant countries go on the field with the moral and vocal backing of thousands of devotees.

What happens in England? Wrangles and disputes, but more often disinterest, among Englishmen, whatever the team picked; a few puny cries of "Come on, England," at Wembley, and the League programme going on just the same.

Manchester United and Wolves supporters could not have cared less whether England beat Scotland last season. Locked as they were in the struggle for the championship, they only cursed the fates that took Billy Wright, Ron Flowers, Peter Broadbent and Bobby Charlton away from their clubs for the day.

Why the apathy?

Arsenal supporters bewailed the loss of Docherty and David Herd to Scotland, and Fulham fans, promotion almost in their grasp, wanted Graham Leggat and Johnny Haynes at Craven Cottage, not at Wembley.

There was more excitement a couple of seasons back, about Manchester United's feats in the European Cup, than ever there has been about an England win.

When Wolves walloped Honved and Moscow Dynamo, among other European club 'giants' under the Molineux floodlights a few winters ago, newspapers and television were full of it.

I'm prepared to wager that more people were talking about Wolves the next day than ever they have about England's international team!

Why, I wonder, this overall apathy to England Soccer performances?

Is it that the majority of our Soccer supporters really believe their own club performances are more important than our national good name?

Or do they feel that the present method of selecting and running the England side leaves so much to be desired that they no longer have any faith in our ability to put the national team back at the top?

And remember, too, so many of the best international fixtures are scheduled for Wembley that the provincial fan feels himself too remote to care very much.

There's a good case for switching more of the top class internationals away from Wembley and staging them on the major provincial grounds like Villa Park or Molineux, Old Trafford or St. James's Park, Newcastle.

These grounds have been selected for home international mid-week games and Football League matches fairly frequently. But more often than not Wembley is the venue.

Two of last season's most attractive fixtures—the games with Russia and Italy, both mid-week affairs, were played on a Wednesday afternoon at Wembley.

How many provincial fans could get tickets? And how many could take time off from work to make the long journey?

In truth, the provinces, especially the North and the Midlands, constitute the very heart of big Soccer in England.

They should be given a better deal in the allocation of the best international matches—particularly those against foreign teams.

Then perhaps the Soccer man-in-the-street would more easily identify himself with the England team, it's hopes, ambitions and plans.

And perhaps the parochial outlook which at present characterises our approach to England's part in international football would be gladly submerged in the country's interests.

I'd like to see that happen. Because not until it does can we seriously start thinking about a real England Supporters' Club.

The England team which met Northern Ireland and gave Joe Baker his first full cap. Back row (left to right): Johnny Haynes (Fulham), Ron Flowers (Wolverhampton Wanderers), Tony Allen (Stoke), Ron Springett (Sheffield Wednesday), Ken Brown (West Ham), and Don Howe (West Bromwich Albion). Front row (left to right): John Connelly (Burnley), Joe Baker (Hibernian), Ronnie Clayton (Blackburn Rovers), Ray Parry (Bolton Wanderers), and Edwin Holliday (Middlesbrough).

(Above): Santos Gilmar, Brazil's great goal-keeper, saves in spectacular fashion.

(Below): Antonio Carbajal, Mexico's world class goalkeeper.

(Above): Germany's Hans Schaefer (left) and Sweden's full-back Sven Axbom in a World Cup tussle.

We must become Continental to win

CHARLES BUCHAN

ON ENGLAND

SINCE that dismal November day six years ago when Hungary trounced England 6—3, our international reputation has sunk to a low ebb.

But not in home games. On our own soil we defeated most of the foreign opposition during our own season and in our own conditions.

Abroad, however, we suffered the humiliating 7—1 defeat in Hungary — only six months after the Wembley affair —World Cup failures in 1954 and 1958, and various Continental and South American tours that flopped badly. All these emphasize our shortcomings.

There is no doubting the fact that our performances at home compared with those abroad are as different as chalk from cheese. There must be some reason.

When you think back only ten to twelve years ago, and browse over outstanding victories like those over Portugal in Lisbon (10—0) and Italy in Turin (4—0), then the poverty of our recent performances stands out more vividly.

Those were the days when Stanley Matthews and Tom Finney were at their best and we had brilliant inside-forwards like Wilf Mannion, Tom Lawton and Stan Mortensen.

And I think the recent talk of curtailing end-of-the-season tours a sign of defeatism.

We expect Continental and foreign teams to come here and meet our best— for instance we have recently lost to Sweden at Wembley and will face Yugoslavia there in May—so it is only just that we should travel at least once a year to oppose them in their own surroundings.

In fact, the more we play abroad, the better it will be for our players. They would be blooded in the tense atmosphere associated with all foreign internationals.

The next World Cup will take place in Chile in 1962. Our youngsters, who will form the backbone of England's team then, must have some experience of the conditions they will encounter in the South American summer months.

The World Cup is now the real criterion of the Soccer worth of a nation. We have a poor record in this great competition and it is time we showed the world our true value.

What are the real reasons for our poor performances against other nations on their soil? There are several.

A dearth of outstanding personalities like the great players I have already mentioned; lack of direction at the top; continuing with out-dated methods, while foreign teams and players have improved by leaps and bounds, notably in team-work and tactics.

There are plenty of fine young players in Britain. In fact, I think there is a bigger crop now than we have had for years.

Youngsters like Bobby Charlton, Jimmy Greaves, Tony Allen, Tony Kay, Ray Wilson and Dave Burnside rank with budding internationals of past generations.

Yet the selectors cannot hit upon an effective combination that practically chooses itself, as it did in former days.

They have tried many players, all up to international standard when playing for their own teams. But very few of them have carved a permanent place for themselves in the National side.

It is not the fault of the players. They are plunged into internationals in teams lacking a strong personality who could encourage them and give them confidence; and they get little guidance as to the tactics and methods of the team.

A personality like Raich Carter or Stan Cullis could bring a great improvement on the field.

But where is he to be found? And a Matt Busby, as team-manager, could inspire the team and introduce workable plans of campaign.

But what I think is the most impor-tant reason for our failure is our persistence in sticking to the British style, fashioned since the change in the offside law in 1925.

These methods, improved by teams like Manchester United, Spurs—in their championship years, Wolves — against teams like Honved and Spartak, and West Bromwich Albion—in Russia, are now hopeless against Continental opposition.

For example, we know full well the Continental methods of man-to-man marking, obstruction whenever possible, and no charging of goalkeepers.

Yet we still persist in trying to overcome these handicaps in our own way.

We will not accept the facts that long wing-to-wing passes and long kicks upfield by full-backs are useless. And that players trying to run, or dribble, round opponents are doomed to failure.

It is clear to me that our modern England teams lack directive from the top. We need somebody in charge of our National side who can introduce new tactics.

The Brazilians have done it with their 4-2-4 formation. We can do it with a blending of our present style and the more modern 'on-the-ground' passing.

We must find something new, not merely revive ideas from the old days.

You see, the Continentals are coached from a very young age in the arts of team-work and positional play. It will take something original to upset their rhythm and balance.

The new scheme, whatever it is, would have to be fully tested against foreign opposition.

Some Continentals — the Hungarians, for one—have already started their preparations for the 1962 World Cup.

Why should we give them a two-year start? Why not start planning now?

I am certain that, if the matter is tackled with all our strength, England can be the next World champions.

LET US GET ON WITH THE JOB STRAIGHT AWAY.

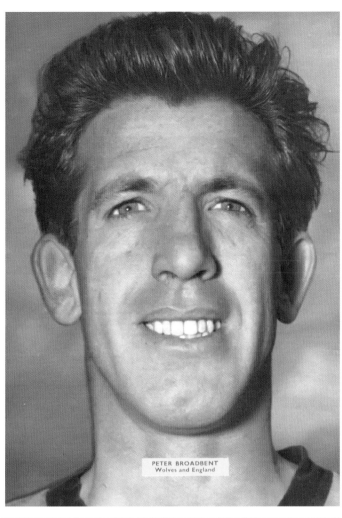

PETER BROADBENT
Wolves and England

DOUG HOLDEN
Bolton Wanderers
and England

GRAHAM SHAW
Sheffield United
and England

BRIAN CLOUGH
Middlesbrough and England

England skipper **BILLY WRIGHT** of Wolves smiles and waves to the crowd as he takes the field for his 100th international — against Scotland at Wembley.

This time Bobby Charlton didn't connect, and goalkeeper Bill Brown punches clear.

Billy Wright is chaired off by his team mates (left to right) Peter Broadbent, Ron Clayton, Don Howe and (in background) Doug Holden.

ENGLAND 1, SCOTLAND 0
(At Wembley Stadium, Saturday, April 11, 1959)

A GOAL brilliantly headed by Bobby Charlton in the 59th minute from a Bryan Douglas centre won England a rather leisurely game and so deprived the Scots of taking the home international championship outright.

England's inside-forwards — Broadbent, Charlton and Haynes—continually cut through the Scottish defence, and but for the fine work of Bobby Evans at centre-half and some magnificent point blank saves by goalkeeper Brown, the score would have been greater.

The Scottish forwards surrendered the initiative rather tamely after half-time and could make little impression on a firm England defence in which Howe and Wright excelled.

Wright, playing in his 100th international and his 88th game as England captain, had a relatively easy match, and what few chances fell to the Scottish forwards were thrown away.

If Scotland had shown a little more punch and thrust and perhaps scored, it might have shaken England out of a comfortable rut.

ENGLAND: Hopkinson (Bolton); Howe (W.B. Albion), Shaw, G. (Sheffield Utd.); Clayton (Blackburn), **Wright** (Wolves), Flowers (Wolves); Douglas (Blackburn), Broadbent (Wolves), Charlton (Manchester Utd), Haynes (Fulham), Holden (Bolton).

SCOTLAND: Brown (Dundee); Duncan McKay (Celtic), Caldow (Rangers), Docherty (Arsenal), Evans (Celtic), David Mackay (Tottenham); Leggat (Fulham), Collins (Everton), Herd (Arsenal), Dick (West Ham), Ormond (Hibernian).

REFEREE: J. Campos (Portugal).
Attendance: 100,000. Receipts: £49,840.

This time Bobby Charlton did connect, with a flying header to beat Bill Brown and score the only goal of the match.

The English and Italian captains, Wright and Segato, exchange pennants before the start of the England - Italy International at Wembley in May.

arises with some
trepidation and declares

The F.A. should take a tip from Churchill

I HAVE taken part in many an international beano in the sacred name of Soccer. All over the world I have sat, too well-fed, and listened to speeches of the most unbelievable drabness from our side and from the other.

I have heard the same Football Association *afficionado* get up five times after five banquets in a row and begin his speech with the well-known opening remark: "I arise with some trepidation . . ."

It got so that I started to say it with him as soon as he had managed to hoist himself to his feet. Even that impudence didn't cure him and to the end of his speaking days he was still 'arising with some trepidation'.

When an England party goes abroad you will find that at least one member of the host party, if not all of them, will make at least part of his speech in the language of his guests, English.

The nearest we have ever got to this catholicity in my own experience has been a quick translation of the host speeches by Raymond Glendenning of the BBC. *I have never heard an England official use even a phrase in his hosts' own language, and that seems to me to be a great pity.*

Surely we have a few linguists in this country one of whom could be co-opted to the touring party to do nothing more than sling the hosts' own lingo back at them.

It isn't that they don't understand our English. Most of them do—including the 'great trepidation'—as well as we do ourselves.

But there is nothing a Frenchman or a German or a Spaniard, an Italian or a Brazilian appreciates more than a foreigner speaking to him in his own tongue.

If that foreigner should happen to be an Englishman (Englishmen being notoriously the greatest language snobs in the world) so much the better.

Winston Churchill—who knows practically everything else anyhow—knows this superlatively well. When he went to Paris during the Liberation, he went to the radio studios and addressed the French nation.

"Prenez garde", he began, *"je vais parler francais!"*

He had warned them that he, the Ultimate Englishman, was going to do battle with not only the hated 'Narzy's', but also with the beautiful French language.

And he battled on throughout his speech and the whole of France rose to him as only the handfuls of *Maquis* had risen during the war.

There was a howl of delighted laughter at his atrocious accent—and a howl of affection that must have warmed the old battler's heart.

In every boulevard café and *bistro* they were drinking his health and doing their best to imitate his accent. He had been an heroic figure. That speech in bad French made him a darling one.

Why cannot the Football Association do something like it?

They don't have to carry a dictionary around with them everywhere they go. But somebody surely could be found—somebody who would have some knowledge of the entirely-different feeling of Continental people, who would have enough feeling not to ride roughshod over local susceptibilities, who

could pack into a speech some local allusions, some references to the history of the country.

Even the guide-books tell you enough for that . . .

The more international Soccer becomes, the more essential it is that the Football Association—and this becomes increasingly the case with the League and the top-ranking clubs here—get themselves somebody who can talk the language wherever they go abroad.

The day has gone when it was enough to be an English footballer: then Continentals just lay down in awe and watched how you went. Now *they* go and English sides stand by and watch *how* they go.

We have seen the passing of the era of the pocket of gold sovereigns and the arrogant manner.

Phineas Fogg could go around the world nowadays in much fewer than eighty days. But he would require more than a bag of English money and the bland assumption that merely because he was an Englishman, the 'natives' would fall over backwards to help him on his way.

Fogg lives, honourably, in the past. So does the time-honoured English speech, half-modest, half-bombastic, that has been the scourge of the Continental banqueting table for so long.

You know the kind of thing . . . "Your fellows were magnificent in defeat and we are proud to have met such gallant sporting foes" . . . "We lost, but at least our chaps were able to demonstrate once more that we English know *how* to lose" . . . "You have gained a victory, but more, you have gained many English friends . . ."

So it has been going on for year after painful year, and all in this frightful clubby English that completely baffles people on the Continent, particularly those in Latin countries who can see nothing but disgrace in defeat.

At a quite recent banquet in London the only foreigner among those present was called on to make a speech.

Everybody sat back to take the opportunity for a short nap—particularly when the gentleman prefaced his remarks with a rather halting preamble in which he apologised aforehand for his imperfect English.

Then he went on and electrified the entire company with a masterly speech on Soccer trends throughout the world—and in perfect English.

This was Ernst Thommen, President of the World Cup Organising Committee, and it was his performance more than any other I have heard, home and abroad, that gave rise to these ruminations.

CAN'T WE FIND JUST *ONE* LIKE HIM?

You must have heard the story of the late J. H. Thomas, famed member of the Labour government of his day, when he found himself alongside Dr. Wellington Koo, the then Chinese Ambassador to London, at a banquet.

To make conversation at the start of the meal, Jimmy Thomas said: *Likee soupee?*, whereat the Chinese beamed and nodded.

That was the end of their conversation, but when Dr. Koo, at the end of dinner had made a delightful speech in his precise Harvard English, he sat down to tumultuous applause and, turning to Mr. Thomas said: *Likee Speechee?*

SEE WHAT I MEAN?

England on Tour...

The lone victory

ENGLAND made amends for a poor first half by slamming in seven goals after half-time to record their only win of the tour.

Even so, England were a goal behind in the 18th minute when Ed Murphy, the American right-winger, beat Hopkinson with a 15-yard-shot.

The England attack played with such little punch and understanding that the result looked wide open until Bradley equalised before the interval.

Charlton, England's star forward, scored a second-half hat-trick including a penalty and Flowers netted twice with 40-yard drives. England's other goals came from Kevan and Haynes.

ENGLAND: Hopkinson (Bolton); Howe (W.B. Albion), Armfield (Blackpool), Clayton (Blackburn), Wright (Wolves), Flowers (Wolves); Bradley (Manchester Utd.), Greaves (Chelsea), Kevan (W.B. Albion), Haynes (Fulham), Charlton (Manchester Utd.).

U.S.A.: Ottobini; Farquhar, Cinowitz; Bachier, Evans, Traina; Murphy, Cameron, Carson, Looby, Zerhusen. Attendance: 14,000.

ANOTHER SLUMP

ENGLAND'S remodelled attack began well enough and in 17 minutes they were a goal ahead through Derek Kevan who headed in when Holden returned a Charlton corner-kick across goal.

In the 23rd minute the game swung Mexico's way when Ponce was replaced by Jasso. When the latter forced a corner three minutes later, right-half Cardenas headed an equaliser which Hopkinson might have prevented.

England slumped badly after this reverse and although they had two 'goals' disallowed by offside decisions after half-time, Mexico deservedly took the lead in the 53rd minute.

Howe missed his tackle and let in Hernandez who beat both Wright and Hopkinson and passed for Reyes to shoot into an empty net.

ENGLAND: Hopkinson (Bolton); Howe (W.B. Albion), Armfield (Blackpool); Clayton (Blackburn), Wright (Wolves), McGuinness (Manchester Utd.) Flowers (Wolves); Holden (Bolton) Bradley (Manchester Utd.), Greaves (Chelsea), Kevan (W.B. Albion), Haynes (Fulham), Charlton (Manchester Utd.).

MEXICO: Carbajal; Bosco, Jauregui; Cardenas, Del Muro, Flores; Del Aguila, Reyes, Gonzales, Ponce, Arellano.

REF.: E. de Queiroz (Brazil). Attendance: 83,000.

A spectacular backwood flip by the Peruvian right-back, Fleming, as England winger, Holden goes for the ball.

And nobody in sight — Julinho scores the first of Brazil's goals without any opposition.

PERU 4 ENGLAND 1

(At Lima, Sunday, May 17, 1959)

ENGLAND were completely mastered by the clever Peru players, who virtually cruised along to a crushing win. In fact, such was the inadequacy of England's performance that it must rank as one of their worst-ever abroad.

More than ever it was clear after this result that England's training and tactics at international level are hopelessly outdated.

It was a mistake by Wright that gave Peru the lead in the tenth minute. He mispassed to Armfield, and the ball went instead to right-winger Montalvo.

From the latter's quick pass, Joya flicked the ball on to Seminario, who scored. In the 40th minute another 'gift' chance gave Peru their second goal.

When Flowers failed to tackle properly, Joya's shot was badly fumbled by Hopkinson, and again Seminario had the easiest of tasks to score.

Half an hour from the end England made it 2—1 when Greaves netted from a Haynes cross to set up an individual record of having scored on each of his Football League, Young England and full international debuts.

Then Montalvo bewildered the England defence for Joya to put Peru 3—1 up, and nine minutes from time Seminario completed his hat-trick from a Joya pass to rub in England's humiliation.

Greaves and Haynes were England's best forwards, but there was little punch on the wings, and the defence had an unhappy afternoon against a magnificent Peru attack.

ENGLAND: Hopkinson (Bolton); Howe (W. B. Albion), Armfield (Blackpool); Clayton (Blackburn), Wright (Wolves), Flowers (Wolves); Deeley (Wolves), Greaves (Chelsea), Charlton (Manchester Utd.), Haynes (Fulham), Holden (Bolton).

PERU: Asca; Fleming, Andrade; Benites, Fernandez, de la Vega; Montalvo, Loya, Joya, Carrasco, Seminario.

REFEREE: Edwin Hieger (Austria). Attendance: 55,000.

BRAZIL 2 ENGLAND 0

(At Rio de Janeiro, Wednesday, May 13, 1959)

ENGLAND fought hard without much luck in this prestige game with the world champions in the packed Maracana stadium, and had most of the play in the second half.

Only ten minutes from the finish, Haynes hit a post, and earlier, Gylmar twice had to save powerful shots from Ron Flowers, who, together with Wright and Clayton, did well.

Brazil went ahead as early as the third minute, through right-winger Julinho, who replaced World Cup star Garrincha just before the game.

Outside-left Canhoteiro began the move with a pass to Pele, and from the centre Julinho easily netted.

Haynes and Broadbent set England on attack, and Haynes went close, but the Brazilians went further ahead in the 29th minute through centre-forward Henrique, who appeared to be offside when Pele centred.

Just before half-time Charlton hit the Brazilian bar with a fierce drive, and when Julinho was hurt, the Brazilian substitute, Formigo, came on and left-half Orlando went off.

England could not break through the formidable Brazilian defence, but at the other end Pele, Canhoteiro and Julinho missed narrowly, and Hopkinson saved brilliantly from Pele right on time.

Armfield did well to hold the dangerous Julinho for most of the second half, but England's other new cap, Norman Deeley, although trying hard, was overshadowed by the huge Nilton Santos.

Brazil were indisputably the masters before half-time, but England's second-half effort merited a goal.

ENGLAND: Hopkinson (Bolton); Howe (W. B. Albion), Armfield (Blackpool), Clayton (Blackburn), Wright (Wolves), Flowers (Wolves), Broadbent (Wolves), Charlton (Manchester Utd.), Haynes (Fulham), Holden (Bolton).

BRAZIL: Gylmar; Djalma Santos, Nilton Santos; Dino, Belini, Orlando; Julinho, Didi, Henrique, Pele, Canhoteiro.

REFEREE: J. Brozzi (Argentina). Attendance: 151,000.

Pele jumps for the ball but Hopkinson has it covered.

★ ★

THE GAME ABROAD

by BILL CROFT

"**D**ON'T be surprised if, in five years' time, Pelé is a back number," writes a fan to me from Santos, the Brazilian port for which the brilliant young coloured inside-forward plays.

"They are wearing him out," he adds. "No man can play as often as Pelé and keep his form for years on end."

The fan sent me a list of seven League and Cup games in which Pelé played in a period of ten days, in four cities. No two games were played consecutively in the same city, so there was a journey between each match.

"Admittedly seven games in ten days was exceptional," my correspondent says, "**but two games a week for Pelé are very common, and three fairly common. He is bound to crack.**"

★   ★   ★

Pelé (real name Edison Arantes do Nascimento) was 17 years and eight months when he won his World Cup medal at Stockholm in 1958.

He has so far kept his cat-like reflexes and speed. But I think they are right who say he is playing better now than he will be at the average international's age.

A Brazilian critic says: "Because of the way Pelé is marked and the extra-vigorous treatment some opponents give him, 90 minutes are as wearing to him as 120 minutes to some."

He is reported to get a "variety star's fee" for each appearance. Rather elastic, that term; but I have heard £100 to £500 per match mentioned. *He may intend to make a pile while the going is good.*

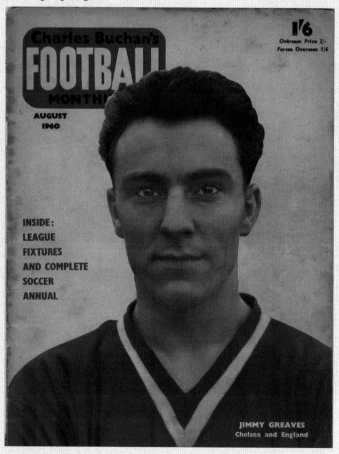

Charles Buchan's FOOTBALL MONTHLY

1'6
Overseas Price 2/-
Forces Overseas 1/6

AUGUST 1960

INSIDE:
LEAGUE
FIXTURES
AND COMPLETE
SOCCER
ANNUAL

JIMMY GREAVES
Chelsea and England

EDISON ARANTES DO NASCIMENTO IS BEING WORN OUT

URGING Russian participation in the European Club Cup competition of 1960-61, a Moscow official said:

"We have stayed out long enough. Arguments that our champion club would be too busy for this competition, do not stand up. Some of our leading teams meet eight or ten foreign sides during a season.

"Teams can't have too much foreign opposition."

★   ★   ★

FRANCE'S new star, 22-year-old centre-forward Francois Huette—first capped against Austria in Paris this season—buys a present for his wife every time his team, the Racing Club, plays away.

It is always a doll wearing regional dress. To a French fan who asked me—a Paris resident—if British professionals often buy presents for their wives when they play away, I had to say: "Sorry; I've no reliable data on that."

Huette was a professional at sixteen-and-a-half. He was going to be a teacher, and was doing well at his studies when the possibility of a Soccer career opened up.

Some thought his father, a schoolmaster, would be furious. But the father, a Soccer fan and old player, and sure his son would make good, said: "Sign, lad, sign."

★   ★   ★

AMERICAN fans applauded Prince Saud Faisal of Saudi Arabia for scoring four goals for Princeton University in one match.

Abebe Abate, of Ethiopia, stated to be "a member of Haile Selassie's Court," scored three in a students' game at Dallas.

The young Aga Khan played for Harvard University during his spell in the U.S.

OPINION

by CHARLES BUCHAN
Former captain of England, Arsenal and Sunderland

THIS WAY WILL NOT WIN NEXT WORLD CUP

RECENT events in the Council chambers of English football make the future prospects of our international Soccer look decidedly grim.

Following the proposal that summer tours abroad by England teams should be restricted to one every two years, I learn that the F.A. International Selection Committee is putting forward to the other United Kingdom Associations and to the Football League a recommendation to suspend the British championship in the season before the 1962 World Cup in Chile.

The reason given is that England will have to play four ties, two away and two at home, in the qualifying round for the World Cup.

That would mean seven internationals in season 1961-62, which is three more than the four allowed in the 1956 agreement with the Football League.

So, to pander to the Football League, the F.A. restricts the opportunity for giving our National side invaluable practice and experience before taking part in the World Cup.

In view of the fact that the Selection Committee have, at least this season, acted boldly and wisely in choosing a young side that can be groomed for the World Cup, I think this is a strange recommendation.

perience it can get before taking part in the World Cup. Yet here are the selectors throwing away the chance three years before the actual event.

The surprising part to me is that, out of nine members on the Senior Selection Committee, only two are not also members of the League Management Committee.

Surely they could have effected some compromise by which the international programme could have gone on as usual.

For instance, if the qualifying World Cup games took place in mid-week, there would be little interference with the League programme if all seven games were played.

After all, the World Cup takes place only once every four years. And a brave showing in this competition does more for our Soccer prestige than the League championship or F.A. Cup.

I am sure the majority of League clubs would not object very strongly against their players being chosen for the extra games. In fact, as they are likely to be young players, I believe they would welcome their selection.

So far this season, the F.A. selectors have stuck to their guns when choosing England teams. I hope they will not be discouraged by the poor displays given in some of the internationals.

backs in the form of defeats like the one by Sweden at Wembley in October. But I am sure it will pay off in the long run.

It is worth remembering that by World Cup time in 1962, youngsters like Joe Baker (Hibernian), Tony Allen (Stoke), Jimmy Greaves (Chelsea), Bobby Charlton (Manchester United) and Eddie Holliday (Middlesbrough) will be mature and experienced campaigners right up to world-class standards.

There is no doubt that England will have the talent to put a bold front in Chile. In fact, I am certain that, if properly groomed, it can come very near to winning the World Cup.

"Selectors must stick to their guns"...

The main reason, in my opinion, why England's international teams have fared so badly in previous World Cup competitions is the poor standard of team-work compared with those of Continental and foreign opposition.

There is no doubt in my mind that our present methods are to blame for our failures. Fast, breakaway attacks with long passes and high centres are futile against the close marking and obstructive defensive tactics of our World Cup rivals.

In the arts of team-work, we should take a leaf out of their book. If necessary, we should employ a coach like George Raynor, who piloted Sweden into the 1958 final in Stockholm, or even a crack Continental to put us on the right road.

They know the ways and means that bring success against any opposition. They could, at least, introduce the right methods.

I know it will be said that our National teams do not have enough time together to assimilate new tactics. But it is not time that is wanted. It is the proper plan.

When the offside law was changed in 1925, I recall Arsenal introducing the 'stopper' centre-half, with a scheming inside-left. The players took to it immediately and were highly successful.

And I remember the Great Britain team that trounced Rest of Europe 6—1 at Hampden Park in 1947. Great players like Billy Steel, Wilf Mannion, Ron Burgess, Jack Vernon and Archie Macaulay had never previously played with some of their colleagues.

Then there was the Rest of Europe eleven that defeated a Great Britain side 4—1 at Belfast in 1956. And the Continental F.I.F.A. eleven that drew 4—4 with England at Wembley in 1954. This team consisted of Johnny Carey, an Irishman, and ten Continentals who, between them, spoke seven different languages.

a day or two together in practice and training. Yet each gave a wonderful exhibition of how the game can be, and should be, played.

Our players are good enough and brainy enough to master any new schemes quickly. And improve upon them considerably. So why should we not pocket our pride and make use of anything that other countries can offer?

At this stage of the season, it is the practice to ponder over the F.A. Cup competition that will engage a lot of our attention during the next few months.

Who will be the 1960 winners at Wembley? One thing can almost be taken for granted. Seeing that the last team outside the First Division to hold the Cup was West Bromwich Albion, way back in 1931, the honours will most likely go to a top-circle club.

In years gone by, teams that were hovering round the bottom half of the First Division table were, in a lot of cases, successful. But in recent seasons that has changed.

Teams like Manchester United, Bolton Wanderers, Nottingham Forest and Blackpool, all recent winners, occupied top-half places while they were engaged on their winning run.

Therefore, in picking out the teams that I expect to figure prominently in this year's competition, I am banking on sides that, though they are unlikely to win the League championship, are absolutely safe from relegation worries.

That limits my choice to about half a dozen clubs. They are West Ham United, Burnley, Preston North End, Bolton Wanderers, Arsenal and Manchester United.

Of the six, the two with the most reliable defences are West Ham United and Bolton. For this reason, I give them preference over the others.

But I should not be surprised if Manchester United came right back to their old form before very long. Once the defence has been tightened up, they will be more like their old selves.

BOBBY CHARLTON (Manchester United)

PETER SWAN
Sheffield Wednesday
and England

DON HOWE
West Bromwich Albion

GERRY HITCHENS
Aston Villa
and England

ENGLAND
V
WALES

'Sharp shooter' Brian Clough shoots wide of the target as keeper Jack Kelsey and his defenders make a desperate attempt to put the striker off.

Yugoslav goal-keeper Soskic dives at the feet of on-rushing Baker, of England.

Agne Simonsson, Sweden's centre forward hurdles over Eddie Hopkinson on his way to goal.

John Connelly opens the scoring from close range against Sweden at Wembley.

The hapless Belyayev is beaten a fourth time as England inside-right Bobby Charlton smashes in an unstoppable shot from the penalty spot. Behind Charlton, Nat Lofthouse, hands on knees, watches approvingly.

ENGLAND 4-2-4 PLAN WORKS AGAIN

Ronnie Clayton leads out England against Yugoslavia at Wembley

Ron Springett in action

With Swan again in attendance, Hodgkinson goes down to check another raid by Cliff Jones.

The acrobatic end of an unsuccessful attempt by Graham Williams, the Welsh left-back, to stop England's fifth goal.

ALL TOGETHER
IN THE
TRIBAL DANCE
(SPANISH STYLE)

PLAYERS of Barcelona, Spanish champions and Cup-holders, are given a terrific pep preliminary for big matches from their French trainer, Helenio Herrara. He stirs them up, mentally and physically, in a vast, bare room at club headquarters. "It looks like a tribal show," said a spectator.

The sustained and strenuous movements just before a game, would alarm some British trainers. But, in fact, it is the oral stuff that is the most surprising.

Herrara shouts questions like: *"Why shall we win this match?"*, and *"What can we expect from you today?"* The players make answers such as *"Count on me!"* and *"We shall play as one man!"*

When one particular session ended, a player kissed a lucky charm. Another prayed. A third looked as though he was in a trance.

Yes, it looked like tribal stuff. The sort of thing which Anglo - Saxons couldn't persuade themselves to do even if their trainer assured them it would help.

Apart from anything else, most of them wouldn't be able to take it seriously.

The thing to remember, though, is that it seems to be good for Spaniards; *that in psychology, as well as in other things, it has paid foreigners to break with British traditional methods.*

HALF of Spain's 16 First Division teams have foreign trainers, including Brazilian, French, Czech and Yugoslav.

The argument in support of them (which I have already mentioned) is that foreign trainers not only introduce useful new methods, but that the players 'have more respect for them'.

A Spanish critic: "Our employment of foreign trainers has surprised fans in Britain. Would not some British clubs, on their form in recent years, benefit by Continental trainers?"

There's another side, however, to the Spanish trainer picture. When things go wrong for a team, in no country in the world is the trainer blamed with more fury than in Spain; in no country does his job seem more uncertain.

"The dance of the damned begins," wrote a Madrid critic when, this season, several sackings seemed to be looming.

WINGS of the Soviet, a well-known Russian club, has been in hot water over alleged demands for excessive fees for exhibition games.

It is fairly common abroad for top-grade sides to play against 'little' teams in towns that otherwise would never see star players.

THE GAME ABROAD
by
BILL CROFT

Wings of the Soviet, according to Russian charges, haggled about their fee (above expenses) just before a kick-off, in such a town, and threatened 'No cash, no play'

They left another town without playing.

The flavour in these Russian complaints about a Russian club is in the fact that professionalism is not recognised in the Soviet.

The criticising newspaper asks : *"Where goes the money that is collected by these dealers in football?"*

* * *

HAS Stanley Matthews an Italian ancestor? An Italian critic says: "I think he hasn't, but had an Italian club been after him in his prime, and he had been willing to leave England, I'm pretty sure an Italian forbear would have been found for him."

Transfer to Italian teams of foreign players above a certain quota can be facilitated if the players have Italian ancestry.

Jokers guarantee to find such a forbear of any foreigner sought by a rich Italian club.

* * *

WHILE France's team was in Sofia to play Bulgaria this season (Bulgaria 1, France 0), the French players sent home 543 picture-postcards.

Goalkeeper Dominique Colonna was top scorer with 60. France's No. 1 player, centre-forward Raymond Kopa, wrote only five.

HERE is an item particularly for treasurers. For every thousand francs paid by spectators at the Parc des Princes, Paris, 387 go to the home team (the Racing Club) and 258 to the visitors.

The remainder: Ground maintenance, 123; taxes, 115; National Federation and the League, 66; organisation expenses, 40; ticket tax-stamps, 11

* * *

COLOMBIA, the South American republic, still makes news by its employment of foreign players (you'll remember several Britons going there years ago).

Teams may employ up to seven foreign players each—and some do it. Most of the non-Colombians are Argentinians but there are 'wanderers' from all over the world.

At one time, Colombian professional clubs employed 250 foreigners between them.

* * *

I HAVE been counting the number of teams in top divisions of some of the foreign leagues, and make them to be:

Argentina, 16; Austria, 14; Belgium, 16; Brazil, 12; Czechoslovakia, 12; France, 20; Holland, 18; Hungary, 14; Italy, 18; Paraguay, 10; Poland, 12; Portugal, 14; Spain, 16; Uruguay, 10; Yugoslavia, 12.

England's First Division beats the lot for numerical strength. Whether the number of League engagements has anything to do with the standard of play, is a point you can argue.

* * *

CONTINENTAL and South American referees and administrators are concerned about the increase of trickery on the field.

It is not sufficient, they say, that calculated offences (deliberate handling, pulling, tripping, and so on) should be punished by a simple free-kick.

"Trickery pollutes the game, and could destroy it," writes a German. *"It must be made non-paying."*

" She believes a wife should always be with her husband ! "

Revenge for England!!!

England v. Spain

No. 1 . . . by Greaves

No. 2 . . . by Douglas

No. 3 . . . by Smith

No. 4 . . . by Smith
(made quite sure by Haynes)

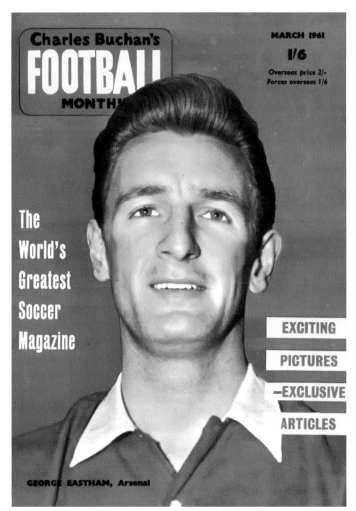

Charles Buchan's
FOOTBALL
MONTHLY

MARCH 1961
1/6
Overseas price 2/-
Forces overseas 1/6

The World's Greatest Soccer Magazine

EXCITING

PICTURES

—EXCLUSIVE

ARTICLES

GEORGE EASTHAM, Arsenal

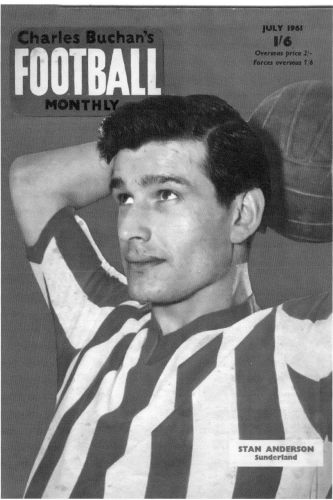

Charles Buchan's
FOOTBALL
MONTHLY

JULY 1961
1/6
Overseas price 2/-
Forces overseas 1/6

STAN ANDERSON
Sunderland

Charles Buchan's
FOOTBALL
MONTHLY

Overseas price 2/-
Forces overseas 1/6
1/6

MAY 1961

BOBBY SMITH
Spurs and England

INSIDE: CUP FINAL SOUVENIR

Charles Buchan's
FOOTBALL
MONTHLY

JULY, 1960

1/6
Overseas Price 2/-
Forces Overseas 1/6

ALAN HODGKINSON
Sheffield United and England

THE GREATEST GLORY

is to be
Captain of England

*(except for
speech making)*

Johnny Haynes is 'chaired' off the Wembley pitch after England had beaten Scotland 9-3—a record—in April, 1961.

by JOHNNY HAYNES

IF I were asked to choose between any of the game's honours I would take that of being captain of England as the greatest of all. Of course, I would like to win the Cup with Fulham. And I would be thrilled to lead, or play for my club in the European Cup Final.

I regard being the captain of England as the greatest honour not merely because I am captain, and the other things seem rather out of reach. In all sincerity, I prize this honour above all others.

And I dare say that any player who has, or has had, the privilege of leading his country would give you the same answer.

I am jealous of England's international reputation, I want it to be of the highest while I lead her. But then so does any player taking part, be he the captain or the newest boy in an international side.

Don't think I am trying to say that I feel I have to give more than the rest of the lads. No player spares himself on international duty. But as captain you feel more responsible—as you should do.

I am a demanding skipper. I ask a lot from players, at country and club level. But I make no apology for this because I demand a lot from myself, and however I am judged in my role as captain and player I would not wish that judgment to be by anything but the highest measure. So, if I find my team-mates failing in

that respect then it is up to me to try to set it right. That is the yardstick I expect to be used on my own performances when they don't come up to scratch.

Billy Wright was an ideal captain, as I came to learn from long experience of serving under him. Billy was a bit quieter than I am when he did the job, but we are not all alike.

I know I do a lot of shouting during a game . . . I always have done. And when things are not going as they should then somebody has to shout. As captain it is my job.

In any case, nobody has ever seen a match without a lot of noise. To most players shouting is instinctive. I make as much noise, often far more, as the rest. But there it is, and I can't see myself changing now.

I am often asked how I feel when my teams, either Fulham or England, come in for heavy criticism . . . and we have had plenty.

Let me say that I respect everybody's right to criticise. I am a critic when I sit and watch a match. But I don't take a lot of notice of criticism. I am my own severest critic. I have been in the game long enough to know when and why things have gone wrong. I accept that we can all have our say, but I believe myself to be the judge of what should be done. I find it easier to captain England than Fulham. With an international

The proudest moment in the life of any British footballer . . . the moment when he meets the Queen at a time of victory. Here, Haynes receives the international trophy after England's 1961 win over Scotland.

captain of Fulham and England

side you don't expect to find the same failings as in a club team. I am not called upon to make changes; all that has been thrashed out beforehand and I would hesitate to alter things, for a most important reason . . .

When a player wins a cap you accept that he has done so because he is thought to be the best in his particular position. Anybody making changes could cause harm to a player's further international chances.

With your club it is different. A captain is more inclined to make changes because it is likely to be just another game, and he probably has a greater knowledge of how his club-mates might react in different positions.

Each job has its worries. As a club and country captain I feel the responsibilities—but I like them—and I worry perhaps a bit more than most. I feel I would not be worth my salt if I didn't.

What used to be one of the hardest jobs attached to leading England was the speech-making at banquets. But I have long since got over that first stage-fright.

I haven't had to make anywhere near as many speeches as Billy Wright, but I have now climbed to my feet often enough to feel more able to tackle this social part of my job. Not for a moment would I dream of trying to tell anybody how to lead a side. After all, I don't suppose I am everybody's cup of tea as captain

Jimmy Greaves completes his hat-trick

MAGNIFICENT ENGLAND

ENGLAND 9, SCOTLAND 3
(At Wembley Stadium, Saturday, April 15, 1961)

A RECORD English victory, Scotland's heaviest defeat in all international matches, and the highest-scoring game between the two countries since the series began in 1872, made this a memorable and historic match.

England's magnificent win was again a triumph for Walter Winterbottom and the 4–2–4 plan. It was also remarkable for the individual success of Haynes and Greaves who have never played so well together.

The Scots fought hard and at one time pulled back to 3—2 after being three goals down in the opening half-hour. But they could not match England for pace and ideas and, above all, for their deadly shooting which brought five goals in 14 minutes, the last four of them in seven minutes late in the second-half.

McNeill, the young Scottish centre-half, was their best player although Law and Wilson tried hard in attack.

Greaves and Haynes scored five of the England goals between them. Charlton, although going near, was the only forward not to score.

Scorers: England—Robson (9 min.), Greaves (19 and 20 min.), Douglas (56 min.), Smith (73 min.), Haynes (78 and 80 min.), Greaves (82 min.), Smith (85 min.). Scotland: Mackay (48 min.), Wilson (53 and 75 min.).

PETER MORRIS.

ENGLAND: Springett (Sheffield Wednesday); Armfield (Blackpool), McNeil (Middlesbrough); Robson (W.B.A.), Swan (Sheffield Wednesday), Flowers (Wolves); Douglas (Blackburn), Greaves (Chelsea), Smith (Tottenham), Haynes (Fulham), Charlton (Manchester Utd.).
SCOTLAND: Haffey (Celtic); Shearer (Rangers), Caldow (Rangers); Mackay (Tottenham), McNeill (Celtic), McCann (Motherwell); McLeod (Hibernian), Law (Manchester City), St. John (Motherwell), Quinn (Motherwell), Wilson (Rangers).
REFEREE: M. Lequesne (France). Attendance: 100,000.

FINAL TABLE

	P.	W.	L.	Goals F.	A.	Pts.
England	3	3	0	19	6	6
Wales	3	2	1	8	6	4
Scotland	3	1	2	8	13	2
Ireland	3	0	3	5	15	0

Charles Buchan's FOOTBALL MONTHLY

SPECIAL TENTH BIRTHDAY ISSUE

SEPTEMBER 1961

Overseas Price 2/–
Forces Overseas 1/6
1/6

BOBBY SMITH, JOHNNY HAYNES, PETER SWAN and RON SPRINGETT

Colour and black and white picture tribute to the Stars of England

WALTER WINTERBOTTOM SUMS UP ENGLAND'S WORLD CUP PROSPECTS

Peter Swan clears against Portugal during England's 2-0 victory in the World Cup qualifier.

A thunderbolt from Bobby Charlton, with England's second goal against Mexico

Johnny Haynes, of England, goes to the aid of Lorenzo Buffon, the Italian goalkeeper, who had collided with Gerry Hitchens. With blood streaming from his broken nose, Buffon was assisted off, and took no further part in the match.

LAZY BIG-HEADS

EUROPEAN trainers who have worked in South America say that Argentina's professionals take the biscuit for casual preparations. Says one trainer who worked with them:

"Technically, they are as talented as the Brazilians, but too many of them are either big-heads, or think that, as 'artists', they should be spared regular and conscientious training.

"That's why several big Argentinian clubs have been scouting for foreign players."

★ ★ ★

PORTUGUESE teams used to take the British style as a model. When they decided to change, they didn't take the methods of the neighbouring Spaniards as an example, despite the deeds of Real Madrid. Nor did they try to copy the Hungarians, though their trainer, Bela Guthmann, a naturalised Austrian, is Hungarian by birth.

Benfica adopted the Brazilian game as a pattern, and National League honours last season, and European Cup feats since, have justified them. Portugal has never had a more popular club. One reason for this is that Benfica relies solely on Portuguese players.

★ ★ ★

THERE is a story about Benfica's centre-forward, 30-year-old José Aguas, twenty times capped by Portugal, which I find hard to believe.

This story says that when a youth, he was a hunter of panthers in Angola (Portuguese West Africa) when Benfica went to play there. Two days before the start of a match, a local team, unexpectedly short of players, invited Aguas to turn out for them, although he had never touched a ball.

He was known only as a great hunter, physically very supple, and with a marvellous eye. Anyway, he played and —so the story goes—was "the best man on the field". So Benfica signed him!

I wouldn't mind wagering, however, that between panther hunts, Aguas had shown a certain prowess with a ball at his feet.

IT WON'T BE TOO HOT IN CHILE

PLAYERS in various countries who have been worrying about the temperatures in Chile at the time of next year's World Cup games, have been told they can be at ease on this point. The temperatures, it is stated, "will be rather cool, and favour Europeans".

Those recorded in June (World Cup month) 1960, for Santiago and Vina del Mar, two of the cities where games will be played next year, show a daytime average of 57 deg. Fahr. In most foreign countries, that is considered an "ideal temperature" for the game.

Latest estimate of the number of Brazilian fans wishing to see some of the matches in Chile is 100,000. Question of hotel accommodation continues to worry the organisers.

I hear that with the certainty of every bed in Santiago, capital of Chile, being occupied, there is considerable activity in buying and making hammocks!

Kopa Defends Auction of Players

CENTRE-FORWARD or outside-right Raymond Kopa, France's No. 1 player, sees "absolutely nothing shocking" in professional players being "bought and sold like objects". He said so after a speaker on the radio had said: "Slavery has long been abolished, but footballers are still sold by auction."

Kopa, a former coal-miner, spoke cold sense. "Who wouldn't rather be a professional footballer than a coal-miner? If a player makes money for a club, why be shocked if he gets a share of it? He's like a cinema star . . ."

I disagree with the last sentence. Cinema stars can get £100,000 or more for a film; they can leave one company for another because fees are better. No one talks of "slavery", or "auction sales" where they are concerned.

A DANGEROUS OCCUPATION

IF reports from San Francisco and Boston are a pointer, referees in America have outsize grievances. Those at San Francisco went on strike recently as "a protest against the mild action handed out to offending players".

Assaults on Boston referees became so frequent that two of them resigned. A report in American "Soccer News" said: "If there should be any more such assaults, the exodus will be on."

Five players of the Lawrence Hungaria team, Boston, were suspended for assaulting an official during and after a game.

'Uncle Sepp' Banks on Youth

GERMANY'S national trainer, Sepp Herberger (known as "Uncle Sepp") hopes to take to Chile "a team young in years but old in experience".

He envisages an eleven of the average age of 23, 24 or 25, "each player having represented Germany about ten times".

Herberger is a great diplomat as well as an ace on Soccer matters. Only a diplomat could have held the tricky job of national trainer for 25 years, as this 64-year-old former international has done.

He is called "the man with a thousand faces"—which also, in a way, suggests diplomacy.

He lives in a village near Heidelberg, and was made a freeman of it three days before Germany won the World Cup in 1954.

That sensational victory made him world famous. His souvenirs of it (his villa is like a Soccer museum) include the ball with which the final was played, and another ball which carries the signatures of the 22 German and Hungarian finalists.

Also on view are examples of the postage stamp, bearing Herberger's portrait, which was issued after the 1954 victory.

He doesn't drink, but keeps 400 bottles of wine in his cellar for visitors.

JOHNNY HAYNES
Fulham

Since May 1960, they

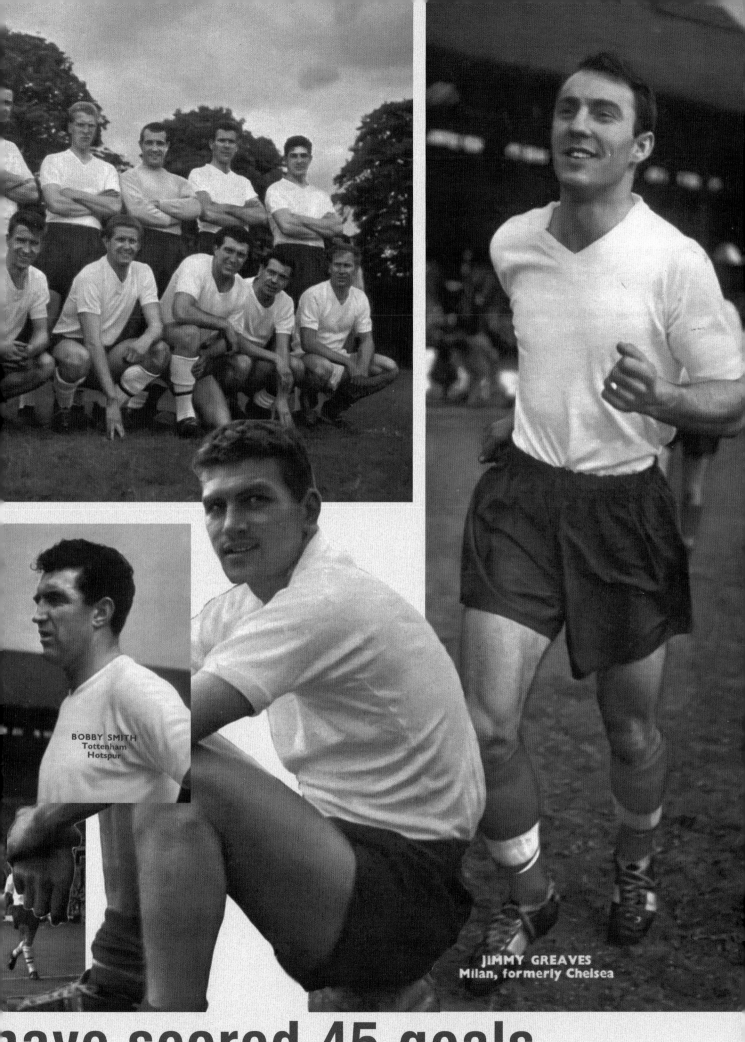

BOBBY SMITH
Tottenham
Hotspur

JIMMY GREAVES
Milan, formerly Chelsea

have scored 45 goals

A NEW LEASE OF LIFE

BOBBY ROBSON, captain of West Bromwich Albion, and his former Fulham colleague, Johnny Haynes, have played most important roles in the revival of England's international fortunes. In this article Robson discusses the 4-2-4 plan which England used last season, and how his conversion from inside-forward to wing-half enabled him to fit into the plan, and started him on a new international career.

THE remarkable success of the England international team in the past season was largely the result of employing the 4—2—4 tactical team plan of team-manager Walter Winterbottom. My part in the plan, as right-half, was to stop inside-forwards scoring, and to link with Johnny Haynes, England's captain and hard-working genius behind the attack.

I linked with Johnny when I was with Fulham, but then I was a goal-scoring inside-forward. It was this link, and the fact that it brought goals, which caused me, originally, to be capped for England.

I am the attacking wing-half in our England scheme whereas Ron Flowers, of Wolves, acts as "double" centre-half with Peter Swan.

But first I want to tell you how it came about that I switched from inside-forward to wing-half, how it has affected my play (and improved it), and to quote a few examples of other notable inside-men who have become even better half-backs.

Because of the "roaming" character of the two jobs, most inside-forwards can play at wing-half, and vice versa. Usually, however, it is the inside-forward who makes a better job of being a wing-half than the wing-half does of the inside-forward position.

Look at some of the inside-forwards who have excelled at wing-half in recent years . . . Don Revie, Bill Slater, Len Phillips, Roy Bentley, Billy Wright, Vic Groves, Archie Macaulay. Bentley, Wright and Slater made even better centre-halves as they grew older.

It was Vic Buckingham who persuaded me to try wing-half. He didn't exactly put it like that because, at the time, he was West Bromwich Albion's manager and the Albion had a serious team problem.

It was during the period when Ronnie Allen and Johnny Nicholls were coming to the end of their highly successful dual "spearhead" role in the attack. At the same time, big Ray Barlow, who had been the constructive "link" behind Allen and Nicholls, lost his speed and it was decided to move him to centre-half.

That left a gap at right-half, which was where I came in. It proved a very good move, indeed.

You see, I had been hardly coming up to expectations at West Bromwich. Albion had paid Fulham £25,000 for me—one of the biggest fees in the club's history, I believe—and I just wasn't fitting in.

Certainly, I couldn't get the goals as I used to at Fulham and, in fact, when Mr. Buckingham suggested the switch to wing-half, I was out of Albion's League side.

At first, I wasn't too keen, and found it hard to adjust myself to my new job. I spent a lot of time in practice games, learning how to "stand off" an opponent, when to tackle or "jockey" and how to "time" a tackle.

As I had always been a good and rapid distributor of the ball, that aspect of the wing-half business didn't particularly bother me—but the tackling part of it did.

You cannot hope to be a good wing-half unless you can get the ball off the other fellow—this is the most important part of the job!

I played my first game as a wing-half for the Albion against Blackpool on Easter Saturday, 1959. I will always remember the match—my wife gave birth to our first child on the same day!

I had been up at four o'clock in the morning to rush her to hospital and I wasn't feeling quite as match-fit as I should have been. But everyone seemed to think I had had a good game and from then on, I settled down more and more each week.

At this stage of my career, I was interested only in establishing myself as a first-team player at West Bromwich. I had virtually forgotten about any further England honours for I had been

out of the national limelight for too long . . . so I thought!

I had last played for England as an inside-forward in the 1958 World Cup matches in Sweden. Frankly, I had not expected to add to my five caps.

But in 1960, I was playing so well at wing-half for the Albion that there were suggestions in the Press that I should be in the England team again.

As I had played for the Football League team at right-half against the Scottish League at Highbury, in March, 1960, it seemed that my new position had become acceptable to the international selectors.

But Ronnie Clayton was holding down the England job and he was also the skipper. I did not see, then, how he could be displaced. However, after the home draw with Yugoslavia, in early May, the England selectors decided to make changes and I was given the right-half berth for the match against Spain, in Madrid.

We lost that game 3—0, but I kept my place for the game with Hungary, in Budapest a week later. Although we were beaten again, that was the start of an unbroken England half-back line consisting of myself, Peter Swan and Ron Flowers.

I can't mention Flowers without paying tribute to the fine way in which he has adapted his game to suit the England 4-2-4 plan.

Ron, by natural inclination, is an attacking half-back, like myself. At Wolverhampton that is the game he plays. Yet in the England team he is required to play a "dual" centre-half role and spend all his time on defence.

So well has he done this difficult job that the success of Walter Winterbottom's 4-2-4 plan was assured last season.

I am perfectly happy in the half-back line now and I wish I had made the switch much earlier in my career.

One of the happiest features of this move was the renewal of my partnership with Johnny Haynes. Surely, he must be England's skipper for many seasons to come!

His display when we beat Scotland 9—3 last April was just great.

What makes the wing-half job so attractive to so many players? I have been asked this question more than once since my conversion.

Well, I'll let you into a secret—when you have the ball, there are more people around you can give it to!

EARTHQUAKES HAVE NOT DAUNTED CHILE

1962 WORLD CUP GOES ON

by

DEREK LIECTY
one of Chile's leading football commentators

IT will take more than earth-quakes to prevent Chile staging the 1962 world Soccer championship. After recovering from the shock of a third of the country being ravaged by nature's rumblings last May, the Chilean Organising Committee, headed by the internationally-known football official, Carlos Dittborn, announced that Chile would proceed on schedule to stage the world tournament between May 30 and June 17, 1962.

This decision was backed by President Jorge Alessandri, who advised FIFA that his government would give all-out support to his country's sporting officials in fulfilling this "great national obligation"

According to modifications approved by the FIFA Organising Committee in August, the Jules Rimet Cup (the world tournament) for 1962 will be played in four principal cities with Santiago, Chile's beautiful capital, the major site and headquarters.

The Port of Arica, 1,300 miles north of Santiago, will stage seven games in a new stadium to be built with municipal funds. It is expected that this city will attract many spectators from neighbouring Peru and Bolivia.

Rancagua, an hour south of Santiago by car, will have its stadium enlarged to accommodate 25,000 at a cost of 170,000 U.S. dollars.

Viña del Mar, is well known for its beach resorts and gambling casino. Only two hours by car or train from Santiago, this attractive city will stage eight games including a semi-final. The city stadium, Sausalito, will accommodate 35,000.

But nothing will surpass the national stadium in Santiago, which is being re-modelled for a capacity of 100,000.

Just a few minutes from the city centre this Soccer setting is surely one of the world's most attractive with its fabulous green turf, and the snow-capped Andes mountains for a background.

Here, seven preliminary games, game for third place, a semi-final, and the final, will be played.

The Chilean Organising Committee has formed sub-committees to cope with every detail of the tournament. Sites are being reviewed for the housing of visiting teams and delegations.

Plan of the National Stadium in Santiago, Chile. It is to be enlarged to accommodate 100,000. The shaded area is to be the new housing project to take 15,000 visitors.

Brazil, automatic qualifier as title-holder, has already sent a delegation, including the team psycho-analyst Dr. Hilton Gosling, to select a suitable training site. The quiet village of Olumé was selected, particularly for its excellent climate and its proximity to Viña del Mar where Brazil will play most of their games.

Thousands of tourists are expected for this important event.

Air transport will be available for those wishing to see games in Arica. Santiago is short of hotel space, but this problem has been solved by the government housing agency which has announced plans for a twelve million dollar "Olympic Village", similar to that constructed in Rome.

It will consist of some 3,000 apartments within walking distance of the National Stadium in Santiago.

Majority of the spectators will come from South America, and the Brazilians may well top the list since a Sao Paulo travel agency already has 3,000 fans signed up. Neighbouring Argentina—almost sure to qualify at the expense of Ecuador—will be supported by thousands of their fanatics.

Efforts will be made to attract as many European fans as possible. One German newspaper has suggested a floating hotel in the form of a steamship to be anchored at Chile's principal port, Valparaiso, which is only ten minutes from Viña del Mar!

Though there will be no snow at the game sites, players and spectators can expect rain, as well as sunshine, in Rancagua, Santiago, and Viña del Mar.

Tickets will soon be made available to the public, and a world-wide travel agency will receive sales authorisation. Prices will be high however.

The Chilean public will be able to buy tickets on a ten-month instalment plan.

There is much activity just now to get all the plans in motion in time for the visit of the FIFA Inspection Committee —including Sir Stanley Rous—in March 1961.

There is little chance that Chile will produce a Cinderella team similar to that of Sweden in 1958. Not since the South American Championship of 1955, when Chile lost the title to Argentina by a point, has Chilean football risen to acceptable international standards.

The national team's recent European tour only served to emphasise that what is most lacking in Chilean football is tactical sense and discipline.

In addition to that unsuccessful tour —they lost five games and drew one —Chile have been beaten recently by Brazil 0-7 and 0-1 for the O'Higgins Cup, and lost 0-4 and 2-4 against Spain on the latter's South American tour.

Now, under Fernando Riera, formerly an outside-left with First Division Rheims, of France, the Chilean World Cup XI will be selected from seventy-one players. The Chilean Football Federation is to construct a football school for intensive training.

The 1962 World Cup will be the largest single event ever to occur in Chile. The Chileans have shown their knack for organisation in the past by successfully staging other international sporting events. But 1962 will be the ultimate test.

Realising that the eyes of the world will be upon them and knowing the Chileans as I do, I am certain this sporting nation will rise to the occasion.

England has not yet qualified for the World Cup tournament in Chile next June. To do so she must first beat Portugal and Luxembourg. But since 1958, the year of the last World Cup, England has been preparing. In this article team-manager Walter Winterbottom explains what has been done, why it has been done, the problems and the results achieved.

We are stronger than in 1958

WALTER WINTERBOTTOM
England team-manager

||||||||||||||||||||||||||||||||||||||||||||||||||||||||||||||

THE World Cup Competition, like the Olympic Games, is held every four years. That presents a problem in team-building, for it is essential that the international players chosen should be welded into a team side and brought to the peak of fitness and match-play in May or June of the year in which the Competition is held.

Several countries have had outstanding international performances during intervening years and then, at the time of the Competition, the standard of their team has suffered because it has been necessary, in some measure, to rebuild the team.

This factor has become increasingly important in World Cup team preparation, and more and more countries have seen the wisdom of starting with young players and gradually giving them international experience in the hope that a strong, fit and co-ordinated team will emerge at the end of the four-year period.

It was for this reason that Sir Stanley Rous planned the introduction of "Under-23" matches. It was felt that here would be an opportunity to find the best young talent, and of exposing it to match-play against Continental teams.

At the time of this introduction it was little realised that so many of the Under-23 players would be selected for the full international team while they were still in the Under-23 age group. Yet in the present England team, Armfield, McNeil, Flowers, Douglas, Greaves, Haynes and Charlton all gained caps while in that age group.

After the World Cup in 1958 it was agreed that young players should be given more experience, and the touring side which went to South America, and suffered defeat, gave it to players like Charlton, Greaves, Armfield and Haynes.

The great difficulty from an international standpoint is to suffer the loss of prestige while team-building goes on. It is felt now that England has at last a nucleus of a team which is stronger than its counterpart in the World Cup of 1958.

You will recall that in international matches during the April and May, and in the World Cup matches of 1958, several members of the team gained their first cap. It was not to be expected, therefore, that the team could have any real depth of understanding.

Even so, the achievement of this team was quite good, considering the strength of the sides competing in England's group: Austria, Russia and Brazil. As one player put it—"We were just beginning to get team-understanding when we were knocked out."

Last season saw a most definite change in circumstances. It had been possible to keep the English international players together throughout the whole time. In addition to the four home international matches, the team also had three useful training sessions in between these matches to help to build a team spirit.

It was most encouraging to see how this understanding stood the team in good stead during the very strenuous summer tour played against Portugal, Italy and Austria.

To qualify for the World Cup, England has first to play against Portugal and Luxembourg in England.

The team must win against Portugal at Wembley on October 25 to make sure of going to Chile. And you may rest assured that the Portuguese international team, based, as it is, on most of the players of the triumphant European Cup winners' club, Benfica, will go all out in preparation and practice to try to win the further honour by gaining a victory or a draw against England.

Should England qualify, the remaining programme for the season is to play matches against Ireland, Wales, Scotland and Austria, and then we are hoping to play Switzerland after the Cup Final in May.

The additional match against Austria in April is an unusual feature. It is to test the England side against a team which has achieved remarkable fame during the last two years by beating so many of the outstanding European sides, including England.

Provided the England team can have its training "get togethers", this programme and preparation, together with League and Cup programmes, should be sufficient to keep the players in peak form.

The only danger is one that all World Cup teams will have to face. The Tournament in Chile comes at the end of the season and it is thought that many players may be feeling the strain.

It is likely that the Competition in Chile will be run on similar lines as that in Sweden, which will mean four groups of four teams playing off to decide which teams go forward to the quarter-finals. This means three matches in seven days, and you can now see the reason why England undertook a similar task this summer.

It is expected that if England qualify, the team will arrive in Chile about a week before the start of the Competition, in order to settle down.

There should be no great problem about climate. The temperature in Chile during June is usually like that in England at the same time. It can even rain and become cold.

The main problem, therefore, will be largely that of avoiding ills which may arise through change of food and drink. But in these days chemical aids are available which should prevent any serious upsets, similar to those experienced when England went to Chile in 1953.

There will also be the problem of travelling long distances between headquarters and venues of matches.

However, by the time of the tournament I expect the World Cup Committee of F.I.F.A., together with the Football Association of Chile, will have resolved these problems.

It is rightly felt that as the tournament is in South America, the South American teams represented in the final sixteen will have the best chance of winning.

Even so, with the constant interchange of experience and matches between South America and Europe, teams are now becoming accustomed to the difference in style and to the atmosphere of playing in strange surroundings, and it may well be that the World Cup will come back to Europe.

IN THE FOOTBALL-DAFT REPUBLIC OF CHILE...

SOCCER IS KING!

BOB FERRIER reports from Santiago, the Chilean capital

THE England footballers who fly to Chile for the World Cup will land in the most football-crazy country in the world.

Here in Chile, a long, slim country squeezed between the Andes and the Pacific Ocean, this great world championship is regarded almost as the greatest event in its history! Some Chileans joke that it is even more important than winning their independence from the old Spanish Empire!

For in Chile, as in the rest of South America, there is only one sport—football is King. Rugby, cricket, hockey, lawn tennis—well, of course, they have heard of such things, and have even produced an occasional champion, like Luis Ayala (at tennis), but sport means *football* and everyone, from the President of the Republic down, is passionately interested.

The England players are likely to be screened off from a lot of the madness. They have a wonderful training spot, in the cool mountains some 50 miles south of Santiago, the capital of Chile, near Rancagua, the town where they will play their early matches against Hungary, Argentina and Bulgaria.

They will stay at Coya, the "rest camp" of the American Braden Copper Company. Believe me, it is a "camp" *without* tents. Braden dig thousands of tons of rich copper out of the mountains, 8,000 feet above Rancagua, at the mines of Sewell.

Halfway down the mountain they have built a little town, Coya, to which their employees go for holidays. It is a wonderful place, in a green valley, with a golf course, swimming pool, perfect training pitch, gymnasium and every other facility. The England players will live, two to a room, and with a bathroom for each room, in a delightful residence in the centre of this little town.

The copper company has a private railway which connects Sewell with Rancagua. It passes through Coya, and whisks down the mountainside to the door of the stadium. Messrs Charlton, Greaves and Haynes will ride in style in the special diesel car reserved for the executives of the Braden Copper Company!

Walter Winterbottom has looked over Coya and the stadium at Rancagua, and visited other centres. The stadium has been built up to a 30,000 capacity, and the pitch is now in perfect condition.

The climate in Rancagua in May and June—the Chilean winter—is likely to be mild, but cold in the evenings, with some rain. It is calculated that of the 18 days of the championship, there are likely to be 12 *with* rain.

If England qualify, their quarter-final match will be in Rancagua, or in Vina del Mar. If they qualify for the semifinal, that definitely will be in Vina del Mar. The only chance England will have of playing in the 100,000-capacity Nacional Stadium, in Santiago, is if they reach the Final.

That would be a tremendous experience for the players, because this fine, big stadium is in a most dazzling setting. The first range of the mighty Andes mountains rises abruptly behind the stadium, 10,000 feet high, and they look as though they are about to topple down on the stadium and the city.

Santiago is a strange mixture of a modern capital and an old Western border town. In the countryside, you are quite likely to see a "huaso", a Chilean cowboy, clopping along on his horse, wearing his flat, black, broadbrimmed hat and "poncho", the "blanket with a hole in the middle", which he slips over his head and which keeps him warm in the chill of the mountain evenings.

Chile is a country of rich mineral deposits, lush farming country, and golden Pacific beaches—and of football fever. The Chilean national team, a total group of 26 players, have been training since January. Every move they have made has been reported in the newspapers and on the radio. Every match abroad concerning the World Cup finalists has been fully reported.

Everyone in Chile knows everything about England's players, from Springett to Charlton, and all the reserves. They think England have no chance. They don't think anyone has any chance—except Chile!

For the hosts of this wonderful championship that is just as it should be. But it would make an England victory in the World Cup, after three attempts in Brazil, Switzerland and Sweden, all the sweeter!

HERE'S ENERGY FOR YOU!

—but how do Wright and Lofthouse replace it?

Like so many other famous sportsmen, Billy Wright and Nat Lofthouse, England players, drink Lucozade to replace lost energy — and so do millions of families all over the country. Lucozade is made with energy-giving Glucose — an invaluable drink in sickness and in health. Always keep some handy in *your* home.

Lucozade

the sparkling GLUCOSE *drink*

replaces lost energy

Poor (rich) Pelé, they won't leave him alone!

by BILL CROFT

"LET my boy live," cried the mother of Pelé, Brazil's famous inside-forward who four years ago won a World Cup medal at the age of 17 years eight months.

It was a general appeal, made because her son has been "harried by admirers, promoters and reporters."

A reporter suggested she should first have appealed to players (Brazilians and other South Americans) who, "eaten up with jealousy of the gentlemanly Pelé, brutally mark him."

Several times we have heard that, because of the stresses of the past four years, Pelé cannot, in Chile, hope to reproduce his Sweden form of 1958. "Only a superman could do it," we have been told.

But we have also heard: "Pelé is a superman." Which reminds us of Alfredo Di Stefano's: "There are no supermen."

Some observers said a few years ago, before his right knee began to worry him, that Pelé was "obviously saturated with stardom."

But even his mother admits there is a great consolation— Pelé has made so much out of the game, as a player and from sidelines, that he could retire in luxury right now.

Nothing sinister

WHEN Russia and Hungary prepared for Chile by training together in Hungary for six weeks, some European critics looked for a sinister motive. I am not surprised they didn't find it.

It is the first time two countries have trained together for the World Cup, pooling resources and experiences, and despite language difficulties (interpreters were, of course, always on hand), I think it an excellent idea, and would have liked to have seen two of the Home Countries adopt it for Sweden in 1958, especially as there would have been no linguistic snag.

The Russians and Hungarians got together at the suggestion of a Russian leader of the game. Had there been anything political in it then Bulgaria, another Chile participant, would have been host to the Russians for a time.

Groups helped

THE World Cup groupings helped in this Russo-Hungarian co-operation, for however well things went for them the two countries cannot meet until the semi-finals.

As England and Hungary are in the same group (plus Argentina and Bulgaria), you can be sure the present state of England's game was a topic at Russo-Hungarian confabs.

Another topic, of course, was Russia's wins over Argentina, Chile and Uruguay in South America last November.

No League worry

DURING their World Cup training, Chile, Colombia, Russia and Uruguay had no League competition to worry them.

Chile and Russia are said to have had five months' pre-paration; Argentina, Brazil and Hungary two months or a little more.

Players of several World Cup countries are listed as "training between League and Cup fixtures."

Very little has been said about Switzerland, who are grouped with Chile, Italy and West Germany, but no country has paid more attention than Switzerland to what has been going on.

A spokesman for Yugoslavia (who are grouped with Colombia, Russia and Uruguay) said: "Don't bother about us. Average age of our players is 23. We're thinking more about the World Cup of 1966."

This makes the Russians all the more wary about the Yugoslavs.

Lion-heart Fontaine

NOTABLE absentee from the Chilean pitches will be Juste Fontaine, French centre-forward, who in Sweden four years ago made a World Cup record by scoring 13 goals in the final stages.

His country still chafe at their defeat by Bulgaria in the preliminaries for the 1962 trophy.

But Fontaine has his own problems, main one of which is to keep fit and efficient after the two fractures which, in the past three years, have immobilised him for 18 months.

The fractures were in the same place, and only a lion-hearted chap could have returned to the game, as Fontaine has done, with the dash that helped to make him famous.

"I'm a lucky man, with two great loves, my wife and football," says Fontaine, who is chairman of France's new Professional Players' Union. He speaks English and Spanish, and sings well.

Back to guards

SHIN-GUARDS made a return among a few players in France towards the end of last season because of an alarming number of fractures.

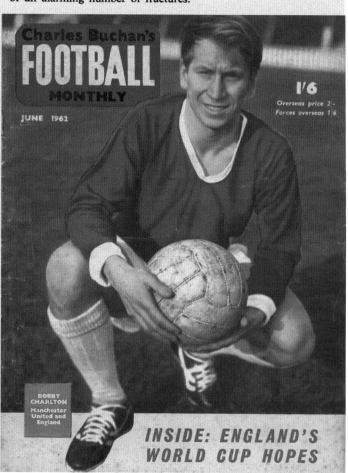

Charles Buchan's FOOTBALL MONTHLY

JUNE 1962

1/6
Overseas price 2/-
Forces overseas 1/6

BOBBY CHARLTON
Manchester United and England

INSIDE: ENGLAND'S WORLD CUP HOPES

WORLD CUP, 1962

IT might have been worse. That was the reaction of England team-manager Walter Winterbottom to the World Cup draw. It seems to be a general feeling—England could have had a tougher draw.

England will have to do battle with Argentina, Hungary and Bulgaria in their table for one of the top two places which will ensure further interest in the competition. It should be possible.

The Bulgarians we know little about, having had experience of their game only at Olympic level. We have not encountered the Argentinians for a decade—the last time for only 20 minutes—but our memories of the Hungarians are still fresh, painfully so.

England's fate will be settled 50 miles from the Chilean capital of Santiago, at Rancagua. It will be a great disappointment if Johnny Haynes doesn't lead his men into the quarter-finals. Less than that and the trip will be considered a failure.

But any advancement must depend upon an improvement in England's international output. So far this season she has yet to move into the smooth, striking stride which brought such a successful run last season.

The Hungarians have been their usual thorough selves about this World Cup business. They have been to see what they can expect in Chile, so the condi-

tions won't be strange to them. On their short tour there they drew with and lost to Chile, and also drew with Uruguay.

They were too good for England at the last meeting, in Budapest, in 1960, and the narrowness of their two defeats by Austria—most improved Soccer country in Europe—is a form-book pointer which would indicate that they are around the same strength as England—the much better England of last season.

The Bulgars are difficult to sum up.

But in the qualifying rounds of this World Cup they accounted for France—semi-finalists in the 1958 series and

third in the rankings—to win their group and a place at Chile. So they command respect.

But form can be misleading. Bulgaria slumped dismally against the moderate Belgians, losing 0—4 to a country which had lost all four games in the qualifying rounds against Sweden and Switzerland.

The last time England met Argentina, rain stopped play. And what rain! The heavens over Buenos Aires opened an hour-and-a-half before the game, and the pitch was under inches of water when the match began.

It was a farce for some 20 minutes. Then referee Arthur Ellis decided that football was impossible and the game was abandoned. That was in 1953.

Two years earlier, Wembley heard the rare noise of an England team being fiercely encouraged by her own crowd . . . but for a reason outside Soccer.

The meeting between the two countries, in May, 1951, came at a time when English tempers smouldered at what was considered to be international robbery by the Argentinians who were asking much more for their meat exports.

That Wembley crowd was in no mood to put down a red carpet for the Argentine footballers. Their feelings were expressed in unusually loud partisan cheers for Stan Mortensen, Jackie Milburn, Tom Finney and the rest of the English side. England won 2—1.

Recently, Argentina ventured into the Old World. Spain and Italy were too good for them, Portugal were beaten, and the Czechs and the Russians were held in meritorious drawn games.

All four groups in the World Cup Finals are well-matched in strength, but even if England's Group 4 is considered the easiest, it would be foolish to underestimate her rivals.

Argentina are joint second favourites with Uruguay for the title after Brazil, the holders.

P. C.

FIRST MATCHES OF THE WORLD CUP

THE World Cup Finals will be played between May 30 and June 17. The two teams which finish at the top of each group will qualify for the quarter-finals. There will be a decider played if two teams are level in second place.

On June 10 the two leaders of each group will play off for places in the semi-finals. They will be between the Arica and Vina Del Mar Zone winners and the Santiago and Rancagua Zone winners, on June 13. Final at Santiago, June 17.

GROUP 1	GROUP 2	GROUP 3	GROUP 4
(At Arica)	*(At Vina del Mar)*	*(At Santiago)*	*(At Rancagua)*
Russia v. Yugoslavia	**Mexico v. Brazil**	**Switzerland v. Chile**	**Bulgaria v. Argentina**
Colombia v. Uruguay	**Spain v. Czechoslovakia**	**W. Germany v. Italy**	**England v. Hungary**

They carry Engla

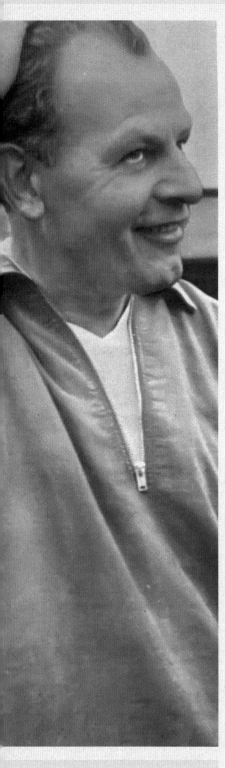

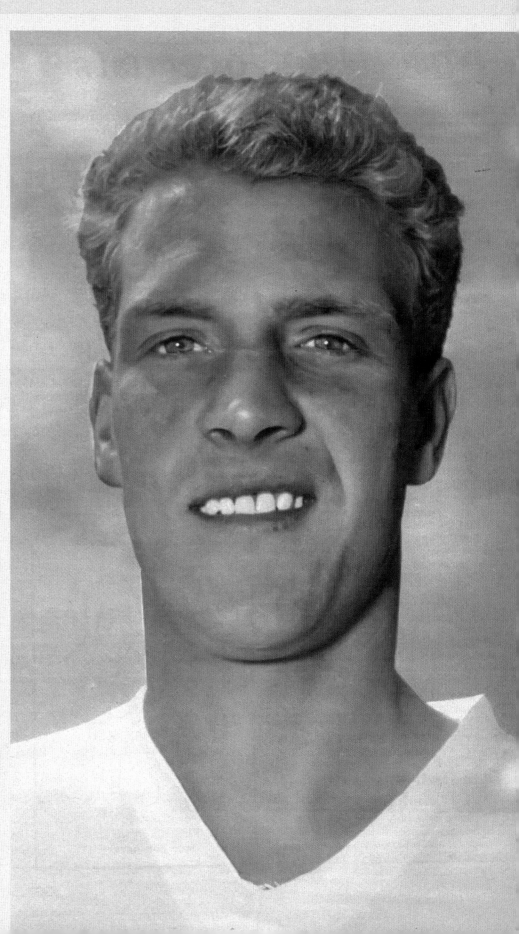

THE BOSS: Walter Winterbottom (above) is not downhearted as he ponders what lies ahead. Nor does Ron Flowers (right) seem overawed.

d's hopes...

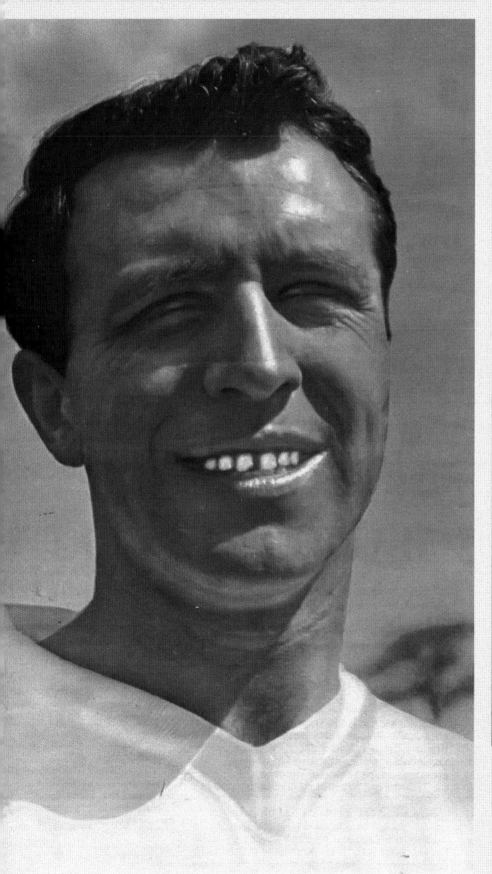

THE CAPTAIN: Johnny Haynes (above) walks off after one of England's last training sessions. (Left) vice-captain Jimmy Armfield.

BILLY WRIGHT SAYS....

BON VOYAGE

and happy hunting to Johnny Haynes and his boys in Chile. As I have led England in her three World Cup quests I know something of the terrific task which faces the skipper and the players he leads.

Every big game in top Soccer severely tests a player's temperament . . . the Cup Final, an international, an important League match. But there is nothing to match the test of meeting the greatest teams and players in the world in the fierce heat of the World Cup.

I suppose the European Cup must come nearest to it for strain, but that tournament is spaced enough to give players time to look round and take stock. And because of its two-leg home and away basis, teams always have a second chance.

But in the final stages of the World's premier competition players have to give everything ALL the time. In Chile there can be no let up and, with world standards levelling up, there are no "soft touches" even for the best teams.

Preparing for the World Cup is not just the usual problem of getting eleven players 100 per cent fit and on top of their game . . . the whole party of 19 must be in top gear.

For there must be changes as the competition unwinds, either to rest one or two players or to improve the team if there are any shortcomings.

There is also the case of resting players from a game you think you can win with a team a little under-strength— to save them for a stiffer one.

That side of the tactical battle was never more clearly shown than in 1954 in Switzerland, when the Germans surprised everybody by becoming World Cup holders.

Then, as now, two teams in each of the four pools had to qualify. Against the Hungarians, Germany fielded a weak team—it included five players who did not appear in their Final side—in order to save the big effort for the play-off against the Turks.

They lost 3—8 to Hungary, but coasted into the last eight by whipping Turkey 7—2.

Then, the teams played two matches in each pool. Now, as in Sweden, there are three games to be played. Each team meets the other three countries in their pool on a League basis, and the two top teams go on.

The tactical battle between team-coaches and managers is never-ending.

In 1958, Brazil beat Sweden in the Final. Now, Djalmar Santos had not been used by Brazil in any match, until the Swedes and their fine wingers, Hamrin and Skoglund, had to be countered.

The experienced Djalmar came in at

England led Switzerland 3—1 at half-time at Wembley, and should have had no worries. But these three have something on their minds. They are Ray Wilson, Peter Swan and Walter Winterbottom, heading for the dressing room at the interval.

"Its a great challenge for the team in South American conditions"...

Continued on next page...

THEY QUEUED TO BUY £35 TICKETS

A FRIEND in Santiago de Chile, where ten games in the World Cup tournament will be played, wrote to me:

"With five pals I queued an hour at a bank for the privilege of paying the first instalment of the dollar equivalent of £35 to see all ten games.

"There was a £43 grade, but it was reserved for members of Chilean football clubs. There were also lower prices for the ten games, down to £8 for standing room. We decided to see the lot in style.

"Anything like £35, cash down, to see football matches, would have frightened us in the ordinary way, much as we love the game. Average fans, however, are lucky if a World Cup series comes their way once in a lifetime.

"Another thing, and the most important, is that the organisers had a brain-wave. We're paying for the seats—we had to book for all the ten matches to be played in the capital—in eight instalments."

The ten games in Santiago are six in the series that will qualify for the quarter-finals, one quarter-final, one semi-final, the final, and the beaten semi-finalists' play-off for third and fourth places.

There will be 32 games in all, 22 of them to be played in three other cities, where booking is not so brisk as in the capital. Everything points, however, to a big financial success, especially as the Government is being very kind about taxation.

More than 20,000 fans are expected to pour into Chile from other South American countries. Estimates of the number who will go from Europe (apart from the competing teams and their officials), vary from 1,000 to 2,500.

GOOD LUCK, ENGLAND!

Continued from previous page...

||||||||||||||||||||||||||||||||||||||||||||||||||||||||||||||||||||||||||||||||||||||||||||||||||

right-back to mark Skoglund. He did a great job. Brazil went on to win the Jules Rimet trophy.

The present system of the World Cup is tougher, but fairer, than that which operated in 1954. Today, teams must see that they have sufficient points to pass on to the quarter-finals.

I am certain England will do better than any of our previous teams. One good reason is that they will have had much more time together than our other World Cup sides.

I have seen the improvement that has been made in the England side, but even so, we in Britain still do not get the preparation together which most other countries have. That is due to our domestic Soccer ties, and we must accept that.

Looking back on England's efforts in the past three tournaments you can see how everybody and everything has to be "on" to get results.

In 1950—England's first entry—the results show how the defence did its job, but the attack failed. England played three games and conceded only two goals. A defence could hardly do better.

But the forwards scored only two goals—against Chile—and out England went. Only the top teams in the four pools went on, and Uruguay became champions by topping the League in

BILLY WRIGHT . . .
captain of England
from 1948 until 1959

which the teams met each other to arrive at the eventual winner.

In Switzerland, in 1954, the competition was the best yet; the standards were superior to any before . . . or since. Then England's attack played its part, but the defence slumped. The forwards scored eight goals, but the defence let in eight in the three games . . . and two of those goals were two too many in the quarter-final against Uruguay.

In Sweden, in 1958, it was back to forward failure. England got four goals in four matches, conceding five. There was a play-off against the Russians and their one goal decided.

You see, the entire team has to click. That's why I say this team are a more competent England outfit. They are much better-balanced than before.

The 1950 campaign in Rio will always be remembered for England's defeat by the Americans in Belo Horizonte, a day described as the blackest and most humiliating in England's Soccer history. I have been taxed about that match more than any other.

I wouldn't even begin to try to make excuses, for the odds were so heavily on England. It was "one of those days". England rattled their post and crossbar, did all the attacking, had unlimited chances of scoring. But THEY did the scoring.

If that game were played ten times again, England would win at least nine times.

Memories of great players come flooding back when I think of my three trips to the Finals . . . players in the 1950 series like Jair and Ademir, the great Brazilian inside-forwards; little Cjaicowski, the Jugoslavian wing-half; Boniperti and Parola, of Italy; Miguez and the then young Schiaffino, of Uruguay.

In 1954 there were the legendary Hungarians, Puskas, Kocsis, Hidegkuti and Boszik; Rahn and the two Walters, Fritz and Ottmar, of Germany; Julhino and Didi, of Brazil; Ocwirk, of Austria, among many others.

In Sweden, in 1958, there were stars like Liedholm, Skoglund and Simonsson from the host country; Kopa and Fontaine, of France; Igor Netto, of Russia; Pele, of Brazil; Hanappi, of Austria.

In the coming weeks the competition will be terrific. And the South American conditions have to be met and mastered. Through it all, only the highest team-spirit and effort will help Haynes and his team to make a good showing.

It is a great challenge. Good luck, England! I am confident that Johnny and the rest will come marching home again having done a good job.

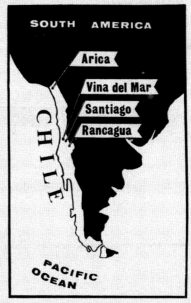

World Cup Venue 1962

THE first World Cup tournament for the Jules Rimet trophy was in 1930. It was named after the Frenchman who was President of FIFA from 1921 to 1954, and who was largely responsible for bringing the competition into being.

There was no British interest in the Cup until 1950, when England took part in Brazil after winning the home international championship, a condition of qualification.

The British Associations have been in and out of FIFA. Final membership was cemented in 1947. Our British insularity kept us aloof from the young, new world Soccer organisation when it was formed in 1904.

We pulled out after the First World War because we refused to entertain football relations with former enemy countries, and again in 1928 after FIFA had recognised "broken time" payments for amateur players in the Olympic Games.

England results:

BRAZIL, 1950

England were in the same pool as Spain, Chile and the United States. Only the winners of the four pools went into the finals which were played on a league table basis.

England 2, Chile 0 (Scorers: Mortensen, Mannion)
United States 1, England 0 (Scorer: Gaetjens)
Spain 1, England 0 (Scorer: Zarra)
Spain won her three matches to top Pool No. 2, England failing to qualify.

SWITZERLAND, 1954

Again there were four pools. Two of each of the four teams in each pool were "seeded". Each team in the pool played only two games, and the two teams with most points went into a knock-out competition of quarter-finals, semi-finals and final. England topped her pool. Results:

England 4, Belgium 4 (Scorers: England—Broadis 2, Lofthouse 2. Belgium—Anoul 2, Coppens, Dickinson own goal).
England 2, Switzerland 0 (Scorers: Mullen, Wilshaw).
Quarter-final: Uruguay 4, England 2 (Scorers: Uruguay—Borges, Schiaffino, Ambrois, Varela. England—Lofthouse, Finney).

SWEDEN, 1958

The same knock-out principle applied, with the last eight composed of the two top teams in their pools. Wales and Ireland reached the last eight after play-offs, but England and Scotland failed, the first-named after a play-off. Results:

England 2, Russia 2 (Scorers: England—Kevan, Finney. Russia—A. Ivanov, Simonian).
England 0, Brazil 0.
England 2, Austria 2 (Scorers: England—Haynes, Kevan. Austria—Koerner, Koller).
Play-off: England 0, Russia 1 (Scorer: Ilyin).

WORLD CUP WINNERS

1930 (In Uruguay)	Uruguay	4	Argentina 2
1934 (Italy)	Italy	2	Czechoslovakia 1
1938 (France)	Italy	4	Hungary 2
1950 (Brazil)	Uruguay. Runners-up, Brazil		

(In this year the Finals were played on a league table basis)

1954 (Switzerland)	Germany	3	Hungary 2
1958 (Sweden)	Brazil	5	Sweden 2

Charles Buchan's
CHILE
WORLD CUP REVIEW

CZECHOSLOVAKIA 1 *Masopust 16min*
Schrojf, Tichy, Pluskal, Popluhar, Novak, Kvasna
Masopust, Scherer, Pospichal, Kadraba, Jelinek

BRAZIL 3 *Amarildo 17min, Zito 69min, Vara 77min*
Gilmore, D. Santos, Mauro, Zozimo, N. Santos,
Didi, Zito, Garrincha, Varva, Amarildo

Thursday June 17th 1962
Attendance 68,679
Venue: National Stadium, Santiago

Now Brazil chase hat-trick

BRAZIL, the holders and hot favourites for the 1962 tournament, duly moved on to their second successive World Cup, in Santiago, and are already planning for the hat-trick attempt in these islands when England stages the 1966 competition.

The Final was tough going against the well-drilled Czech defence, but the result was a triumph for their smooth, imaginative game as opposed to the too-defensive outlook of so many of the teams in Chile.

As a spectacle the competition fell below the standard of Sweden (1958), and even more so Switzerland (1954), the finest of the tournaments so far. The reason was the grim, give nothing away, defensive game. Only results counted.

Such was Brazil's strength that they succeeded even without Pele, the world's greatest forward, who was injured and out of action for the last decisive matches.

The only consolation for England and Scotland is that the teams which defeated them, Brazil and Czechoslovakia, became the eventual Finalists. But that is small consolation.

A valiant defence was the English contribution to the world Soccer jamboree in Chile, but sterile and stereotyped attacking ideas won no new admirers for the British game.

Most countries had their moments . . . the Yugoslavs were bright and aggressive; the Russians earlier moved as if they might storm through to the Final; Mexico looked great in beating the Czechs; even little Colombia surpassed themselves in their 4—4 draw with Russia.

And who would have rated Chile as third best in the world before the start of the tournament?

Sadly, from England there was only the expected defeat of Argentina. There was nothing memorable in its achievement.

Here are the results of the Finals:

GROUP 1

Uruguay 2 (Cubilias, Sasia), Colombia 1 (Zuluaca); Russia 2 (Ivanov, Pondelejnik), Yugoslavia 0; Uruguay 1 (Carbrera), Yugoslavia 3 (Skoblar, Galic, Jerkovic); Russia 4 (Ivanov 2, Chislenko, Pondelejnik), Colombia 4 (Aceros, Coll, Rada, Klinger); Russia 2 (Manykin, Ivanov), Uruguay 1 (Sasia); Yugoslavia 5 (Galic 2, Jerkovic 2, Melic).

GROUP 2

Chile 3 (Sanchez L., 2, Ramirez), Switzerland 1 (Wuetrich); W. Germany 0, Italy 0; Chile 2 (Ramirez, Toro), Italy 0; W. Germany 2 (Bruells, Seeler), Switzerland 1 (Schneiter); Chile 0, W. Germany 2 (Syzmaniak, Seeler); Italy 3 (Bulcarelli 2, Mora), Switzerland 0.

GROUP 3

Brazil 2 (Zagallo, Pele), Mexico 0; Spain 0, Czechoslovakia 1 (Stibranyl); Brazil 0, Czechoslovakia 0; Spain 1 (Peiro), Mexico 0; Brazil 2 (Amarildo 2), Spain 1 (Andelardo); Czechoslovakia 1 (Masek), Mexico 3 (Diaz, Del Aguila, H. Hermandez).

GROUP 4

Argentina 1 (Facundo), Bulgaria 0; England 1 (Flowers); Hungary 2 (Tichy, Albert); Argentina 1 (Sanfilippo), England 3 (Flowers, Charlton, Greaves); Hungary 6 (Albert 3, Tichy 2, Solymosi), Bulgaria 1 (Asparoukov); Hungary 0, Argentina 0; England 0, Bulgaria 0.

...razil found themselves one goal down ...nly after 16 minutes when Masopust ...cored. Amarildo (The White Pele) ...qualised from an acute angle. The scores ...emained level until the 69th minute when ...ito headed home a cross from Amarildo.

...he game was settled after a mistake by the ...zech goalkeeper Schrojf, when he allowed ... high ball from Djalma Santos to slip ...rough his fingers and Vava stabbed home ...om close range.

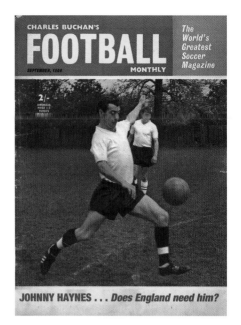

JOHNNY HAYNES . . . *Does England need him?*

Over a hundred countries now entered the tournament at the qualifying stages. The highest entry yet, although with boycotts from Africa and much of Asia it still wasn't the global competition we know today.

England had been awarded the tournament in 1960 and despite all the prestige this would bring, there was little in the way of Government support, or even widespread enthusiasm amongst the public until the tournament reached its latter stages. In fact tickets for every game, including the final were available right up until the last moment.

Stadiums that were only just adequate for our League football, certainly wouldn't be for the World Cup Finals where more seating and press facilities would be required. Wembley Stadium at that time, was the largest arena, not only used for football, but also for greyhound racing and speedway, plus it had hosted athletics for the 1948 Olympic Games. Open to the elements at both ends it was decided to re-roof the whole arena, although a more ambitious project to install extra seating behind the goals was dismissed as too costly.

More progressive clubs such as Sheffield Wednesday and Manchester United decided to use the opportunity to build impressive new grandstands, those at United incorporating luxury boxes and entertainment suites, whilst other clubs such as Aston Villa and Sunderland contented themselves with temporary extra seating and others did nothing at all.

However all this was in the future, more pressing for the Football Association was the need to sort out the England manager's position. Surprisingly, considering the hostile reception for Walter Winterbottom and the players from the media and fans after failure in Chile, the F.A were in no rush to dismiss him.

Walter Winterbottom was a highly respected figure within the game, particularly abroad. Alongside his responsibilities as team manager, he also oversaw the growth and development of coaching in this country and he was to inspire a generation of younger men such as Malcolm Allison and Ron Greenwood. He was also the 'right sort' for the F.A. and he could be relied upon to not rock the boat, preferring evolution to revolution. Therefore it was a surprise when Winterbottom handed in his resignation. He himself had been looking for a change and was very disappointed when he was overlooked in favour of Dennis Follows for the position of F.A. secretary when Stanley Rous moved on to Fifa, although he agreed to stay on as manager until his replacement was found.

The England manager's position had subtly changed over the years, expected to coach a team he hadn't picked and take the flak when it went wrong. Even the affable Winterbottom was upset by hostile media criticism and this was becoming a whole new element to the job. Initially it was thought that Jimmy Adamson would take over, he had been an assistant in Chile and was considered a good choice, recommended by Winterbottom, but when he decided he didn't want the job, the F.A were forced to consider other options. The most obvious choice would have been either Bill Nicholson of Spurs or Stan Cullis of Wolves, but they both distanced themselves from the position, preferring to stay in club football without the extra pressure and expectation that would come at this moment in time.

Meanwhile Alf Ramsey had been quietly learning his trade in rural Ipswich, where over a number of years he had managed a small team with a tiny budget, not only taking them into the top division, but then winning it at the first attempt. Alf Ramsey stood out as an ideal candidate, a player with considerable international experience, firsthand knowledge of competing in a World Cup and also a captains role with the successful Tottenham team. Indeed Tottenham, by having the unusual distinction (for the time) of a tactical plan, had won the Division One title in 1951, using manager Arthur Rowe's 'push and run' method. Even with all those credentials you would have found little talk of him even being considered for the job at that time.

However, although he wasn't among the fifty nine applicants for the job, Ramsey was approached and offered the position in September 1962. At this time even he seemed reluctant to take up the offer, after all Ipswich were playing in the European Cup and he was enjoying the lifestyle and the day to day involvement with the players, not to mention the loyalty he felt for the club. In the end, the pride and love for his country probably swayed his decision, but he was astute enough to negotiate the terms that he wanted. Firstly, he would continue as Ipswich manager until May of 1963, managing England in a part time capacity until then and most importantly for the national team, he alone would be the sole selector of players, there would be no interference from amateur committee members. These terms were agreed and on the 25th October 1962 it was officially announced that Alf Ramsey would be the man to take England through to the next World Cup.

In an interview with Brian James of the Daily Mail, Alf Ramsey laid out his philosophy. "If any player, no matter how clever an individual, is not prepared to accept the discipline of the team's method, then I can see no advantage in selecting him".

Although not mentioning anyone by name, one player for many years had polarized opinion. Johnny Haynes, generally loved by the southern press, but not liked by northern football supporters who had rarely seemed to see him perform well. As it turned out, Alf Ramsey never picked him for any of his squads. Haynes undoubtedly had talent, but in the two previous World Cups he had not made an impression, his style was negated by continental opposition and he often didn't endear himself to his colleagues with his shows of exasperation whenever they made a mistake.

In the meantime Walter Winterbottom would continue in a 'caretaker capacity' until the new regime's first game away in Paris, the return game in the European Nations Cup. The first game being a mind numbing 1-1 draw. The 'Ramsey' era couldn't have got off to a worse start, three goals down by half-time, they salvaged some pride but still fell to a heavy 5-2 defeat. Jimmy Armfield recalls the players being locked in the dressing room for thirty minutes after the match whilst the manager reminded the players of their responsibilities when they pulled on the 'white shirt'. The game itself could have been closer, the usually reliable Ron Springett had a nightmare performance, spreading uncertainty amongst the defence.

After another loss, to Scotland, Ramsey was to get a prolonged period with his players to begin instilling his philosophy. Beginning with a home draw with Brazil, followed by a summer tour into Europe and another three games. Springett paid the price for his poor performances and was replaced by Gordon Banks and there was a recall for full back Ray Wilson. Wilson recalls his feelings about the manager, "I thought it was a good appointment and also because he had played international football himself, he understood the different pressure that the players were under".

The tour started with a 4-2 demolition of Czechoslovakia, the previous year's World

Cup runners up. Although when Greaves was replaced by Roger Hunt for the next game in East Germany, the press took this as a sign that the manager preferred hard work and reliability over quality, though the statistics will show that if Greaves was scoring, he stayed in the team and he was back in for the 8-1 thrashing of Switzerland that brought the tour to a close.

After spending time with his players, Ramsey had decided to model the team around Bobby Charlton. At this time Charlton was not always fully appreciated, not a conventional forward nor midfield player, he could play wide but often struggled to impose himself on a game. Under this manager he was to be given license to roam and his shooting, especially from dead balls was considered vital by a manager who realized chances would be few and far between at the highest level.

It was at this time that Alf Ramsey made his famous declaration, "I believe that England will win the World Cup in 1966. We have the ability, strength, character and perhaps above all, players with the right temperament". Ray Wilson recalls the surprise felt by the players, was this putting too much pressure on the team? Although if the manager had this much confidence, perhaps we should have as well. England were at that time in the middle of a twelve match unbeaten run, was this a case of the manager getting carried away, only time would tell.

The confidence that the manager had in his players appeared fully justified in the game against the Rest of the World in October 1963. Putting aside the 'exhibition' nature of the encounter, it was, as the Guardian described, "The finest exhibition from an England team for many years". High praise and Bobby Charlton in particular stood out in his free role, comparable to anyone on the pitch. This was followed up with an exhilarating 8-3 victory over Northern Ireland but to Ramsey's dismay, it was to be 143

days before the next international and by that time centre forward Bobby Smith had disappeared from his plans and Johnny Byrne, now at West Ham was given the chance to stake his claim.

Ramsey's stock was now at its highest, within a short period of time he had turned a dysfunctional dispirited team into a cohesive unit but just as quickly, fortunes changed and after a very poor tour to South America it looked like it was back to square one, as the team's shortcomings were exposed. In truth it confirmed to the manager that England would not win the World Cup playing open attacking football, but would need to modify their game to suit the opposition.

This tour also gave Ramsey the opportunity to lay the law down to the players about the standard of behaviour he expected. Ray Wilson recalls the night the squad met up at Hendon Hall before travelling. "The players were all making their own way to the hotel. On arriving, Bobby Moore told a few of the lads he had been invited to a restaurant opening and we could go along. I think seven of us went, including Jimmy Greaves and Gordon Banks, we weren't late back and certainly weren't drunk but on going up to our rooms we found our passports laid on our beds, our absence had been noted. We expected to be in trouble but next day nothing was said, in fact it was the day after that when training had finished, Alf said he believed several players wanted to speak to him. He handled the situation brilliantly, pragmatically he didn't want to have to leave behind any players but he left me in no doubt about what would happen in the future". By keeping this 'in house' the manager retained the trust of the players.

The tour that England were about to embark on included a four team tournament in Brazil along with Argentina and Portugal. However the tour began with a meaningless friendly in New York, which resulted in a 10-0 victory, but it meant that the team would be playing Brazil only thirty six hours

Brothers JACK and BOBBY CHARLTON

later. Poorly prepared and jet lagged, it was no surprise when they ran out of steam after an hour and lost 5-1.

If Alf Ramsey needed any further confirmation about the true nature of international football, it came in the final game against Argentina, who only needed a point to clinch the trophy. After dominating possession as Argentina dropped deep, England were able to create little and in fact lost to a quick breakaway goal. The manager was now convinced more than ever that games at the top level would be tight affairs won by the teams that made the least number of mistakes. Strengths were less important than weaknesses.

Alf Ramsey had certainly not bothered to cultivate a friendly relationship with the press and all progress made the previous year was quickly forgotten as they turned on him. Danny Blanchflower writing for the Sunday Express was particularly scathing, "He (Ramsey) might very well know what he is looking for, but it seems to me he certainly doesn't know how to find it".

This tour was a turning point in the build up to 1966, the manager knew that we couldn't always compete on skill, but he felt let down by the attitude of certain players and from this moment on, 'character' played as great a part in his team selection as talent. 442 had also been exposed as unsuitable, there was no room for a defensive midfield player if two wide men were used.

The next international against Northern Ireland gave the manager the chance to further experiment with tactics and there was a slight move to a 433 formation. England raced to a 4-0 half time lead before letting

Ireland back into the game, hanging on for a 4-3 victory.

Once more the press sharpened their knives. The Daily Mail picked up on unrest in the camp and declared, "Ninety minutes of shambles in Belfast ought to be enough to end the eighteen month reign of amiable Alfred".

Things were not to improve as another unimpressive three performances followed to end the international year of 1964. The public had become so disillusioned that attendances at Wembley for the games against Wales and Belgium were played out in front of less than 45,000 fans.

Another concern for the manager at this time was the choice of captain. Jimmy Armfield had missed several games injured and it had seemed certain that Bobby Moore was a definite to replace him in this role, but Ramsey was concerned that Moore was picking up bad habits and sometimes didn't always give the impression that he was taking his role seriously enough. Bobby's big pal was Jimmy Greaves and they could often be heard taking the mickey out of the manager's accent. There was no evidence that this was malicious but Ramsey could not afford his authority to be undermined in any way and Moore realizing what an opportunity he had, toned down the act.

By the time of the next international against Scotland in April 1965, the team and in particular the defence was taking on a more recognizable look. Despite misgivings in the press, debuts were given to Nobby Stiles and Jack Charlton, identified by the manager as having the character and attributes that he needed and two games later Alan Ball was introduced against

Yugoslavia. Despite several forced changes it was becoming clear that England were trying to adjust their playing formation. With Nobby Stiles playing just in front of the back four, they were already looking a solid outfit and spirits were high after another win in Nuremberg over Germany, followed up with a victory in Sweden. Perhaps the press would now leave Alf Ramsey to concentrate on the job in hand.

No chance, the knives were out once more after a 3-2 home defeat to Austria in October. In reality it was undeserved, but to the manager's critics that didn't matter. Greaves had missed a host of chances (it turned out he was suffering from jaundice) before two late goals turned the game on its head.

Just as despair was setting in, the team produced their best and most efficient display for years, winning in Spain. Definitely no wingers on show, a rock solid performance with two hardworking forwards, the Spanish full backs were left bemused with having no-one to mark. Alf Ramsey had been working towards this flexibility for years and now that he had found it, all that remained was to finalise the right players to carry this out. There were still forty players vying for selection in the final squad of twenty two but within that, only six places were still realistically up for grabs.

It is now widely forgotten that just five months before the World Cup Final, England played and beat West Germany in a friendly game at Wembley, a match that also saw a debut for Geoff Hurst. It was a cagey affair, one goal from Stiles (confusingly wearing the number nine shirt) was enough to stretch England's unbeaten record against the

Germans to twelve matches.

As part of the World Cup build up, the trophy had arrived in England and surprisingly Stanley Gibbons Collectables, were allowed to 'borrow' it for an exhibition they were putting on at Westminster Central Hall. The trophy was insured for £30,000 and the police were supposed to provide round the clock surveillance. However in a comedy sketch that could have been written by Peter Sellars, on Sunday March 20th, one of the guards on walking past the cabinet, noticed the Trophy was missing. So began a nationwide hunt and the story was to get even more incredible with ransom notes and messages in the personal column of the 'Evening News'. A rendezvous with the blackmailer led to the Flying Squad making an arrest, but he claimed to be the go-between and have no idea where the trophy was.

Four days later, on the Saturday, David Corbett and his dog Pickles were returning home to Beulah Hill in London, when Pickles sniffing in the hedge came upon a package wrapped in newspaper. It was the World Cup, no damage done, apart from that to the country's reputation. Pickles was now officially the first hero of the competition. No-one was ever charged with the theft.

After an uncharacteristically open encounter, resulting in a 4-3 victory over Scotland at Hampden, the build up to the finals began in earnest with a victory over Yugoslavia that saw a surprise debut for Martin Peters. On the Monday after that game, the squad of forty players was reduced to twenty eight, who were told to report to Lilleshall on June 6th, for a training camp, before the squad would be further

reduced to the final twenty two. This time there would be no allowances made for anyone who stepped out of line. Ramsey made it clear that the next eight weeks would define the careers of this squad and any deprivation was surely a small sacrifice.

As it turned out, only twenty seven players attended, Brian Labone dropped out with injury, before Ramsey announced the five unlucky players would be Peter Thompson, Gordon Milne, Bobby Tambling, Keith Newton and Johnny Byrne, although they were all told to maintain their fitness in case of injuries.

The squad then set off for a series of matches in Scandinavia, where a variety of formations were used. Ramsey still hiding his true intentions, chose a deliberately tough final fixture in Poland, where the team were told in no uncertain terms to win. This was the team likely to start the tournament and Ramsey surprised by picking newcomer Peters in midfield. The team carried out their instructions to the letter, a determined and gritty performance in the industrial city of Chorzow was the perfect way to end their match preparations. On their return the squad were given a couple of days off to see families, a decision thought to be one of the best by the players who were by now raring to go.

At last there were signs of World Cup fever in England, as countries from around the world began arriving. This was perhaps the last 'normal' World Cup where players were allowed some freedom to mingle with supporters. It was a common sight to see Brazilians and Portuguese around Liverpool, whilst the North East took the exotic Koreans to their hearts, open training sessions were

fertile grounds for autograph hunters.

As the first round of matches began, the tournament was by no means a sell out, you could walk up on the day for the opening ceremony and England's first game against Uruguay. The press reacted badly to a dull goalless draw, showing that they just couldn't understand the pressure the 'home' team are under in a World Cup. Alf Ramsey was not displeased with the result, he had emphasized the fact that you must not lose the first game and considered Uruguay to be the hardest rivals in their group. He also knew that the team would need to play a different, more attacking game in the next two matches to progress.

Two changes were made to the line-up that faced Mexico, Peters and Paine replacing Connelly and the injured Ball. Once more England were faced with a ten man defence and for long periods looked to have little idea about how to break it down. It was not until Bobby Charlton scored one of the best goals ever seen in the stadium after thirty eight minutes, that the pressure was released and England largely controlled the game after that, adding another goal for a 2-0 victory. Again the English press were unimpressed, 'This will not win the Cup' they trumpeted.

England's final group game was against France, a draw would probably be enough, but against a distinctly average French side nothing less than victory was expected. The right wing position once more saw a change, Ian Callaghan stepping in and for once England were not faced with a blanket defence. A decent game was won with two goals from the unsung Roger Hunt, but the manager would have been pleased with the

defensive performance, especially for the fifteen minutes after half-time when they came under sustained pressure for the first time in the competition. The first objective had been achieved and better news was to follow. England were expected to play their quarter final, if they qualified at Goodison Park, Everton, but the organizing committee decided that the ground would not be big enough and for financial reasons announced they would play all their matches whilst they remained in the tournament, at Wembley and as a result they wouldn't need to change their training base either.

Whilst England were progressing, there was controversy and romance in the other groups. In Group Three an ageing Brazilian side, were over reliant on Pele and he was singled out for brutal treatment in every game, surprisingly the worst offenders were Portugal who came to the competition with a reputation for skill and fair play and the holders were knocked out with Portugal and Hungary progressing.

In Group Two Argentina had set their stall out, for a skillful side, they were the most cynical team in the tournament, defensive minded and prepared to do almost anything to get a result, they also had Antonio Rattin who apart from being a very good player, fancied he could referee the game at the same time. Along with West Germany they qualified for the second stages, but in a foretaste of what was to come, they were forced to play with ten men after Albrecht was sent off against Germany.

The romance came in Group Four, where the unheralded North Koreans beat Italy and drew with Chile to set up a quarter final with Portugal, Pak Doo Ik attaining immediate cult status with the winner against Italy. For a footballing hot spot, the attendances at Sunderland and Middlesbrough were

particularly disappointing, the lowest crowd of the tournament saw only 13,792 witness the Chile-North Korea encounter at Ayresome Park.

England were now set to face Argentina on Saturday 23rd July in the quarter finals. Alf Ramsey had long considered them to be England's fiercest rivals for the Cup and he knew the best chance of getting the right result, lay in keeping cool in the face of what was going to be a highly charged atmosphere. His first task was to ensure that he had his best players available. In the group match against France Nobby Stiles had not only been cautioned but was lucky not to be sent off after a late and dangerous challenge on Jacky Simon. The competition's disciplinary committee met and warned the player about his future conduct, whilst members of England's F.A. questioned the wisdom and policy of playing 'that sort' of player in a potentially volatile game and the damage it might due to our reputation. After asking the player himself whether it had been a deliberate foul, the manager received the answer he wanted, that it had just been mistimed and decided to stand alongside his player, declaring that if Stiles wasn't available nor would he be. This stance was greatly appreciated by the players, who knew that they could depend on their manager. In the meantime Ramsey asked coach, Harold Shepherdson to have a quiet word with the player and remind him how much he owed the manager and not to let him down. As it turned out, Nobby was professionalism personified as the South Americans predictably lost their heads.

Ramsey by now was ready to make the necessary changes to the system to get the right result. In came Alan Ball on the right side but the manager was faced with replacing Jimmy Greaves who hadn't

recovered sufficiently, after having stitches after the France game. Geoff Hurst was given the nod to resume his partnership with Roger Hunt and the aerial threat he offered was a different challenge to the Argentinians. Greaves had not had a good tournament, unlucky not to score maybe, but offering the team less when they were under pressure. This change certainly turned out well for the manager.

A hot sunny day at Wembley, with the other quarter finals taking place at the same time and by a quirk of fate or conspiracy, England's game against Argentina was refereed by a German, whilst Uruguay against West Germany was refereed by an Englishman, more of that later.

The game panned out exactly as Alf Ramsey had predicted, body checks and tripping were the order of the day from Argentina, alongside moments of genuine skill. After half an hour, three Argentinians had already been cautioned, Artime, Solari and inevitably Antonio Rattin, but it was still a surprise when referee Kreitlein finally ran out of patience and sent the Argentinian captain off with ten minutes of the first half remaining. This was the cue for all hell to break loose as Rattin refused to leave the pitch and at one point it looked like the whole team would follow their skipper off. After seven minutes order was finally regained and the game continued in much the same fashion, Argentina falling deeper and goal scoring chances were at a premium. Two more South Americans went into the book, whilst the Charlton brothers also joined them. It was not until thirteen minutes from the end that England got their breakthrough, a beautiful flighted cross from Peters found club team mate Geoff Hurst and he guided an unstoppable header passed Roma for what turned out to be the winning

The gamble
of Greaves

goal. Alf Ramsey had got his tactics spot on and his players did him proud, though the game finished with further incidents when Ramsey refused to let his players exchange shirts and several Argentinian players tried to get into the English dressing room to continue the argument. Back to Uruguay who at the same time had two players sent off by referee Jim Finney against Germany, leading to allegations of a conspiracy by the South Americans.

Alf Ramsey caused further controversy and almost an international incident in an interview after the game. Clearly still upset at what his players had faced he said "We haven't produced our best football, it is not possible until we meet the right type of opposition, a team which comes out to play football, not as animals as we have seen in this World Cup". Ramsey also relented and allowed the players a couple of drinks to celebrate.

In the other quarter finals, West Germany had crushed nine man Uruguay 4-0, Russia beat Hungary 2-1 and North Korea were beaten 5-3 by Portugal, but not before they had given them an almighty scare, racing into a three goal lead before Eusebio hit back with four goals. Now at last it looked as if the tournament might settle down and produce some entertaining football.

The first semi-final featured West Germany and Russia at Goodison Park, a lively encounter settled by a Franz Beckenbauer strike in a 2-1 win, so England knew who their opponents would be if they reached the final.

So the stage was set for what turned out to be the best game of the competition, played in a fine sporting spirit giving the referee the opportunity to let the game flow. England were unchanged from the Argentina game, Greaves was still not considered fit enough

for selection, whilst Stiles was handed the job of marking the dangerous Eusebio.

Another warm summer's evening, saw the first half belong to England, playing their most fluent football yet, but it took a rebound after thirty minutes to present Bobby Charlton with the chance to put them ahead and despite other chances, 1-0 was the half-time score. The second half was a different story as Portugal gained control and forced England back, though at times they overelaborated allowing England to regroup. Ten minutes from time it looked as if the game was clinched after Hunt had made a fine run and after holding up the ball he spotted Charlton steaming up in support and rolled the ball perfectly for him. Bobby without breaking stride, powered the ball home, but within two minutes it was game on again as Jack Charlton punched the ball off the line and Eusebio scored his eighth goal from the penalty spot. Sustained pressure from Portugal followed, several scrambles and a fine save from Banks before the whistle blew and England were through to the final.

Tears from Eusebio but it was a fine advert for European football and the two best teams were to meet to decide who would lift the Jules Rimet Trophy.

In the build up to the final, the newspapers were full of the Greaves conundrum, should he return to the side, after all it would have been almost unthinkable only months before to consider England lifting the trophy without him in the team. Unknown to the press the real story was whether Bobby Moore would be fit having contracted tonsillitis, luckily the team doctor had spotted the symptoms and was able to treat it, but it was touch and go.

July 30th 1966 had arrived and the rest is history.

AS ALWAYS, THE NAVY'S THERE!

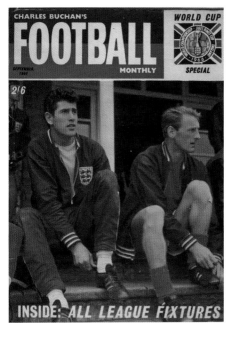

ALF RAMSEY . . .

the right man
at the right hour
for the right job

by PAT COLLINS

IT is not long since I expressed here my sympathy for the man who would take over as England's team manager. Now Alf Ramsey is installed, and so much in connection with the job has changed that I realise my sympathy was entirely misplaced.

England now have a team boss who is actually to be allowed to pick HIS team without worrying about the recommendations of an over-blown selection committee.

That was the big victory Ramsey won before he agreed to take the job. So it should be. So it should always have been. But better late than never. England are now moving into more enlightened days.

The general acclaim of the choice of Ramsey was also tinged with relief that the F.A. had managed to get a real professional for the job. At one stage one wondered where they would turn, for it seemed that none of the men most qualified was interested.

There is no doubt that few, if any, are more qualified for the position as England team-manager than the man who led Ipswich Town out of the wilderness.

Of course, there will still be some who doubt the choice.

On the day of the announcement a famous critic had reservations. "I don't know, I'm not sure he is the right man," he said. "After all, Ipswich were fortunate to win the League title, the way they are struggling this season proves that."

Such reasoning beats me. Not for a moment do I believe that all England's Soccer ills suddenly will be given a magic prescription by the new man. But surely nobody can doubt the worth of Ramsey's work at Ipswich, on a shoe-string budget, which showed results long before last season. After all, he built teams which took Ipswich from the Third to the First Division championship in six seasons. How, then, can anyone doubt him now before half the present term is through?

What IS important for England is that this man Ramsey has ideas on how this game should be played . . . and has been successful with them at club level. He has already said that he must devise a plan for England. Be sure he will.

There will be no rigid, inflexible dogma which cannot be bent or reshaped for individuals, but a plan which will meet the needs of the players he has at hand—just as it was with his club sides.

I know Alf Ramsey as a man of high purpose, not given to saying the easiest and most popular thing that comes to mind. He will care nothing of personal criticism if he believes he is doing the right thing. He is a demanding character, but a scrupulously fair one.

Best of all, for England's sake, he is a strong man who knows, as an ex-player, when he is being sold short of the effort he expects.

I recall an example of this. A few years back Ipswich Town were unexpectedly defeated in the Cup by the then non-League Peterborough. It had been a tight finish and somebody was foolish enough to say: "Hard luck, Alf."

"Hard luck?" he echoed coldly, "it was nothing of the kind. Peterborough played as we should have done, as a team with something to play for. Today my players let down the fans, my directors, my club and myself."

Future England players are warned: if after a game your shirt does not have to be wrung out—then you are not matching Alf Ramsey's idea of the required effort.

fascinating . . . argumentative

OTHERS may be brave, or precocious enough, but few are qualified to attempt what Ivan Sharpe, a Press colleague over the years, has attempted in his fascinating new Soccer book.

In "Soccer Top Ten", friend Ivan lists his idea of the ten leading players in the seven positions from goalkeeper to winger, whom he has seen or played against in half-a-century of playing and writing about the game. It will start the biggest argument since the penalty kick was introduced.

Classing full-backs, wing-halves, inside-forwards and wingers each as one position—and not considering whether left or right—Sharpe mentions just on 400 players, past and present.

At times he makes light reference to a particular playing quality, a short sentence which nevertheless is sufficient to rekindle old and warm memories. In his staccato style he whisks us swiftly round the English playing scene, or to some memorable match abroad in a vivid line or two.

Of course, his findings will be challenged. That is the beauty of the book. For every spectator is a Soccer selector — for pub, club, or country side.

Sharpe's selections are oblivious to record books and cap-collections. For instance, Jimmy Adamson, of Burnley, not honoured by England, gets in among wing-halves such as Veitch, McWilliam, Duncan Edwards, Grimsdell and McMullan. I would have had Archie Macaulay, Alex Massie and Ronnie Burgess among them. And I can imagine a cry for such as Cliff Britton, Matt Busby and Roy Paul.

Sharpe rates Vivian Woodward as THE greatest inside man. He is followed by Clem Stephenson, Bloomer, Alex James, Joe Smith, Charles Buchan, Doherty, Law, Greaves and McIlroy.

It is good to see the moderns so well-represented. They will seldom get higher or more worthwhile assessment.

I am sure fans, young and old, will denounce, discuss and decry, but all will delight in this eminently readable book.

P.C.

(Soccer Top Ten, Stanley Paul, 18s.)

BOSS ON THE BALL!

No desk man, Alf Ramsey, the new England team-manager. He looks a bit out of condition, but at least he has his eye on the ball—which is more than can be said for Bryan Douglas, during indoor training.

JOHNNY BYRNE
West Ham and England

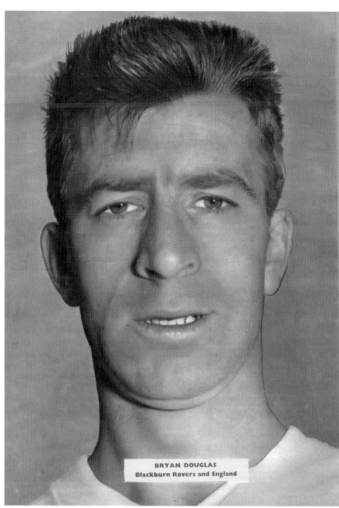

BRYAN DOUGLAS
Blackburn Rovers and England

RAY CRAWFORD
Ipswich Town
and England

BOBBY MOORE
West Ham United

You are wishing for the moon, Mr. Richards!

by PAT COLLINS

TO make a better showing in the World Cup of 1966, right here in our own backyard, England must, apparently, do the following: sack Winterbottom; sack Haynes; make England players more dedicated; keep them together longer; bring in a League club manager, or managers; let Stanley Matthews and Tom Finney take charge of the international sides.

ALSO, AS MR. JOE RICHARDS SAYS, PUT COUNTRY BEFORE CLUB.

Don't stop me if you have heard any or all of this before. It's the remark from the League President-cum-Chairman of the England selectors which makes me smile.

For on the day we were wondering about the news from Rancagua and England's fate against the tough Argentinians, I was smog-bound in the thick haze of cigar and cigarette smoke which hung over the League's A.G.M. in London.

Maybe it had no real part in the business on hand—club business—but I thought it would have been nice to hear a well-wisher there make some goodwill comment about England's game, to show that the gathering was in Chile in spirit, at least.

But it was not given a thought. And in the two hours of talk . . . procedure, plaint and proposal . . . not a syllable was uttered about improving England's football, from the playing or watching angle.

The only time England were mentioned there was a smug satisfaction that the F.A. had agreed to pay the wages of players on representative duty. Then followed a request for the League to do likewise for inter-League games!

Mr. Bob Lord, of Burnley, and Mr. John Moores, the Everton chairman, almost a double-act in which they were continually bobbing up and down, teamed-up on the above.

Country before club? I wonder if they realise how their clubs benefit DIRECTLY from calls which put their players in the "star" class.

Willingly or otherwise, clubs have accepted this "star" system, as shown by the different pay scales which now operate. It is on the international and representative field that names are made, not at Turf Moor, Goodison, Molineux, or anywhere else.

Last season, the Football League lost 639,852 customers. We may sometimes sigh that there are not more personalities in the game, but the international-tag does help to boost gates, especially in away games. However, as always, the clubs want it both ways.

My thoughts went back to that League meeting when I heard of the play-safe, defensive games which marred the World Cup as a spectacle in Chile. For who could be more cautious than English League clubs?

Even those sobering figures of a further attendance slump could not make them take the plunge and try the four-up and four-down proposal of the Management Committee. This proposed broadening of the competition may not be entirely the magic wand needed to bring back the crowds, but it DOES merit a trial.

Perhaps the play-safe clubs knew they were flouting the hopes of many in turning it down, and that would explain the decision to hide their votes under the cloak of the secret ballot, a decision which justly angered Mr. Richards.

I don't see any patriotic lead coming from League clubs to aid England's international cause. It will still be "club before country" come what may.

One of the things I regret—while appreciating what is behind it—is the first opposition to the F.A.'s decision to let clubs sign youngsters still at school. England have envied other countries who have taken boys from the cradle and brought them along in a club social atmosphere. Might not the idea work here? I feel that with earlier coaching and training, England—and Scotland, Ireland and Wales—could go a long way towards turning out more athletic youngsters, particularly in the way of speeding them up. For one of the things I believe we most lack in our British game is speed. It shows at top-level competition.

I don't want a brood of sprinters. I know there is not much point in moving fast without the ball. But one of the reasons why Jimmy Armfield is among the best full-backs in the world is his speed. He goes where he wants to, fast. And he has an attacking flair because he has the speed to recover.

It is also because of his speed that I would have liked to have seen John Connelly on England's right wing in Chile.

The Continentals often score over England where all else is equal, when pace, just pure pace, comes into the reckoning.

If they are taken at an earlier age it should be possible to sharpen up the youngsters. The skills, ball control, heading and the rest, are matters for later coaching.

Two final thoughts on the last World Cup. First, wing-half Ron Flowers, with two penalties, was England's top-scorer—the biggest indictment of a woe-begone attack.

Second, the strange twist by the men on the spot when they acclaimed Bobby Charlton as England's only world-class forward. Just a few weeks before he left for Chile the majority were of the opinion that he was lucky to be in the England side.

Strange, isn't it?

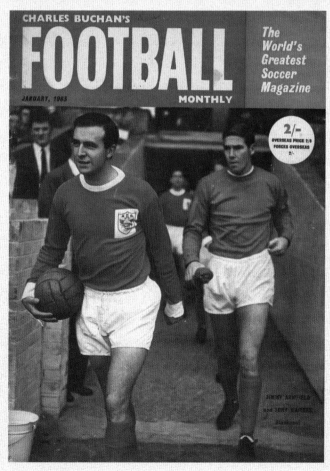

GORDON BANKS
Leicester City and England

JIMMY ARMFIELD
Blackpool

TONY KAY
Sheffield Wednesday

ROGER HUNT
Liverpool

Naughty, naughty ! Ney, inside-left of Brazil, probably didn't realise that the all-seeing eye of the camera was watching. That's why we have a nice shot of him doing a Harlem Globetrotters' basketball act with Gordon Banks, of England.

Jimmy Armfield with Brazilian goalkeeper Gilmar.

OUR CAMERAS CAPTURE THE ACTION AT WEMBLEY FOR ENGLAND V BRAZIL

Bryan Douglas tussles with Brazilian Tavares.

CAPTAIN MOORE WAS GREAT

CZECHOSLOVAKIA 2, ENGLAND 4
(At Bratislava, May 29, 1963)
Scorers: Czechoslovakia—Scherer, Masek. England—
Smith, Greaves 2, Charlton

THE Czechs were runners-up in the last World Cup and so victory over them was a fine English achievement.

With Jimmy Armfield injured, Moore took over to become England's youngest captain (21). He was great—as were the rest of the English defence which stood up manfully to the Czechs' opening onslaught.

ENGLAND—Banks (Leicester); Shellito (Chelsea), Wilson (Huddersfield); Milne (Liverpool), Norman (Spurs), Moore (West Ham), Paine (Southampton), Greaves (Spurs), Smith (Spurs), Eastham (Arsenal), Charlton (Man. Utd.).
CZECHOSLOVAKIA—Schroif; Lala, Novak; Pluskal, Popluhar, Masopust (Bubernek); Stilbranyi, Scherer, Kadraba, Kvasnak, Masek.

Massacre of the Swiss

SWITZERLAND 1, ENGLAND 8
(At Basle, June 5, 1963)
Scorers: Switzerland—Bertschi.
England—Charlton 3, Byrne 2, Kay, Douglas, Melia

ENGLAND, with seven changes, took just enough time for the team to get to know each other . . . then the massacre of the Swiss was on. It was never a test for an England side which produced goals almost at will.

Kay had an inspiring match for his first cap, and Charlton rounded off a thoroughly satisfactory personal tour with his hat-trick. The experiment of Moore and Flowers as two centre-halves, while not highly tried, still looked impressive.

SWITZERLAND—Stettler; Grobety, Tacchella; Weber, Schneiter, Leimgruber; Allemann, Odermatt, Kuhn, Bertschi, Pottier.
ENGLAND—Springett (Sheff. Wed.); Armfield (Blackpool), Wilson (Huddersfield); Kay (Everton), Moore (West Ham), Flowers (Wolves); Douglas (Blackburn), Greaves (Tottenham), Byrne (West Ham), Melia (Liverpool), Charlton (Man. Utd.).

England defence let down by attack

ENGLAND 1, BRAZIL 1
(At Wembley, May 8, 1963)
Scorers: England—Douglas. Brazil—Pepe

AN untidy, scrambled equaliser by Douglas in the last five minutes was in keeping with the previous efforts of the English attack which, with a monopoly of the ball, fumbled and faltered before a packed, disciplined defence.

Truest after-match comment was that such a grand England defence did not deserve the attack it had in front of them. Moore had a great game. Milne's first cap was worn with high honour, and the almost unemployed Banks apart, the other defenders, came through splendidly.

After Pepe's "banana" shot had fooled Banks, the Brazilians, without Pele and Zito, injured in a Hamburg car crash 4 hours earlier, pulled back to hold on to their lead.

For the most part they looked what they were, a young, experimental side, none too convincing in attack, but with much of the usual efficiency in defence.

The big England failure was the lack of ideas and resource when all too-orthodox moves were easily countered.

ENGLAND—Banks (Leicester). Armfield (Blackpool), Wilson (Huddersfield); Milne (Liverpool), Norman (Spurs), Moore (West Ham); Douglas (Blackburn), Greaves (Spurs), Smith (Spurs), Eastham (Arsenal), Charlton (Man. Utd.)
BRAZIL—Gilmar; Lima, Eduardo, Diaz, Rildo, Zequinha, Mengalvio; Dorval, Coutinho, Amarildo (Ney), Pepe.

KAPUT!

England poised, masterful

EAST GERMANY 1, ENGLAND 2
At Leipzig, June 2, 1963
Scorers: E. Germany—Ducke P.
England—Hunt, Charlton

ENGLAND handsomely maintained their improvement, with Charlton at his best, Eastham, a thin, frail general of the attack and Paine making an even stronger claim to be England's No. 1 right-winger.

Greaves was ruled out through tonsilitis and seven of the side had been treated for a stomach ailment. But having survived the early German pressure the English always looked the more poised, more masterful side.

The English were unrecognisable as the side who had struggled at home. Their discipline and fighting heart was a tribute to Alf Ramsey's managership which had welded them into a team to command the respect of the best of the Continental sides.

EAST GERMANY—Fritzsche; Kaiser, Heine, Liebrecht; Urbanczyk, Krampe; P., Noeldner, Ducke R.; Nachaigall, Frenzel, Ducke
ENGLAND—Banks (Leicester); Armfield (Blackpool), Wilson (Huddersfield); Milne (Liverpool), Norman (Spurs), Moore (West Ham); Paine (Southampton), Hunt (Liverpool), Smith (Spurs), Eastham (Arsenal), Charlton (Man. Utd.).

Roger Hunt hurdles the desperate lunge of the East German defender during the countries historic first ever meeting.

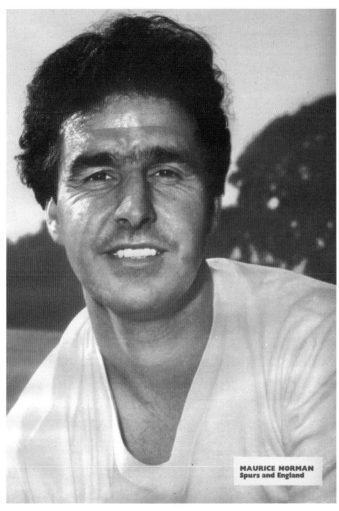

MAURICE NORMAN
Spurs and England

RAY POINTER
Burnley and England

RON SPRINGETT
Sheffield Wednesday

RAY WILSON
Huddersfield Town
and England

GEORGE COHEN
Fulham

JIMMY GREAVES
(Spurs and England)

GORDON BANKS
Leicester City

BOBBY CHARLTON
Manchester United

Clifford Webb

England, under the managership of Alf Ramsey, made one of her most successful close-season tours last June, winning all three games. In this article, Guest Writer CLIFFORD WEBB, B.B.C. commentator and one of Fleet Street's most experienced sports journalists, analyses that tour with an eye on the 1966 World Cup.

A FEW weeks ago we witnessed the greatest transformation scene in the history of English Soccer—a magical switch from the greyest gloom to whiter-than-white.

It is easy to recall the sequence of events. England humiliated by France in Paris and eliminated from the European Nations' Cup. England humbled by Scotland at Wembley—a narrow defeat, but one which revealed nothing on which hopes for the future could be pinned.

Then, England in a lack-lustre draw against Brazil, at the Empire Stadium. On paper, not a bad performance, remembering that Brazil are the World Cup-holders; in fact, a completely uninspiring, unimaginative display by England against a half-pace Brazilian team.

They were obviously not up to strength because of injuries and, more important, because the process of shedding some of the older stars and blooding the new was taking place.

Everybody—well, nearly everybody—was so sorry for team-manager Alf Ramsey. What a load of trouble he had been landed with! How could he possibly build a World Cup team out of that lot?

Remember the newspaper quotes? After Scotland: "This was the worst England team I have ever seen, and the shabbiest, poorest England display I can remember . . ."

"We remembered how Lawton and Mannion and Matthews and the others in white shirts used to ride majestically over the Scots. Now there were these white mice in their places."

And, after Brazil: "The plain fact is that our football, at international level, is slipping farther and farther away from the peak attained by other countries".

I must confess that, to an extent, I shared these views. Meeting Alf Ramsey at the Footballer of the Year dinner in London's West End, I told him I didn't envy him his task, but wished him well.

Alf smiled wryly and replied that the sentiments I expressed were the same as had been put forward by many others that evening . . . "but don't write us off".

Then came the announcement of the England party to make the tour embracing matches against Czechoslovakia, East Germany and Switzerland.

Nobody was wildly enthusiastic, even though some new names appeared . . . Ken Shellito, the Chelsea full-back, Tony Kay, the expensive Everton half-back, Terry Paine, the lively Southampton winger.

England transformed

- BUT THERE'S STILL A LONG WAY TO GO

WEBB
Continued from above

The Soccer bombshell burst in a cascade of glowing tributes after England had walloped the Czechs 4—2 in Bratislava, under the captaincy of West Ham's Bobby Moore, with new caps Ken Shellito and Terry Paine contributing man-sized performances.

"England, wearing an all-scarlet rig like a battle banner, crushed the mighty Czechs . . ."

After clearing your ears to make certain you heard aright on the radio, you had to rub your eyes to take in all the fulsome praise heaped on the "Ramsey Raiders".

On to Leipzig . . . East Germany 1, England 2. By now there was a frenzied searching for adjectives; a positive hysteria of bubbling praise.

Don't get me wrong. That Leipzig win was a great one. So many things had piled up against England.

Tummy trouble for eight players (and some of us who attended the World Cup series in Brazil in 1950, and who queued, groaning, with the players outside the door of "Doctor-trainer" Jimmy Trotter's hotel room, know how lowering this can be); goal-cracking Jimmy Greaves down with tonsilitis; a big, pre-match political build-up for East Germany . . .

I was glad that the man of the match turned out to be George Eastham, whose snaky skill I always thought England could ill afford to ignore. But Eastham was no isolated hero. That was a team fit to carry the England label.

And so to Switzerland, a place of happy memories for England players, particularly in the years just after World War II when a plane whisked us from the rationed austerity of post-war Britain to a land flowing (literally) with milk and honey. And meat and eggs and fish.

Never has an England Soccer tour finished so triumphantly. 8—1 for England, in Basle—and there was Ramsey after that resounding victory standing with a grin wider than the Thames estuary and saying:

"The thing that thrilled me was that even when we were 6—1 up, the boys were still fighting for the ball and chasing chances. This is the spirit and outlook I have always wanted to see from England players."

And so say all of us.

As I have said, a complete, almost miraculous transformation. As if some football fairy godmother had waved a magic wand. And therein lies the danger.

You can't win the World Cup with a magic wand. The basic necessities are between 20 and 24 magic players.

Has England got them? Not yet. On this three-match, three-win tour England took 19, and of that happy band we should remember that by the next World Cup year, 1966, some of them will be slightly over the top.

Ray Wilson, for instance will be 31, so will Ron Flowers and Brian Douglas. Maurice Norman will be 30, Bobby Smith 32.

But we can lick our lips and grease our rattles in pleasant anticipation when we check the ages of some of the others.

Ken Shellito is just 21, so is Bobby Moore. Terry Paine 23, Roger Hunt 24, Jimmy Greaves 22, Johnny Byrne 24, George Eastham, Jimmy Melia, Bobby Charlton, all are 25.

Yes, the nucleus seems to be there. And backing up the boys in possession come the "Under-23s", with stars like Alan Hinton (Wolves), Ernie Hunt (Swindon), Derek Stokes (Huddersfield), Brian Labone (Everton).

One could be excused for imagining that all the young players I have named suddenly appeared towards the back-end of last season. We all know it was nothing of the sort. They had been there for some time: it was merely a question of how best to use them.

That is where Alf Ramsey comes in. Quietly—Alf was always the quiet one, anyway—Walter Winterbottom's successor as England's team chief changed the national side's pattern of play.

He hasn't finished yet, but already there is more than a glimpse of a modern formation—a definite four-two-four set-up which gives a side much-needed elasticity, freedom to experiment, to extemporise and to gear tactics to the need of the moment.

I think that it has been made clear that to win a World Cup a nation must be able to place in the field a team of eleven complete footballers.

Frankly, I was amazed that Hungary missed the World Cup in Switzerland in 1954 because Puskas and Co., in my opinion—based on two Soccer visits to South America and a long round of international games in all parts of Europe—impressed me as the greatest team I have ever seen.

Far more than the Brazilians, the Argentinians and the great Uruguayans of that period, they had a team of footballers so complete it was breathtaking to watch them swing from tight defence to gloriously open attack in the flicker of an eyelid.

My respect for Ramsey grows. I am beginning to believe he is a wily old bird who is not going to be overawed by smooth Latin rhythm, but who keeps the Hungarian image in the back of his mind.

I believe, too, that the success of England's recent European tour has earned him the profound respect and admiration of all his players. And that is more than half the battle.

Summing up, I would say England still have a long way to go, much hard work to do, and the whole-hearted co-operation of every one of the 92 League clubs to seek.

But I like to recall the undisguised envy in the voice of one of Europe's best-known coaches who, after seeing the Leipzig game said:

"With such players, England's future can only be good."

England on top of the World

ENGLAND 2, REST OF WORLD 1
(At Wembley, October 23, 1963)
Scorers: England—Paine, Greaves
Rest of World—Law

ENGLAND rose magnificently to the challenge from some of the greatest players in the world, and fittingly celebrated the Centenary of the F.A. by this victory.

Greaves was in wonderful form, standing out even in this illustrious company. It was unfortunate for him that his wonderful second half effort, when he "scored" after being twice fouled, was ruled out by the referee who had awarded a free-kick to England before Greaves shot.

The greater team-work of the home side more than off-set the individual skill of the Rest. In fact, the Rest were very lucky to get off as lightly as they did.

But for Yashin's great goalkeeping in the first half England would have won far more comfortably.

ENGLAND—Banks (Leicester); Armfield (Blackpool), Wilson (Huddersfield); Milne (Liverpool), Norman (Spurs), Moore (West Ham); Paine (Southampton), Greaves (Spurs), Smith (Spurs), Eastham (Arsenal), Charlton (Manchester U.).

REST OF WORLD—Yashin (Russia); Santos (Brazil), Schnellinger (W. Germany); Pluskal, Popluhar, Masopust (Czechoslovakia); Kopa (France), Law (Scotland), Di Stefano (Spain), Eusebio (Portugal), Gento (Spain). Soskic (Yugoslavia), Eyzaguirre (Chile), Baxter (Scotland), Seeler (W. Germany) and Puskas (Spain) were second half substitutes.

REST OF WORLD—Standing: Puskas (Spain), D. Santos (Brazil), Schnellinger (W. Germany), Yashin (U.S.S.R.), Popluhar (Czechoslovakia), Pluskal (Czechoslovakia), Baxter (Scotland), Masopust (Czechoslovakia), Eyzaguirre (Chile), (behind him, Soskic, Yugoslavia), Seeler (W. Germany). Kneeling: Kopa (France), Law (Scotland), Di Stefano (Spain), Eusebio (Portugal), Gento (Spain).

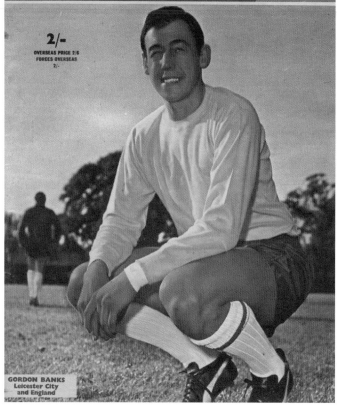

CHARLES BUCHAN'S
FOOTBALL MONTHLY
The World's Greatest Soccer Magazine

JANUARY, 1964

2/-
OVERSEAS PRICE 2/6
FORCES OVERSEAS
2/-

GORDON BANKS
Leicester City
and England

CHARLES BUCHAN'S
FOOTBALL MONTHLY
The World's Greatest Soccer Magazine

MARCH, 1964

2/-
OVERSEAS PRICE 2/6
FORCES OVERSEAS
2/-

BRYAN DOUGLAS
Blackburn Rovers
and England

CHARLES BUCHAN'S
FOOTBALL MONTHLY
The World's Greatest Soccer Magazine

JULY, 1964

2/-
OVERSEAS PRICE 2/6
FORCES OVERSEAS

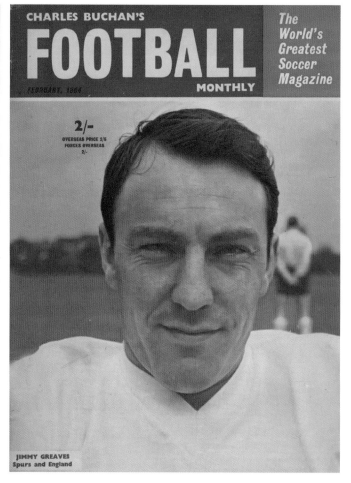

CHARLES BUCHAN'S
FOOTBALL MONTHLY
The World's Greatest Soccer Magazine

FEBRUARY, 1964

2/-
OVERSEAS PRICE 2/6
FORCES OVERSEAS
2/-

JIMMY GREAVES
Spurs and England

Italian clubs £7 million in the red

ITALIAN League leaders, worried by some of the clubs' "enormous deficits", ordered them to present balance-sheets, then threatened to make the chairmen responsible for part of the debts.

The League bitterly criticised "colossal bonuses paid to players for a single victory," and "huge transfer fees paid for foreign players, some of whom had never been seen in action by the clubs that acquired them."

Between them, 36 of Italy's professional clubs are said to be owing £7 million. Only one club in each of the two Leagues owes nothing.

A group of M.P.s has called for an inquiry.

★　　　★　　　★

ITALIAN fans don't get much for their money in goals, for the average scored in the First Division last season was only 2.11 per match.

Returns made for 12 European countries' top Leagues showed Switzerland heading the average scoring with 4.09 goals a match. Between Switzerland in the lead and Italy at the bottom came Luxembourg, Scotland, Austria, England, West Germany, Holland, Portugal, France, Spain and Belgium in that order.

Counts were not made for countries that have a big weather break in their seasons.

On a single day in Italy's First Division, last season, four games were goalless, and five others produced only 13 goals.

★　　　★　　　★

FRANCE is wondering how centre-forward Nestor Combin will fare with Juventus, to whom he was transferred from Lyons for a reported £63,000 this summer.

Combin, aged 23, was born in Argentina. He failed to make good there and went to France, took French nationality and in his 64 "official" matches last season, scored 62 goals.

"We've been looking for another John Charles," a Juventus official said at Combin's signing, "and now I think we've got him."

When Frenchmen warned Combin he would find Italian club officials, trainers and crowds the most exacting in the world," he said:

"I know all that. I'm going because I can't resist the money. Even if it's hell it will be only for a slice of my life, and the money will help to heal the burns—if any."

The game abroad
by Bill Croft

DIDI GOES BACK—HE MAY ADVISE BRAZIL

THAT great Brazilian inside-forward, Didi (real name Waldira Pereira), winner of two World Cup medals and aged 36, is back with Botafogo of Rio de Janeiro after serving two years in Peru as a club trainer.

He left Botafogo over a pay problem, coached a Peruvian team twice into second place in the National League, but played only in friendlies because of a ban Botafogo imposed on him.

He returned to the Botafogo club with a smile, is playing for them, and is strongly tipped as an adviser of the Brazil team for the World Cup of 1966.

Didi's colourful career includes an unsuccessful year with Real of Madrid, where his ideas often clashed with Alfredo Di Stefano's.

★　　　★　　　★

DI STEFANO as you know is now with Espanol, of Barcelona, following what has been called Real of Madrid's "surprising decision that they can get along without him."

He was 38 on July 4, played well last season, and has said he wants to go on playing. Several Spanish, Italian and other teams have made offers for his services as player, manager or coach.

While I write, it looks as though Di Stefano has little intention of realising a dream he was said to be nursing a few years ago. "When my playing days are over," he was then reported to have said, "I'll gladly retire from top Soccer's nerve-wracking stage, return to my native Argentina, and administer the property I've bought there with my earnings.

"Houses and farms will be easier to manage than footballers, and they won't watch me with the hard piercing eyes of the usual club president—though I must say I've had none of that from Real's chiefs."

A few months ago, the great Alfredo was quoted as saying he felt "much too fit for retirement yet." A likely job for him seemed to be the managing of Real of Madrid's new "Sports City".

His earnings in eleven years with Real, including the huge bonuses awarded by the world's most glamorous and successful club, have been put as high as £350,000.

★　　　★　　　★

SIGNED on by Real to succeed Di Stefano is 27-year-old Emilio Morollon, for six seasons centre-forward for Valladolid. Numerous offers were received for this player during that period, but Valladolid turned them down, as he was considered to be "half the team".

He could not, however, prevent their relegation, and it was this which speeded his departure.

★　　　★　　　★

ASKED if he would be playing next year, inside-forward Ferenc Puskas, still, at 37, a star of Real of Madrid, said "Yes—if the ball continues to travel faster than the players."

A Spanish critic writes of Puskas: "No player in the world anticipates better than he, where the ball is going next, or makes better use of it when he gets it.

"Some foraging, however, is vital and, for that reason, my bet is Real won't have room for Puskas after the current season."

" Do that again, mate, and I'll have you for parking your Jaguar outside!"

TALKING POINT

JOHNNY HAYNES...
does England need him ?

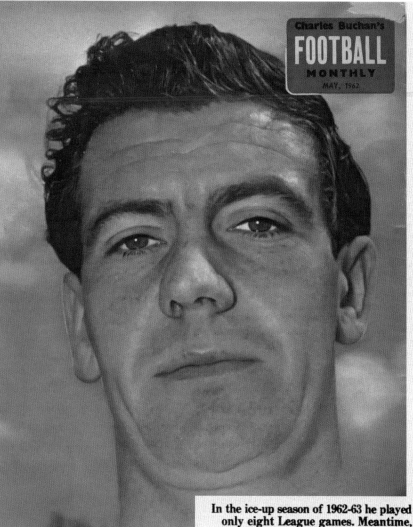

ON Saturday, October 3, ten years after looking very much the new boy in a side in which he had colleagues such as Billy Wright, Stanley Matthews, the late Roger Byrne and Nat Lofthouse, Johnny Haynes may return to Windsor Park, Belfast, in an England shirt.

If he does, it will be his 57th cap—and will bridge a wait of two years in the Soccer wilderness.

Two years ago he was England's captain, for the 22nd time. His side had been tossed out of the World Cup by Brazil, the champions. From Chile a storm blew up, threatening to blow Haynes out of further England reckoning.

As captain, Haynes was bracketed with team-manager Walter Winterbottom as the main cause of that World Cup flop. He was criticised on all sides for his "too stereotyped ideas", lack of real ball control, his captaincy. Nobody had a good word for him.

Lamented the official "F.A. News" . . . "Haynes and Greaves, on whom so much depended, had poor championships".

Such criticism was nothing new for Haynes. No forward caused more controversy. Most of his critics were in the North, but there were plenty, too, in the South.

You are either for him or against—there is no in-between.

Looking back, an observer wrote: "It was all too evident in Chile that his once-telling passes were no longer capable

IT'S SKIPPER HAYNES AGAIN

In the ice-up season of 1962-63 he played only eight League games. Meantime, Alf Ramsey took over as England manager and one-man selection panel.

There was some campaigning for the return of Haynes last season. Others felt that Ramsey already had his ideas about the Fulham player . . . and didn't see him fitting into an England side playing HIS way.

England's failure in Brazil last June brought out the headlines and demands for the return of Haynes.

DOES ENGLAND NEED JOHNNY HAYNES?

If, as Ramsey has admitted, some of England's failings were due to inaccurate passing, who better than Haynes, the most precise, most telling distributor in the game?

If her need is a link-man to assemble and deliver from defence, to polish and prime and supply the attack—who has more suitable qualifications?

He will be 31 by the time England stages the World Cup. He is keen to win back his place. The question of whether he returns as captain is not really important.

What is important is to find an answer to the question . . . does England need Johnny Haynes, the player?

England face South American opposition once again! ...

FOOTBALL ASSOCIATION INTERNATIONAL MATCH
WEDNESDAY, MAY 6th 1964
KICK OFF 3 P.M.

ENGLAND
v
URUGUAY

WEMBLEY
EMPIRE STADIUM

OFFICIAL PROGRAMME — ONE SHILLING

England skipper Bobby Moore and Uruguay's Martinez
exchange pennants before the match at Wembley in 1964

14

Johnny Byrne opens the scoring from close range against Uruguay

ENGLAND WERE TOO RIGID

SCOTLAND 1, ENGLAND 0
(Hampden Park, Glasgow, April 11, 1964)
Scorer: Scotland—Gilzean

ALTHOUGH it did not reach memorable playing heights this match was interesting because of the marked difference in method between the teams. England were rigid, disciplined, stick-to-the-plan; the Scots had belief that their undoubted skill would lift them above all planning.

The Scots had their plans, of course, but they left it to individuals to direct events as the game unfolded. England stuck stiffly to briefing, yet they had chances enough to have won.

Greig, of Rangers, in his first international, was a big success. He gave the Scottish half-back line a solid look, and was a fine foil to the attacking urge of club-mate Baxter on the other flank.

Henderson, another Ranger, was a menace to England, giving Wilson a worrying time. He might have been even more of a threat had he had better service.

England lost their early grip on a game they could have dictated had Hunt done better with two good chances in the first 10 minutes. This victory, won by Gilzean's header at 72 minutes, was a hat-trick for the Scots in these encounters.

SCOTLAND—Forsyth (Dundee), Kennedy (Celtic) (Kilmarnock); Hamilton (Celtic), Baxter (Rangers); Greig (Rangers), McNeil (Tottenham), Gilzean (Dundee), Henderson (Rangers), White (Rangers).
ENGLAND—Banks (Leicester); Armfield (Blackpool), Wilson (Huddersfield); Milne (Liverpool), Norman (Tottenham), Moore (West Ham); Paine (Southampton), Hunt (Liverpool), Byrne (West Ham), Eastham (Arsenal), Charlton (Man. Utd.).

Irish deserved a draw

N. IRELAND 3, ENGLAND 4
(At Windsor Park, Belfast, Oct. 3, 1964)
Scorers: N. Ireland—Wilson, McLaughlin 2.
England—Pickering, Greaves 3.

SLOW hand-clapped by an Irish crowd which turned against them when the score was 4-0 to England in less than half an hour, the Irish side made a magnificent fight-back against the odds. They deserved at least a draw.

Within minutes they were handicapped when McLaughlin fell and injured a wrist. Three times he went off for attention, but he was no passenger. It was McLaughlin's pluck which lit the fuse to an Irish team which took all the second-half honours.

Greaves' first half hat-trick, a wonderful effort in which he scored all three within 11 minutes, seemed to have put Ireland out of the reckoning. But the home side threw back the taunts of their own fans in a most incredible fashion.

Wilson first, then two from the heroic McLaughlin, put the Irish in with a

ENGLAND BEWILDERED

ENGLAND 2, BELGIUM 2
(At Wembley, Oct. 21, 1964)
Scorers: England—Pickering, Verblest o.g.
Belgium—Cornelis, Van Himst.

A BEWILDERED English side chased shadows for most of the first half. The Belgians, well on top, moved quickly and shrewdly into positions which always gave them a spare man to pass to. When England got into the game in the second half it was more by extra physical effort than by improvement in skills.

It was a tough debut for Venables. The more experienced players around him never got going, so to ease the load of his first cap. But he came more into the run of things as the game went on.

The teamwork of the Belgians, with half the side coming from Anderlecht, was far superior to England's. Especially lacking was some strong captaincy by Moore in the earlier moments, when the tide flowed against his men.

ENGLAND—Waiters (Blackpool); Cohen (Fulham), Thomson (Wolves); Milne (Liverpool), Norman (Spurs), Moore (West Ham); Thompson (Liverpool), Greaves (Spurs), Pickering (Everton),

England still have no blend

HOLLAND 1, ENGLAND 1
(At Amsterdam, Dec. 2, 1964)
Scorers: Holland—Moulijn. England—Greaves.

THERE were just five minutes left when Greaves side-stepped a Dutch defender and hammered home England's face-saving goal. But that goal only partially hid the failure of the expected winners to match the tactical skill of the unfancied home side.

England's defence got through a lot of dogged resistance—it had to. Charlton, in spasms, gave the England attack some bite, but there were no real triumphs in an England team yet to show any effective blend.

HOLLAND: Graafland; Flinkevleugel, Israel, Schrijvers, Fransen; Nuninga, Muller, Van Nee, Bouwmeester, Moulijn.
ENGLAND: Waiters (Blackpool); Cohen (Fulham), Flowers (Wolves); Mullery (Spurs); Norman (Spurs), Thomson (Wolves), Wignall (Nottm. F.), Thompson (Liverpool), Greaves (Spurs), Charlton (Man. U.), Venables (Chelsea).

England 2, Wales 1
(At Wembley, Nov. 18, 1964)
Scorers: England—Wignall 2.
Wales—Jones.

ENGLAND were without the first-choice inside-forwards Greaves and Venables—Hunt and Byrne deputised. Great effort was made by the winners, but it was not allied to a particularly skilful performance.

Most home attacks were pressed down the left where Hinton troubled Stuart Williams with his speed. Both English goals came from a Nottingham Forest tie-up between Hinton and centre-forward Wignall, who came out reasonably well with two goals in his first international.

Millington started shakily in the Welsh goal, but later made some fine saves to deny England superiority. Waiters at the other end, in the few times he was tested, showed high-class work.

Wales kept doggedly to their task. Rees was their best forward, keeping Thomson fully occupied.

A less than half-filled stadium generated little of the international atmosphere which can lift players above themselves.

ENGLAND—Waiters (Blackpool); Cohen (Fulham), Thomson (Wolves); Bailey (Charlton), Flowers (Wolves), Young (Sheff. Wed.); Thompson (Liverpool), Hunt (Liverpool), Wignall (Nottm. For.), Byrne

Charles Buchan's on tour with...

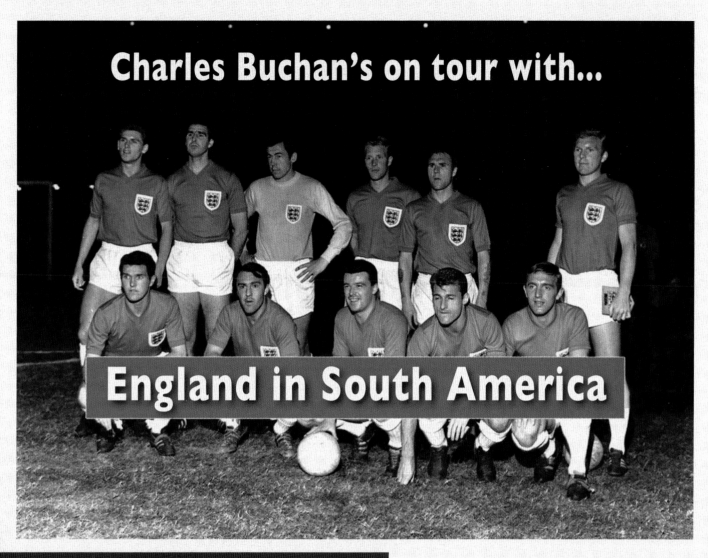

England in South America

big game details ||||||||||||||||||||||||||||||||||||||||||||||||||||||||||||||||||||||||||||||

ENGLAND'S FAULT —AS USUAL

FINAL TABLE

	P	W	D	L	F	A	Pts
Argentina	3	3	0	0	6	0	6
Brazil	3	2	0	1	9	5	4
England	3	0	1	2	2	7	1
Portugal	3	0	1	2	2	7	1

ENGLAND 1, PORTUGAL 1
(Sao Paulo, June 4, 1964)
Scorers: England—Hunt.
Portugal—Flowers, o.g.

WHAT seemed to be perfectly good goals by Hunt and Byrne were disallowed . . . Torres, the giant Portuguese centre-forward, was sent off for disputing a decision minutes from time . . . Greaves hit the bar—but Portugal, with only eight fit men, held out.

Eusebio was dangerous until he was hurt, but it was the usual tale of England not taking their chances. Banks was unlucky to be beaten, he had a shot by Perez covered until the ball struck Flowers and changed direction. Byrne was receiving attention when the goal was scored.

Hunt, a great trier, took his chance splendidly for the equaliser.

ENGLAND: Banks (Leicester); Thomson (Wolves); Wilson (Huddersfield); Flowers (Wolves), Norman (Spurs), Moore (West Ham); Paine (Southampton), Greaves (Spurs), Byrne (West Ham), Hunt (Liverpool), Thompson (Liverpool).
PORTUGAL: Americo; Festa, Gomes; Mendes, Vicente, Batista; J. Carlos, Eusebio, Torres, Coluna, Perez.

BRAZIL 5, ENGLAND 1
(Rio de Janeiro, May 31, 1964)
Scorers: Brazil—Rinaldo 2, Pele, Julinho, Dias.
England—Greaves

ENGLAND had no answer to Pelé. Just when Greaves had got an early second-half equaliser and there seemed to be some chance of a surprise, the great Brazilian inside-left took charge of the game.

Within minutes England were shattered by three goals . . . and Pelé figured prominently in each, scoring the second himself.

Hard as England fought they were mostly chasing second-half shadows . . . to chants of "Brazil, Brazil". Accompanied by exploding firecrackers, the world champions sailed serenely home.

BRAZIL: Gilmar; Alberto, Brito; Dias, Joel, Rildo; Julinho, Gerson, Vava, Pelé, Rinaldo.
ENGLAND: Waiters (Blackpool); Cohen (Fulham), Wilson (Huddersfield); Milne (Liverpool), Norman (Spurs), Moore (West Ham); Thompson (Liverpool), Greaves (Spurs), Byrne (West Ham), Eastham (Arsenal), Charlton (Manchester Utd.).

ARGENTINA 1, ENGLAND 0
(Rio de Janeiro, June 7, 1964)
Scorers: Argentina—Chaldon

ENGLAND—Banks (Leicester); Thomson (Wolves), Wilson (Huddersfield); Milne (Liverpool), Norman (Spurs), Moore (West Ham); Thompson (Liverpool), Greaves (Spurs), Byrne (West Ham), Eastham (Arsenal), Charlton (Manchester United).
ARGENTINA—Carrizo; Delgado, Vidal; Simeone, Viertes, Rattin; Rendo, Omega, Prospitti, Chaldon, Rojas, Pelch.

U.S.A. 0, ENGLAND 10
(New York, May 27, 1964)
Scorers: England—Hunt 4, Pickering 3, Paine 2, Charlton

ENGLAND—Banks (Leicester); Cohen (Fulham), Thomson (Wolves); Bailey (Charlton), Norman (Spurs), Flowers (Wolves); Paine (Southampton), Hunt (Liverpool), Pickering (Everton), Eastham (Arsenal), Thompson (Liverpool).
U.S.—Schwart; Borobiak, Racz; Rick, Garcia, Horvath; Noha, Chysowych, Mate, Murphy, Wild.

FRANCE UNDER-23 0, SCOTLAND UNDER-23 2
(Nantes, May 24, 1964)
Scorers: Scotland—Martin, Robertson

SCOTLAND—Davies (Dundee Utd.); King (Kilmarnock), Shevlane (Hearts); Bremner (Leeds), McGrory (Kilmarnock), Murray (Motherwell); Johnstone (Celtic), Martin (Hibs), Sharkey (Sunderland), Gibson (Middlesbrough), Robertson (Spurs).
FRANCE—Landi; Brucato, Polny: Desgoerges, Sillou, Simon; Guino, Destrumelle, Guy, Rodighiero, Roy.

URGENT !

To: Alf Ramsey, Esq.

Dear Alf...

PAT COLLINS is getting worried about England's chances in the 1966 World Cup, to be held here. So, he has written this letter to Alf Ramsey, the England team-manager . . .

❝When you became England team-manager I welcomed the appointment. I felt you could handle the job as capably as any, better than most. Now, two years and 19 internationals later, you have my sympathy.

Here you are at the beginning of a four-month break from action by your team—until the match with Scotland at Wembley in April.

And you haven't much time, have you, between now and the World Cup?

We have been talking about the World Cup for so long, and July, 1966, may still sound quite a way ahead.

But I say that you MUST have your team ready for the start of our home international programme NEXT season.

And, barring accidents and the very minimum changes, the team must play together, stay together, if England are to make a show in 1966.

Right now I think you have only HALF a team to count on. And I'd be surprised if you didn't think the same way.

In 19 games you have rung the changes 44 times. A sour critic of those changes remarked that the current boast of a player is that he DIDN'T have an England cap.

On the other hand, few can say they haven't had a chance.

England are still a long way from shaking down into a settled—and satisfying—combination.

The usual moans are going up that although the England hopefuls should be meeting regularly and plotting the future, League football and the clubs' affairs are put before country. And that something should be done about it.

Of course, something should be done . . . but it won't!

It's useless to thump tables—and typewriters—and point to the set-ups of rivals who will be descending upon us in the summer of next year.

Club interests DO come first. That is final, established and immovably so. It will be so in our time. It's one of the reasons for my sympathy for you.

When you took over, remember, you said England could win the World Cup. Well, if you manage to find a team to do that you will be the Sportsman of next year and every other year!

Fortunately, England are in the final rounds as the host country. The Scots, Irish and Welsh have still to make it.

I've been trying to sort out players who look most certain to figure in England's World Cup Pool. It turned out to be a very short list.

Greaves . . . Waiters . . . Charlton (I'd consider him at centre-forward, too, Alf!) . . . Peter Thompson (because he can play either wing) . . . a fit Bobby Moore . . . Bobby Thomson (because he, too, can switch) . . . Banks (second goalkeeper) . . . Ray Wilson, a "must" if fully recovered . . . Venables (he will have matured).

I couldn't stretch my list beyond that. Only in goal and at full-back, definitely at full-back, do I see you having free choice.

How you must envy Ian McColl with Denis Law, Jimmy Baxter and Willie Henderson! Or the Irish with Georgie Best!

When Len Badger, of Sheffield United gets his chance at right-back, I expect to see him stay. The same goes for John Sissons, of West Ham. These are the two most exciting youngsters I've watched this season.

I'm not trying to tell you anything . . . you have already noted them, and centre-forward Mick Jones, Badger's club-mate, and Alan Ball, of Blackpool.

Young men all, but growing rapidly each week as more experience comes their way. I'd like to see them "blooded" in the big time as soon as possible.

Then, if they show signs of matching, next season they can start in, or on the fringe of, the England team you feel is going to be near enough the one for the World Cup.

As I say, Alf, time is running out. You have to find the right link-up at inside-forward and wing-half. And you have to decide soon whom you see as the best in those positions so that they get as much playing together as possible.

I don't envy you your job. Good wing-halves or inside-forwards are hard to find. In fact, it is not now a case of finding but of deciding on the men from those you have tried, either in the full England or Under-23 team.

The search is over now. And time is short. When we go into the same barren international waste next season we must know what England's team will be for the following summer.❞

Sincerely,
PAT COLLINS.

IT IS WITH DEEP REGRET that we record the death of Billy Walker, Jimmy McMullan, John Nibloe, Ralph Hunt and Frank Buckley.

Walker and McMullan were old rivals on the field. Billy gained 18 caps from England, captained his country and starred for Aston Villa before managing Sheffield Wednesday and Nottingham Forest.

Jimmy, a great wing-half for Manchester City, also led Scotland. He succeeded Billy as Wednesday manager. They both died on the same day in November.

John Nibloe was a centre-forward for Sheffield United, Doncaster Rovers and Stockport County. He died following County's match with Newport County in November. He was the son of the old Scottish international full-back.

Ralph Hunt, a centre-forward with eight League clubs, was injured in a car accident with three other Chesterfield players and died from his injuries in December.

Major Frank Buckley, 82, died just before Christmas. He had been ill for some time. A professional for Aston Villa, Birmingham and Derby, he became manager of six clubs. But it was for his success with Wolves, with the "Buckley Babes" of the thirties, that he will be most remembered.

CHARLES BUCHAN'S

FOOTBALL

JULY, 1965   MONTHLY

The
World's
Greatest
Soccer
Magazine

2/-
OVERSEAS PRICE 2/8
FORCES OVERSEAS
2/-

Hungarian goalkeeper
Jozef Gelei foils Terry Paine,
for the defeat of 1953

Billy McNeill and Bobby Moore lead out the teams at Wembley

Mr. Denis Howell (left), Minister for Sport, with Mr. Eric Taylor, of Sheffield Wednesday, whose ground will put on World Cup matches.

Pat Collins Says...

WHY DON'T WE GET CRACKING?

AT long last some positive Government help is promised for the staging of the World Cup here in England next year. Now we have a chance of putting on a good show. But are we too late? Almost! Such backing should have been guaranteed at least a year ago. It would have gilded the efforts of the clubs putting on the matches. It would have broadened their financial horizons.

The tardy political recognition of the greatest international sporting event after the Olympic Games is almost unbelievable. Countries like Brazil, Switzerland, Sweden and Chile have staged the finals since the first British participation in the Jules Rimet Cup – and all had Government backing from the word go!

●

It was, and still is, astonishing to read the quoted Statement of Sir John Lang, principle advisor on sport to the Government, last month: "I don't think Her Majesty's Government were aware of the dates until comparatively recently. At least, we had nothing official about it"

We are now going into the argument of who-should-of-told-who, but the facts are that we were allocated this tournament as early as 1960.

In February, 1963, the F.A. chose the grounds they wanted, and the only change was that Ayresome Park, Middlesbrough, took over from St. James's Park, Newcastle.

Now, perhaps, after the promise of Government aid, the world may believe that we intend to do something about this greatest of all soccer occasions – a sporting extravaganza to catch the holiday mood, and meet the needs of thousands of tourists.

For them it will be a football carnival and a pilgrimage to the birth-place of the game. For us, it will be a great national test, with prestige, commercial interest and our name as hosts all tied up in it.

Time, which should and could have been an ally, is now an enemy. We have risked being made a laughing stock... a world-wide joke. A right gesture at the right time could have avoided the present scurry to put a better face on things.

We will be more highly judged than any previous host nation, for we, the British gave the game to the world, produced its laws and standards of legislature.

The standard we have to match is that of the Japanese who so magnificently organized the last Olympic Games, a vastly more complicated undertaking than the World Cup.

The eyes of the world will be on Manchester and Middlesbrough, Sheffield and Sunderland, on Birmingham, Liverpool and London, where the games will be played. On all of us.

For our visitors won't be watching football ALL the time they're here. And the hundreds on visiting journalists will not be writing only of the games they see.

Our hotels, entertainment, offerings, cultural Centre's, transport facilities, parks, restaurants, we, when stopped in the street and asked the way, will all be a part of the parade that will come under their critical eyes.

Radio and TV coverage will be on a scale vaster than anything dreamed of when we last put on such a sporting spectacle- The Olympic Games of 1948.

Mr. Denis Howell, the Minister for Sport, who many of us know as a very capable ex-Football League referee, has made his recommendations after visiting the selected grounds. We will now await the result.

Anything will be better than nothing, but we would have been more confident about the picture we will present in July, 1966, if it had not been left so late, late, late.

LET'S GET CRACKING!

Star Strip — BOBBY CHARLTON

IN OCTOBER **1956** A NERVOUS 18-YEAR-OLD CENTRE-FORWARD MADE HIS FIRST DIVISION DEBUT AGAINST **CHARLTON ATHLETIC** — AND SCORED TWO GOALS! WITHIN SIX MONTHS **BOBBY CHARLTON** HAD HELPED **MANCHESTER UNITED** TO THEIR SECOND SUCCESSIVE LEAGUE CHAMPIONSHIP.....

THE SPLENDID GOAL HE SCORED IN THE F.A. CUP SEMI-FINAL AGAINST **BIRMINGHAM** THAT SAME SEASON IS STILL **CHARLTON**'S MOST TREASURED MEMORY...A GOAL WHICH TOOK **UNITED** TO WITHIN REACH OF A FABULOUS DOUBLE....

BUT, DISAPPOINTMENT.... INJURY HIT, **UNITED** LOST AT WEMBLEY TO **ASTON VILLA**..

...1958 SAW **UNITED**'S SECOND EUROPEAN CUP VENTURE, AND **CHARLTON** HAMMERED TWO FINE GOALS PAST THE **RED STAR** GOALKEEPER IN BELGRADE...

...IN THE FEW MONTHS AFTER MUNICH, **BOBBY CHARLTON** BECAME VERY MUCH A NATIONAL HERO. FOOTBALL LOVERS WERE PLEASED WHEN **UNITED**'S PATCHED UP SIDE REACHED THE CUP-FINAL AGAIN....

GOOD OWD BOLTON!

SEMI-FINAL
FULHAM BEATEN
CHARLTON HITS
GLORIOUS GOAL

NEXT DAY, NEWS OF A PLANE CRASH SHOOK THE WORLD...

...SYMPATHETIC WHEN YOUNG **BOBBY** AND HIS COLLEAGUES WERE ONCE MORE BEATEN...

...A COMPLETE FOOTBALLER, HE WAS *OUTSIDE-LEFT* IN **ENGLAND**'S BRILLIANT 1960-61 TEAM WHICH BEAT **SCOTLAND** 9-3, **MEXICO** 8-0 AND WHICH ALTOGETHER SCORED 40 GOALS IN SIX OUTINGS....

...DELIGHTED WHEN **CHARLTON**, REMARKABLY RECOVERED, WAS PICKED TO PLAY AGAINST **SCOTLAND**, AND WHEN HE MARKED HIS INTERNATIONAL DEBUT WITH A MAGNIFICENT GOAL IN **ENGLAND**'S 4-0 WIN...

...A DESCENDANT OF SOCCER'S MOST RENOWNED FAMILY, THE **MILBURNS** OF ASHINGTON, **BOBBY CHARLTON** GOT HIS CUP-WINNER'S MEDAL AT THE THIRD ATTEMPT WHEN **UNITED** CRUSHED THE FAVOURITES, **LEICESTER** IN 1963....

I PLAYED EACH OF MY THREE FINALS IN A DIFFERENT POSITION — INSIDE-LEFT IN THE FIRST, CENTRE-FORWARD AGAINST BOLTON, AND NOW OUTSIDE-LEFT IN THE THIRD...

BUT THIS VERSATILE YOUNG MAN WAS TO BE SWITCHED AGAIN, SAYS MANAGER **MATT BUSBY**....

I MUST PLAY WHERE MY CLUB NEEDS ME MOST, REGARDLESS OF MY ENGLAND FUTURE

BACK IN THE NUMBER NINE SHIRT, **CHARLTON** PROMPTLY FIRED IN A GREAT WINNING GOAL IN THE CUP WINNERS' CUP-TIE WITH **SPURS**!

NATURALLY BOBBY WASN'T GETTING THE GOALS LIKE HE USED TO DO, IT SEEMED SUCH A WASTE, AND SO WHEN LAW WAS SUSPENDED AT CHRISTMAS, I WAS ABLE TO MAKE THE MOVE WHICH I'D CONSIDERED FOR SOME TIME....

LAST APRIL HE PLAYED IN HIS SEVENTH SUCCESSIVE **ENGLAND-SCOTLAND** CLASH, ALTOGETHER IN OVER 50 INTERNATIONALS **BOBBY** HAS HIT MORE THAN 30 GOALS

R. BOND-64

JACKIE CHARLTON
Leeds United

JOE BAKER
Arsenal and England

PETER THOMPSON
Liverpool

JOHN CONNELLY
Burnley and England

The game abroad

CENTRE-FORWARD Jose Altafini, the Brazilian who a few months ago was transferred from Milan to Naples, scored 120 goals in his 205 appearances with the former team.

It was because of his decision to leave Milan that the club's trainer, Gipo Viani, lost his job after nine years' service.

Altafini (Brazil's reserve centre-forward in the 1958 World Cup finals) fell out with Viani when the trainer styled him a "rabbit" for alleged timidity on the field. Nothing could heal the quarrel.

Altafini played superbly for Milan, and scored both goals when they beat Benfica 2—1 in the European Club Cup Final at Wembley in 1963.

FOR his part in the 5—1 win of Benfica (Portugal) over Real Madrid in the first leg of their European Club Cup quarter-final at Lisbon, several neutral critics paid centre-forward Da Silva Ferreira Eusebio a compliment by describing him as "another Pelé".

Eusebio's two goals were part of a consummate display by this dusky native of Portuguese West Africa, where he was discovered by a former Portuguese international.

Benfica got him "for a song", but have richly rewarded him. He lodges with other bachelor players of Benfica in a club-house. On the walls of his room are photos of Pelé.

Jazz records, films and motoring are his hobbies after Soccer. He invests his handsome savings in property in his homeland.

He gives his club no trouble. "His combination of Soccer skill, sportsmanship, good temper and good conduct," says a Benfica official who has known him for several years, "seems too good to be true."

Italy and Spain want more foreigners

HELENIO HERRERA says that after the World Cup next year, Italy and Spain will open their doors wider to foreign players.

"Far from hindering the development of a specific country's players," he says, "foreigners help the home talent."

He cites Italy-imported stars Amarildo, Angelillo, John Charles, Jair, Sivori and Suarez as contributors to the fame of Italy's own current native best.

"Foreign players," he argues, "add variety to matches and increase gate receipts."

Other views of the great "H.H.":

"There are many different ways of playing football, but I, of course, think Inter-Milan's way in the past few years is the best.

"Having chosen a method, a trainer should stick to it. Many trainers have only their impatience to blame for losing their jobs."

A listener to that last comment might add: ". . . and the impatience of their club directors".

AFTER Norway's remarkable 3—0 win over Yugoslavia in the World Cup at Oslo, there were new appeals for the frank adoption of professionalism.

Norway stands by amateurism (though there are said to be "certain modest rewards"), and her players were at work the day after their well-merited win.

Writes an Oslo critic: "It is unfair, in these fiercely competitive days in sport, and in view of the national prestige supposed to be involved, to expect amateurs to compete successfully with professionals.

"If we don't go modern, there will be irresistible offers to our best players from foreign professional clubs."

Foreign captures of Swedish amateurs were cited. But Sweden, too, now looks like openly adopting professionalism, or at any rate "semi-professionalism", which seems to work well in Holland.

Sweden may make the decision at a congress next March.

"WHERE are the stars of 1965?" asked Leopold Gernhardt, formerly of Rapid of Vienne and now assistant trainer of Austria's team.

Echoing Hidegkuti, he said: "Austria's 'wonder team' of the early 1930s had half-a-dozen super-stars. In recent years we have not only been short of great players; we haven't even kept up-to-date.

"Our 1965 game often looks old-fashioned, and players jib at the severe training for the modern high-speed game.

"Too many players expect too much money. The financial sense of some of them is more pronounced than their football intelligence."

During the winter break in Austria's season, several teams pick up useful money from indoor matches in Vienna and Innsbruck. There's a tip (if it's needed), if ever a winter break is introduced in the British Isles.

SALUTE to "veterans"! Centre-half Bellini and wing-half Orlando, of Brazil's World Cup winning team in 1958, but not in that of 1962—are now ranked as Probables for Brazil's party in her bid to retain the trophy in England next year.

Orlando (30) and Bellini (34) are back in favour because Brazil has found that young defenders, however brilliant with their clubs, are more likely than seasoned campaigners to disappoint in vital matches.

Orlando returned to Brazil a few months ago after a spell in Argentina. Critics say he has improved, as he "now combines the best qualities of Brazilian and Argentinian defenders".

Bellini, captain of the 1958 World Cup winners, is a natural leader. Because of a dip in his form, he was a reserve in the 1962 World Cup finals, but this year he returned to the national team and played in seven consecutive games in which Brazil conceded only one goal.

Bellini was once captaining Brazil when a temperamental member of the team, playing badly, had a fit of nerves, stopped playing, and started to cry. Bellini "brought him back to his senses by cracking left and right smacks to the face".

GERMANY PRESSES FOR WORLD CUP

WEST GERMANY now has 12 stadiums with a capacity of 50,000 to 95,000, and two others holding 45,000. Excellent road, rail and air networks link the great Soccer centres.

The national federation, called the Deutscher Fussball - Bund, groups 15,000 clubs and 2,200,000 registered players.

Germany underlines those and other advantages (including an abundance of permanent and general sports training centres "where teams would be lodged better than in hotels") in her application to be World Cup host in 1974 (in 1970 it will be Mexico).

Spain is also a candidate for 1974, but Germany looks like winning.

★ ★ ★

"LET us give back to football some of its charm as a game ; let us fight against its degradation to a competition of rigorous and ruthless combat," said an article in a recent Bulletin of the Union of European Football Associations.

The article, dealing with the effect of defensive tactics on gate receipts, said that in one country only 306 goals were scored in the first 153 national League games.

An average of two a match doesn't look so terrible—but in more than half of the games the score was 1-0, 1-1, or 0-0.

About the way TV can affect gates, the article cited the Yugoslavia v. Union of European Football Association team, played in Belgrade in aid of the Skopje earthquake relief fund. Though the match was to be televised, 35,000 tickets were sold.

But it rained—and only 17,000 turned up.

MONEY NO WORRY TO BRAZIL

DURING part of their collective training for the World Cup Finals next year, Brazil's players will use three different types of boots suitable for three types of pitch surface.

Forty players will be assembled at Rio de Janeiro on April 1, 1966, for medical and psychological examinations. At the end of May, the 22 for the journey to England will be named.

Brazil's preparations for the World Cup tussles are so comprehensive, thorough and costly, that most of the competing countries could afford nothing like them.

Finance needn't worry the Cup-holders, however. The country's Football Confederation, the Government and several commercial concerns will help.

Brazil's World Cup preparation really begins in earnest this year. One team of possibles will play eight matches in various parts of South America in June. Another will play six games overseas (at Beirut, Damascus, Algiers, Casablanca, Oporto and Stockholm), also in June.

Main aim of the overseas six-match circuit is to widen the Brazilians' acquaintance with other peoples' Soccer.

AFTER Brazil's summer tour, many foreign critics either made her World Cup (1966) favourites or bracketed her with England as likeliest winner.

The Brazilians beat Algeria 3—0 at Oran, drew 0—0 with Portugal at Lisbon, beat Sweden 2—1 at Stockholm, and Russia 3—0 at Moscow.

Including three games played in Brazil before the team's departure, only one goal was scored against the World Cup holders in seven consecutive tussles.

The tour was a fine feat. The win over Russia alone, before a crowd of 103,000, made Brazil look like a 1966 menace.

★ ★ ★

Russia used three substitutes, Brazil two. Of Brazil's 13 players, four (D. Santos, Bellini, Pelé and Garrincha) were in the World Cup Final of 1958, and only two (D. Santos and Garrincha) in that of 1962.

★ ★ ★

A Russian critic said Pelé (who scored two splendid goals and "made" the third) played right up to his reputation, and "seemed to have a sixth sense".

A neutral critic underlined the contrast between Russia's "disciplined, solid, regu-

SIDELIGHTS on the game in Russia . . . Players number about two and a half million. To meet the travel problem—two of the national First Division clubs are nearly 3,000 miles apart), teams sometimes play several games on flying circuits which may extend to six weeks.

Russia's size handicaps her in the world football struggle because her talent (playing and administrative) is so scattered.

When severe frosts stop normal play, an indoor version is staged in some cities, and friendlies are occasionally played on beaten snow.

In the central region of the country the season for normal play extends from April to October.

Though the word "professional" isn't used, several thousand high-class players benefit either by broken-time pay, housing advantages, Army promotions, and jobs that are not too exacting. Most players thus rewarded have to teach the game to boys.

A problem at the start of the year was the ageing of certain famous players and coaches. A shake-up has been going on— some say it is too late—in view of the

I have already seen three World Cup Final events – 1954 in Switzerland; 1958 in Sweden; and 1962 in Chile. I thoroughly enjoyed myself as a spectator. But although I enjoyed all three trips they were not entirely pleasure jaunts. I went officially, on behalf on my club, Sheffield Wednesday, with two definite objects in view.

First, I, and my club, wanted first-hand knowledge of how the game was progressing in other countries; to discover for myself how their administration worked; how they planned and organized their big events.

For it was obvious that the World Cup finals would come to Britain, and because our ground at Hillsborough had been chosen to stage many big matches – F.A.Cup semi-finals, international, inter-league games – we felt that we were in with a chance of taking an active part in this important event.

The foresight of my board has been justified, for we have been allocated four matches. But, before we knew this, we went ahead with ground improvements, the biggest single part being our magnificent new 10,000-seater North stand, build on the cantilever principle, which means no pillars to obstruct the view.

We also added one inch to what has become the accepted width of seats in soccer stands, and it is amazing how much extra comfort this single inch allows and to do it we had to sacrifice 2,000 seats. But we know we have done the right thing, not only for the World Cup visitors but for our own faithful spectators.

We have also improved refreshment

Writes Eric Taylor
General Manager and Secretary
Sheffield Wednesday FC

Association in the promotion of this 'once in a life-time' Soccer Festival to the tune of half-a-million. A magnificent gesture. But it is a pity that the move and offer did not come earlier.

After all, we in England have known about this prestige event since the decision by F.I.F.A. in the summer of 1960 and it was on my return from Chile in 1962 that I wrote an article published in the F.A. News the following October under the heading '1966... and all that', stressing that Government Aid was vital to the success of staging World Cup

club and municipal officials, Press, police, hoteliers etc. The job of this committee is as vital as that of any club actually staging games.

Accommodation has to be found for visiting teams, and training quarters. And apart from local spectators, visitors from all over Britain, and in fact the whole world are expected.

Transport to and from the grounds will have to be available. Extra car-parking space will be needed. Restaurants will be expected to provide suitable menus for overseas visitors. And I am sure that

THERE IS SO LITTLE TIME!

and toilet facilities in our original stand. And have added a cosy, licensed bar, and with minor improvements and alterations here and there we feel that we are ready to play our part in this vital, prestige event of the World Cup.

We would of liked to of done even more, to have extended our new stand to all four sides of the ground. That is completely beyond our financial capabilities at this time, but it is still in our minds for the future.

Which brings me to and important point. The Government, as a result of the probings, enquiries, surveys and negotiations sponsored by the Minister for Sport Mr. Denis Howell, M.P. – a very capable and well know Football League referee – is known to assist the Football

matches here in 1966.
But let's be thankful, even though time appears to be against us.
Switzerland, Sweden... their club's had government backing for the magnificent stadia and facilities which were available. Yet here, already it is being said that the staging clubs are LUCKY to receive the tax payers' money to improve THEIR OWN GROUNDS.

Of course we are, but let no one forget that the rest of the cost – something between one and a quarter and one and a half million pounds – has to be found by the SAME SIX CLUBS to complete the job before the first ball is kicked in July, 1966.

A liaison committee has been formed, comprising F.A. councillors,

shops will want to provide them with souvenirs.
Accommodation should not be too big a problem as fortunately most games are played in university towns and cities. While the series is being played, most 'varsities will be enjoying summer vacation, so perhaps overseas parties could be accommodated in their Halls of Residence.

Yes, the World Cup may primarily be a Soccer event, but I for one would like to see it treated as an important national event in the broadest possible sense.

LET US NOT ONLY SELL BRITISH SOCCER, BUT BRITAIN.

STAR STRIP — GORDON BANKS

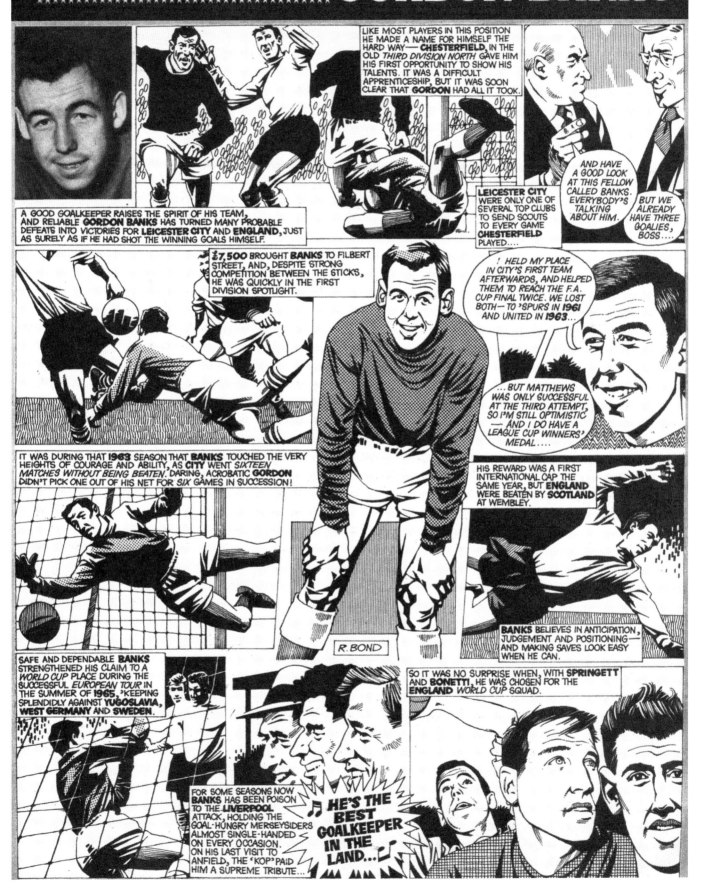

LIKE MOST PLAYERS IN THIS POSITION HE MADE A NAME FOR HIMSELF THE HARD WAY — **CHESTERFIELD**, IN THE OLD *THIRD DIVISION NORTH* GAVE HIM HIS FIRST OPPORTUNITY TO SHOW HIS TALENTS. IT WAS A DIFFICULT APPRENTICESHIP, BUT IT WAS SOON CLEAR THAT **GORDON** HAD ALL IT TOOK.

A GOOD GOALKEEPER RAISES THE SPIRIT OF HIS TEAM, AND RELIABLE **GORDON BANKS** HAS TURNED MANY PROBABLE DEFEATS INTO VICTORIES FOR **LEICESTER CITY** AND **ENGLAND**, JUST AS SURELY AS IF HE HAD SHOT THE WINNING GOALS HIMSELF.

LEICESTER CITY WERE ONLY ONE OF SEVERAL TOP CLUBS TO SEND SCOUTS TO EVERY GAME **CHESTERFIELD** PLAYED....

AND HAVE A GOOD LOOK AT THIS FELLOW CALLED BANKS. EVERYBODY'S TALKING ABOUT HIM.

BUT WE ALREADY HAVE THREE GOALIES, BOSS....

£7,500 BROUGHT **BANKS** TO FILBERT STREET, AND, DESPITE STRONG COMPETITION BETWEEN THE STICKS, HE WAS QUICKLY IN THE FIRST DIVISION SPOTLIGHT.

I HELD MY PLACE IN CITY'S FIRST TEAM AFTERWARDS, AND HELPED THEM TO REACH THE F.A. CUP FINAL TWICE. WE LOST BOTH — TO 'SPURS IN 1961 AND UNITED IN 1963...

...BUT MATTHEWS WAS ONLY SUCCESSFUL AT THE THIRD ATTEMPT, SO I'M STILL OPTIMISTIC — AND I DO HAVE A LEAGUE CUP WINNERS' MEDAL....

IT WAS DURING THAT *1963* SEASON THAT **BANKS** TOUCHED THE VERY HEIGHTS OF COURAGE AND ABILITY, AS **CITY** WENT *SIXTEEN MATCHES WITHOUT BEING BEATEN*. DARING, ACROBATIC **GORDON** DIDN'T PICK ONE OUT OF HIS NET FOR *SIX* GAMES IN SUCCESSION!

HIS REWARD WAS A FIRST INTERNATIONAL CAP THE SAME YEAR, BUT **ENGLAND** WERE BEATEN BY **SCOTLAND** AT WEMBLEY.

R. BOND

BANKS BELIEVES IN ANTICIPATION, JUDGEMENT AND POSITIONING — AND MAKING SAVES LOOK EASY WHEN HE CAN.

SAFE AND DEPENDABLE **BANKS** STRENGTHENED HIS CLAIM TO A *WORLD CUP* PLACE DURING THE SUCCESSFUL *EUROPEAN TOUR* IN THE SUMMER OF *1965*, 'KEEPING SPLENDIDLY AGAINST **YUGOSLAVIA**, **WEST GERMANY** AND **SWEDEN**.

SO IT WAS NO SURPRISE WHEN, WITH **SPRINGETT** AND **BONETTI**, HE WAS CHOSEN FOR THE **ENGLAND** WORLD CUP SQUAD.

FOR SOME SEASONS NOW **BANKS** HAS BEEN POISON TO THE **LIVERPOOL** ATTACK, HOLDING THE GOAL-HUNGRY MERSEYSIDERS ALMOST SINGLE-HANDED ON EVERY OCCASION. ON HIS LAST VISIT TO ANFIELD, THE 'KOP' PAID HIM A SUPREME TRIBUTE...

♪ HE'S THE BEST GOALKEEPER IN THE LAND... ♫

AUSTRIA THE THIRD

ENGLAND 2, AUSTRIA 3
(At Wembley, Oct. 20)
Scorers: England—R. Charlton, Connelly.
Austria—Floegel, Fritsch 2.

TWICE in the lead, England were caught and then overtaken by a rebuilt Austrian side who joined Hungary and Sweden as the only foreign countries to win in England. So ended a 16-month unbeaten run of ten matches for the home side.

The English crowd howled in derision at their defeated team. They had seen a game, which England dominated for so long, tossed away. They had seen victory spurned time and again.

Bridges returned—and failed. Stiles was right out of touch. Greaves missed chances and made no impact on the game. Paine was checked. Only Bobby Charlton, a fine display, and Connelly worried the Austrian defence.

Fritsch, 18-year-old right-winger playing in his first international, got two of the Austrian goals. His second came through slack English marking following a free-kick. His winner, beautifully taken, caught Springett off his line.

ENGLAND—Springett (Sheff. Wed.); Cohen (Fulham), Wilson (Everton); Stiles (Man. Utd.), J. Charlton (Leeds), Moore (West Ham); Paine (Southampton), Greaves (Spurs), Bridges (Chelsea), R. Charlton, Connelly (Man. Utd.).

AUSTRIA—Fraydl; Sara, Frank (sub. Dirnberger); Stamm, Ullmann, Ludescher; Fritsch, Buzek, Hasil, Floegel, Macek.

ENGLAND'S SHAME

While Northern Ireland sailed to glory, England fumbled to shameful defeat against Austria at Wembley. Above, Bobby Charlton gets England's first goal after four minutes. Below, count them - there are six English players standing still as Fritsch scores Austria's equaliser. Austria are the third Continental country to win in England.

Joe Baker, England's centre-forward (white shirt), breaks through five Spaniards during the match in Madrid, but was foiled. He got the first of the two goals, though.

UNDOUBTEDLY the best England display in a long time. The Spaniards were bemused by refreshing and novel English tactics which produced the tactician's dream . . . that of always having a man spare in defence and attack. It calls for team-work and intelligent positioning.

England had that and more.

The goals proved the understanding and flow of this almost new-style England. Left-back Ray Wilson made the first for Baker, and Moore—up in support more than usual—crossed the ball for Hunt's goal.

Banks was seldom troubled. Stiles, Bobby Charlton and Eastham worked out the openings while Hunt, Baker and Ball were spearheads. The whole thing worked like a charm and gave England a much-needed boost.

SPAIN: Iribar; Reija, Sanchis; Glara, Olivella, Zoco; Ufarte, Rodriguez, Ansola, Martinez, Lapetra. Martin (sub.).
ENGLAND: Banks (Leicester); Cohen (Fulham), Wilson (Huddersfield); Stiles (Man. Utd.), J. Charlton (Leeds), Moore (West Ham); Ball ((Blackpool), Hunt (Liverpool), Baker (Arsenal), Eastham (Arsenal), R. Charlton (Man. Utd.). Hunter (Leeds) (sub.).

ENGLAND'S BEST...

And here's the second by which the Spaniards were beaten - being scored by Roger Hunt.

SPANIARDS BLIGHTED !

THE GAM(

SIDELIGHTS on the game in Russia . . . Players number about two and a half million. To meet the travel problem (two of the national First Division clubs are nearly 3,000 miles apart), teams sometimes play several games on flying circuits which may extend to six weeks.

Russia's size handicaps her in the world football struggle because her talent (playing and administrative) is so scattered.

When severe frosts stop normal play, an indoor version is staged in some cities, and friendlies are occasionally played on beaten snow.

In the central region of the country the season for normal play extends from April to October.

Though the word "professional" isn't used, several thousand high-class players benefit either by broken-time pay, housing advantages, Army promotions, and jobs that are not too exacting. Most players thus rewarded have to teach the game to boys.

A problem at the start of the year was the ageing of certain famous players and coaches. A shake-up has been going on— some say it is too late—in view of the World Cup 1966.

AFTER Norway's remarkable 3—0 win over Yugoslavia in the World Cup at Oslo, there were new appeals for the frank adoption of professionalism.

Norway stands by amateurism (though there are said to be "certain modest rewards"), and her players were at work the day after their well-merited win.

Writes an Oslo critic: "It is unfair, in these fiercely competitive days in sport, and in view of the national prestige supposed to be involved, to expect amateurs to compete successfully with professionals.

"If we don't go modern, there will be irresistible offers to our best players from foreign professional clubs."

Foreign captures of Swedish amateurs were cited. But Sweden, too, now looks like openly adopting professionalism, or at any rate "semi-professionalism", which seems to work well in Holland.

Sweden may make the decision at a congress next March.

SALUTE to "veterans"! Centre-half Bellini and wing-half Orlando, of Brazil's World Cup winning team in 1958,—but not in that of 1962—are now ranked as Probables for Brazil's party in her bid to retain the trophy in England next year.

Orlando (30) and Bellini (34) are back in favour because Brazil has found that young defenders, however brilliant with their clubs, are more likely than seasoned campaigners to disappoint in vital matches.

Orlando returned to Brazil a few months ago after a spell in Argentina. Critics say he has improved, as he "now combines the best qualities of Brazilian and Argentinian defenders".

Bellini, captain of the 1958 World Cup winners, is a natural leader. Because of a dip in his form, he was a reserve in the 1962 World Cup finals, but this year he returned to the national team and played in seven consecutive games in which Brazil conceded only one goal.

Bellini was once captaining Brazil when a temperamental member of the team, playing badly, had a fit of nerves, stopped playing, and started to cry. Bellini "brought him back to his senses by cracking left and right smacks to the face".

CENTRE-FORWARD Jose Altafini, the Brazilian who a few months ago was transferred from Milan to Naples, scored 120 goals in his 205 appearances with the former team.

It was because of his decision to leave Milan that the club's trainer, Gipo Viani, lost his job after nine years' service.

Altafini (Brazil's reserve centre-forward in the 1958 World Cup finals) fell out with Viani when the trainer styled him a "rabbit" for alleged timidity on the field. Nothing could heal the quarrel.

Altafini played superbly for Milan, and scored both goals when they beat Benfica 2—1 in the European Club Cup Final at Wembley in 1963.

"WHERE are the stars of 1965?" asked Leopold Gernhardt, formerly of Rapid of Vienne and now assistant trainer of Austria's team.

Echoing Hidegkuti, he said: "Austria's 'wonder team' of the early 1930s had half-a-dozen super-stars. In recent years we have not only been short of great players; we haven't even kept up-to-date.

"Our 1965 game often looks old-fashioned, and players jib at the severe training for the modern high-speed game.

"Too many players expect too much money. The financial sense of some of them is more pronounced than their football intelligence."

During the winter break in Austria's season, several teams pick up useful money from indoor matches in Vienna and Innsbruck. There's a tip (if it's needed), if ever a winter break is introduced in the British Isles.

AFTER Brazil's summer tour, many foreign critics either made her World Cup (1966) favourites or bracketed her with England as likeliest winner.

The Brazilians beat Algeria 3—0 at Oran, drew 0—0 with Portugal at Lisbon, beat Sweden 2—1 at Stockholm, and Russia 3—0 at Moscow.

Including three games played in Brazil before the team's departure, only one goal was scored against the World Cup holders in seven consecutive tussles.

The tour was a fine feat. The win over Russia alone, before a crowd of 103,000, made Brazil look like a 1966 menace.

★   ★   ★

Russia used three substitutes, Brazil two. Of Brazil's 13 players, four (D. Santos, Bellini, Pelé and Garrincha) were in the World Cup Final of 1958, and only two (D. Santos and Garrincha) in that of 1962.

★   ★   ★

A Russian critic said Pelé (who scored two splendid goals and "made" the third) played right up to his reputation, and "seemed to have a sixth sense".

GERMANY PRESSES FOR WORLD CUP

WEST GERMANY now has 12 stadiums with a capacity of 50,000 to 95,000, and two others holding 45,000. Excellent road, rail and air networks link the great Soccer centres.

The national federation, called the Deutscher Fussball - Bund, groups 15,000 clubs and 2,200,000 registered players.

Germany underlines those and other advantages (including an abundance of permanent and general sports training centres "where teams would be lodged better than in hotels") in her application to be World Cup host in 1974 (in 1970 it will be Mexico).

Spain is also a candidate for 1974, but Germany looks like winning.

★   ★   ★

"LET us give back to football some of its charm as a game; let us fight against its degradation to a competition of rigorous and ruthless combat," said an article in a recent Bulletin of the Union of European Football Associations.

The article, dealing with the effect of defensive tactics on gate receipts, said that in one country only 306

goals were scored in the first 153 national League games.

An average of two a match doesn't look so terrible—but in more than half of the games the score was 1-0, 1-1, or 0-0.

About the way TV can affect gates, the article cited the Yugoslavia v. Union of European Football Association team, played in Belgrade in aid of the Skopje earthquake relief fund. Though the match was to be televised, 35,000 tickets were sold.

But it rained—and only 17,000 turned up.

MONEY NO WORRY TO BRAZIL

DURING part of their collective training for the World Cup Finals next year, Brazil's players will use three different types of boots suitable for three types of pitch surface.

Forty players will be assembled at Rio de Janeiro on April 1, 1966, for medical and psychological examinations. At the end of May, the 22 for the journey to England will be named.

Brazil's preparations for the World Cup tussles are so comprehensive, thorough and costly, that most of the competing countries could afford nothing like them.

Finance needn't worry the Cup-holders, however. The country's Football Confederation, the Government and several commercial concerns will help.

Brazil's World Cup preparation really begins in earnest this year. One team of possibles will play eight matches in various parts of South America in June. Another will play six games overseas (at Beirut, Damascus, Algiers, Casablanca, Oporto and Stockholm), also in June.

Main aim of the overseas six-match circuit is to widen the Brazilians' acquaintance with other peoples' Soccer.

Italy and Spain want more foreigners

HELENIO HERRERA says that after the World Cup next year, Italy and Spain will open their doors wider to foreign players.

"Far from hindering the development of a specific country's players," he says, "foreigners help the home talent."

He cites Italy-imported stars Amarildo, Angelillo, John Charles, Jair, Sivori and Suarez as contributors to the fame of Italy's own current native best.

"Foreign players," he argues, "add variety to matches and increase gate receipts."

Other views of the great "H.H.":

"There are many different ways of playing football, but I, of course, think Inter-Milan's way in the past few years is the best.

"Having chosen a method, a trainer should stick to it. Many trainers have only their impatience to blame for losing their jobs."

A listener to that last comment might add: "... and the impatience of their club directors".

FOR his part in the 5—1 win of Benfica (Portugal) over Real Madrid in the first leg of their European Club Cup quarter-final at Lisbon, several neutral critics paid centre-forward Da Silva Ferreira Eusebio a compliment by describing him as "another Pelé".

Eusebio's two goals were part of a consummate display by this dusky native of Portuguese West Africa, where he was discovered by a former Portuguese international.

Benfica got him "for a song", but have richly rewarded him. He lodges with other bachelor players of Benfica in a club-house. On the walls of his room are photos of Pelé.

Jazz records, films and motoring are his hobbies after Soccer. He invests his handsome savings in property in his homeland.

He gives his club no trouble. "His combination of Soccer skill, sportsmanship, good temper and good conduct," says a Benfica official who has known him for several years, "seems too good to be true."

SLAZENGER FOOTBALLS
Chosen for
THE 1966 WORLD CUP

—and for the 1965 European Cup Winners Cup Final

—and for the 1965 F.A. Cup Final

Jules Rimet Cup for the World Cup Competition 1966

Slazenger OF COURSE!

Get in now for tickets

IF you are still thinking of being at the World Cup games then stop thinking and start acting . . . NOW! Books of ten-, seven-, four- and three-match tickets are on sale . . . and going fast.

There is no shortage of tickets, but the demand will rocket when the various countries know their fate. And the draw is made in January.

No individual tickets will be on sale until March or April. And there will be NO individual tickets for the Final—and hardly likely to be any for the semi-finals.

Here are the grades and prices for season tickets:

Season	Grade 1 (seating)	Grade 2 (seating)	Grade 3 (standing)	Grade 4 (standing)
10-match	£25 15s.	£15 15s.	£7 7s. 6d.	£3 17s. 6d.
7-match	£15 2s.	£7 15s.	£4 10s. 0d.	£2 12s. 6d.
4-match	£8 16s.	£4 15s.	£2 12s. 6d.	£1 10s. 0d.
3-match	£6 6s.	£3 0s.	£1 17s. 6d.	£1 2s. 6d.

The ten-match season ticket: from July 11 to 30, covers all eighth final matches in any one group (A, B, C or D) together with the quarter final in the same group, one semi-final, the third and fourth place final and the Final itself.

Seven-match season tickets cover all eighth final matches in any one group, and the quarter final in the same group.

Four-match: These will be for all eighth final matches played on a particular ground, together with the quarter final in the same group.

Three-match: These will be for all eighth final matches played on a particular ground.

●

Every ten-match season ticket-holder is guaranteed his place at the Wembley Final on July 30. The intention is to have a ballot for any remaining places at Wembley among the seven-, four- and three-match ticket holders.

●

How to apply: Applications for season-tickets can be made on the official application forms which can be obtained either from the offices of the World Cup Organisation, White City Stadium, London, W.12, from your local club or box office.

Ten- and Seven-match applications should be made direct to the office of the World Cup Organisation; Four- and Three-match applications to the Box Offices at the grounds where matches are to be played. All applications must be accompanied by cheque or money order to the total cost of tickets ordered, plus postage.

Receipt vouchers will be sent to buyers

GEOFF HURST
West Ham Utd.

OUR COLOUR CA

RON SPRINGETT
Queen's Park Rangers

ERA CAPTURES ENGLAND'S STARS

World Cup!

CAN

ALF RAMSEY
... the Man on the Spot.

BRITAIN'S top managers believe, like team-boss Alf Ramsey, that England CAN win the World Cup . . . but they are not prepared to go along with Alf's reported view that England WILL lift the Jules Rimet trophy.

This conclusion I have reached after conducting a Soccer census of club managers across Britain. Some did not want to be quoted by name; others seemed to take the view that miracles CAN happen . . . but that England would be hard-pressed to produce one.

One of the unnamed managers—"I don't want anyone to think I am knocking Alf, or the England team . . . but if I give my opinion, it must be an honest one"—virtually dismissed England's chances of glory.

"This will be the supreme test of greatness—and the world's finest footballing nations will be parading their talents. I'm afraid I just don't think England are great enough to prove that they are the peers of them all . . . much as I would like to see this happen," he said.

Move north of the Border, to JOCK STEIN, who so narrowly failed to steer Scotland into the final stages of the tournament. Listen to this Soccer-wise Scot as he says:

"So much depends on so many things . . . you need a bit of luck and the run of the ball on occasions. *Given both these things, England could do really well.*"

WILL England win the trophy? Jock's diplomatic reply: "The answer to this question is contained in what I have just said."

JOHN PRENTICE, Scotland's team-manager, and the man who could be in charge of Scotland's next tilt at world greatness: "I wouldn't rule England out completely. They must have a fair chance, for Alf Ramsey is working on the right lines to find his best tactical formation." But

WILL England win that trophy?— "*I don't think so.*"

Manchester United's MATT BUSBY, the acknowledged "king" among managers in Britain: "Certainly Alf Ramsey knows what he is aiming for, and England COULD do well . . . but my feeling is that they will have to find more striking force up front.

"*The defence seems pretty well settled, but unless England find that attacking flair, I am afraid they will have a struggle to get through to the final and win.*"

Only a few days to go — July 11—then the world's greatest Soccer tournament will be on. England, Argentina, Bulgaria, Chile, France, Hungary, Italy, Mexico, North Korea, Portugal, Russia, Spain, Switzerland, Uruguay, West Germany — all will strive to take the Cup from Brazil, holders. IAN DAVID reports what some of our managers think.

DON REVIE, young and dynamic boss of Leeds United, who gave a great account of themselves in European competition last season: "Yes, England CAN take the trophy —but I would not say they WILL win it.

"It should help them to find that little bit extra to be playing in front of their own fans and under conditions with which they are familiar—and I hope the work Alf Ramsey has put into his job will pay off, with the players blending together to carry out his plans. *I repeat . . . they CAN win the World Cup—but I won't say they WILL.*"

ALAN BROWN, no-nonsense boss of Cup-finalists Sheffield Wednesday: "Barring early upsets — and there usually are some—I believe England CAN win the World Cup. Let's acknowledge that England are good enough to go a long way, given the luck . . . and whoever wins the trophy will need a ration of THAT."

Miracles CAN happen!

ENGLAND DO IT?

WILL England win, though: "Ah . . . *let's say it's a tall order.*"

TONY WADDINGTON, manager of Stoke City, knows about upsets—his team highly fancied in the Potteries to do well in the F.A. Cup, were shock losers . . . at home . . . to Walsall.

Waddington said: "This is probably England's best chance for a long time —and I have great respect for Alf Ramsey's judgment, in spite of the carping critics. But the greatest danger —through no fault of Alf's — *is that we have not got sufficient players of world class*, although we ARE getting nearer to the number required.

"Remember, if you have four or five players of that calibre, you are in Brazil's category. This, I believe, is the reason Alf Ramsey has resorted to the tactical formation we have seen . . . because of the lack of world-class players at his disposal.

All in all, however, I am not sure we have yet reached that level that will make people believe this is the team to win the World Cup."

And here's one man who WILL be quoted . . . as saying that England will NOT carry off the Jules Rimet trophy . . . BERT TRAUTMANN, who won fame as Manchester City's goalkeeper and is now general

manager of Stockport County.

Bert arrived in England as a German paratrooper prisoner of war, stayed to win the hearts of countless thousands of Soccer fans. He knows the European Soccer set-up as well as Britain's—and says, bluntly:

"Obviously, England CAN win— but I don't think they will . . . not when I consider the other top foot-balling nations who will be fighting for supremacy in the world's greatest tournament. And I remember especially Brazil — the holders — Russia, whatever may have been said about their chances, and Italy.

"England's chances will be better if the grounds are heavy, if there is plenty of rain.

"West Germany? Well . . . they could reach the quarter-finals. But while Brazil must still be the favour-ites, *I have a sneaking fancy for the Italians.*"

So there you have it. CAN England pull it off? WILL England do it?

As D-Day draws near, Alf Ramsey has ONE consolation to mull over: No-one is going so far as to say "England WON'T . . . but Brazil, or Italy, or North Korea WILL." Yes, it's as open as that. *So good hunting, Alf Ramsey and England!*

JOHN PRENTICE . . . "England won't win."

DON REVIE . . . "being at home will help."

BERT TRAUTMANN (left) . . . "England want rain.'

JOCK STEIN . . . "England could do well."

KARL SCHNELLINGER
West Germany

OUR COLOUR CAMERA CAPTURES S

GARRINCHA
Brazil

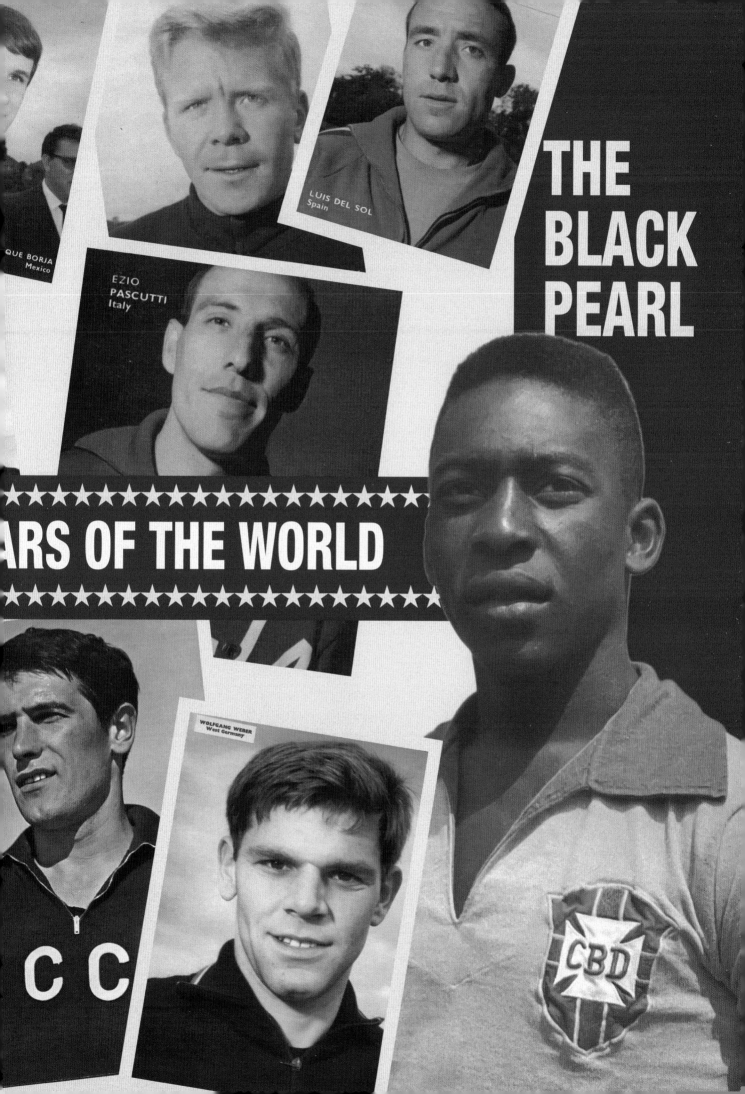

LUIS DEL SOL
Spain

QUE BORJA
Mexico

EZIO
PASCUTTI
Italy

THE
BLACK
PEARL

★★★★★★★★★★★★★★★★★★★★★★★
ARS OF THE WORLD
★★★★★★★★★★★★★★★★★★★★★★★

WOLFGANG WEBER
West Germany

C C

CBD

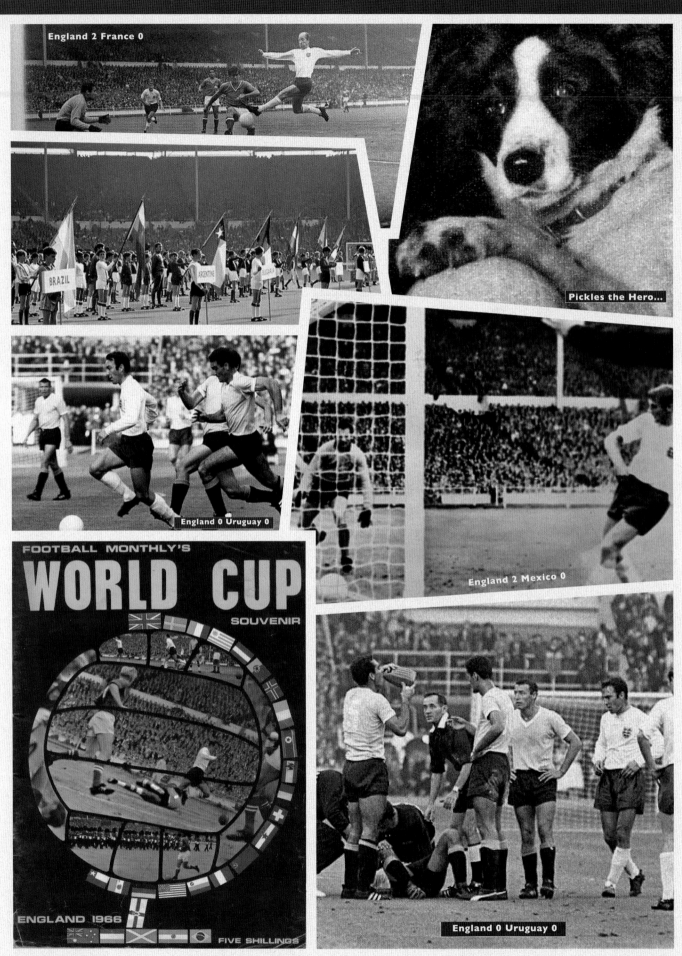

England 2 France 0

Pickles the Hero...

England 0 Uruguay 0

England 2 Mexico 0

FOOTBALL MONTHLY'S
WORLD CUP
SOUVENIR

ENGLAND 1966

FIVE SHILLINGS

England 0 Uruguay 0

ENGLAND Pause for a pose before an England squad starts training. Standing: Cohen, Stiles, Baker, Thompson, Banks, Eastham, Springett, Milne, Flowers, Wilson, Reaney, Greaves, Harris, Hunter, Hunt, Trainer Harold Shepherdson. Squatting: Jackie Charlton, Newton, Ball, Hurst, Bobby Charlton, Moore.

IT'S HURST...
AS ENGLAND TAME ARGENTINA!

OFF!

EMPIRE STADIUM
WEMBLEY

ENTER AT
A
TURNSTILES

WORLD CHAMPIONSHIP
1966
Jules Rimet Cup
QUARTER FINAL

ENTRANCE
23

EAST

SECRETARY,
THE FOOTBALL ASSOCIATION

STANDING
ENCLOSURE

SATURDAY JULY 23
KICK-OFF 3 p.m.

STANDING   7/6
(SEE PLAN & CONDITIONS ON BACK)
TO BE RETAINED

CHARLES BUCHAN'S FOOTBALL MONTHLY
TUESDAY 26th JULY 1966

GREAT!
ENGLAND'S GLORY BOYS
Through to the Final by 2-1

EMPIRE STADIUM
WEMBLEY

ENTER AT
J
TURNSTILES

WORLD CHAMPIONSHIP
1966
Jules Rimet Cup
SEMI-FINAL

D. Follows. SECRETARY.
THE FOOTBALL ASSOCIATION

ENTRANCE
52

TUESDAY JULY 26
KICK 7.30 p.m.

WEST
STAND
STANDING
ENCLOSURE

(SEE PLAN OF LOCATIONS ON BACK)
TO BE DETERMINED

17/6

SEMI FINAL

ENGLAND'S GOLDEN DAY . . .

White-shirted Weber falls after his 89th minute equaliser, leading to extra-time.

ABOVE: After ... Stiles and Greaves in victory embrace. RIGHT: Before ... the teams line-up with England in unfamiliar dark shirts.

BELOW: Emmerich shoots past Cohen (left) and Peters but Banks saved.

ENGLAND'S GOLDEN DAY . . .

On July 30, 1966, England won the World Cup when they beat West Germany 4-2 at Wembley after extra time. Here are some of the unforgettable moments . . .

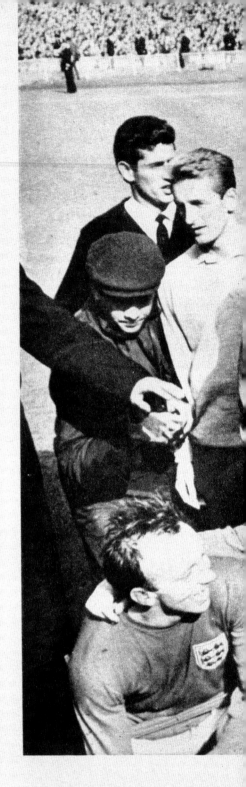

Bobby Moore obviously treasures England's new trophy. (Right) Ball hugs Hurst, scorer of that last-kick fourth goal.

The team, trainer Shepherdson and some of England's reserves . . . and it's smiles all round for a job well done.

Haller's delight as he scores the first German goal.

ENGLAND'S GOLDEN DAY...

The biggest crowd of a tournament which set an aggregate attendance record for the World Cup, saw only the second extra-time FINAL of the eight so far played.

The toast is ENGLAND ... from Bobby Charlton at the victory banquet.

ABOVE: England relax waiting for the start of extra-time. For Jack Charlton (5) and Moore a chance to rest their legs.

BELOW: The wives celebrate: Left to right: Mrs. Moore, Mrs. Peters, Mrs. Hurst, Mrs. Springett and Mrs. Bonetti.

ENGLAND

S GOLDEN DAY

The Royal Box wears a wide, approving smile as the Queen presents the World Cup to England's captain. Bobby Moore.

This was the moment Alf Ramsey (left) had planned-and prophesied... With Jack Charlton in support, Martin Peters rams in England's second goal from the corner which Alan Ball (far left) had just taken. England were on the way... On the way to the celebration scene (right) with Nobby Stiles jigging for joy on the lap of honour with Bobby Moore, Geoff Hurst (holding Cup) and Peters. This was the day Ramsey had promised would be England's

THE MAN WHO HAD FAITH IN THIS DAY

Charles Buchan's
ENGLAND
WORLD CUP REVIEW

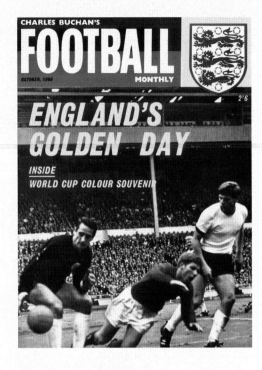

CHARLES BUCHAN'S
FOOTBALL MONTHLY
OCTOBER, 1966

2'6

ENGLAND'S GOLDEN DAY

INSIDE
WORLD CUP COLOUR SOUVENIR

GROUP 1

July 11: Wembley Stadium, London
England **0 - 0** Uruguay

July 13: Wembley Stadium, London
France **1 - 1** Mexico

July 15: White City, London
Uruguay **2 - 1** France

July 16: Wembley Stadium, London
England **2 - 0** Mexico

July 19: Wembley Stadium, London
Uruguay **0 - 0** Mexico

July 20: Wembley Stadium, London
England **2 - 0** France

	P	W	D	L	F	A	Pts
England	3	2	1	0	4	0	5
Uruguay	3	1	2	0	2	1	4
Mexico	3	0	2	1	1	3	2
France	3	0	1	2	2	5	1

GROUP 2

July 12: Hillsborough, Sheffield
West Germany **5 - 0** Switzerland

July 13: Villa Park, Birmingham
Argentina **2 - 1** Spain

July 15: Hillsborough, Sheffield
Spain **2 - 1** Switzerland

July 16: Villa Park, Birmingham
Argentina **0 - 0** West Germany

July 19: Hillsborough, Sheffield
Argentina **2 - 0** Switzerland

July 20: Villa Park, Birmingham
West Germany **2 - 1** Spain

	P	W	D	L	F	A	Pts
West Germany	3	2	1	0	7	1	5
Argentina	3	2	1	0	4	1	5
Spain	3	1	0	2	4	5	2
Switzerland	3	0	0	3	1	9	0

GROUP 3

July 12: Goodison Park, Liverpool
Brazil **2 - 0** Bulgaria

July 13: Old Trafford, Manchester
Portugal **3 - 1** Hungary

July 15: Goodison Park, Liverpool
Hungary **3 - 1** Brazil

July 16: Old Trafford, Manchester
Portugal **3 - 0** Bulgaria

July 19: Goodison Park, Liverpool
Portugal **3 - 1** Brazil

July 20: Old Trafford, Manchester
Hungary **3 - 1** Bulgaria

	P	W	D	L	F	A	Pts
Portugal	3	3	0	0	9	2	6
Hungary	3	2	0	1	7	5	4
Brazil	3	1	0	2	4	6	2

GROUP 4

July 12: Ayresome Park, Middlesbrough
Soviet Union **3 - 0** North Korea

July 13: Roker Park, Sunderland
Italy **2 - 0** Chile

July 15: Ayresome Park, Middlesbrough
Chile **1 - 1** North Korea

July 16: Roker Park, Sunderland
Soviet Union **1 - 0** Italy

July 19: Ayresome Park, Middlesbrough
North Korea **1 - 0** Italy

July 20: Roker Park, Sunderland
Soviet Union **2 - 1** Chile

	P	W	D	L	F	A	Pts
Soviet Union	3	3	0	0	6	1	6
North Korea	3	1	1	1	2	4	3
Italy	3	1	0	2	2	2	2
Chile	3	0	1	2	2	5	1

QUARTER-FINALS

July 23: Wembley Stadium, London
England **1 - 0** Argentina

July 23: Hillsborough, Sheffield
West Germany **4 - 0** Uruguay

July 23: Goodison Park, Liverpool
Portugal **5 - 3** North Korea

July 23: Roker Park, Sunderland
Soviet Union **2 - 1** Hungary

SEMI-FINALS

July 25: Goodison Park, Liverpool
West Germany **2 - 1** Soviet Union

July 26: Wembley Stadium, London
England **2 - 1** Portugal

THIRD-PLACE PLAY-OFF

July 28: Wembley Stadium, London
Portugal **2 - 1** Soviet Union

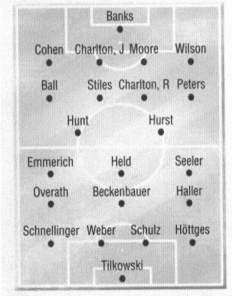

THE FINAL

ENGLAND	(1) 4
WEST GERMANY	(1) 2

(AET: 2-2 AT 90 MINS)

DATE Saturday July 30, 1966
ATTENDANCE 93,802
VENUE Wembley Stadium

Banks

Cohen   Charlton, J   Moore   Wilson

Ball   Stiles   Charlton, R   Peters

Hunt   Hurst

Emmerich   Held   Seeler

Overath   Beckenbauer   Haller

Schnellinger   Weber   Schulz   Höttges

Tilkowski

Postscript

Over the past fifty years, with the continuing disappointment of the England national football team, the summer of '66 and in particular the 30th July has grown in mythology to reach almost mystical status. The players have been lionised with calls for them all to be knighted, even posthumously. But even allowing for hyperbole, there is no doubt that this was a great occasion for English football.

The post war years had seen a decline, not only in the quality of the England team but also in our position within the world football order.

A decline that seemed terminal after humiliation by Hungary in 1953 and subsequent disappointing performances in three World Cups, was gradually reversed and under the inspired leadership of Alf Ramsey, we were on top of the world once more.

It was hoped that victory in 1966 would lead to a new 'Golden Age' for the England team, but this was not to be. Defending their title four years later in Mexico they were unfortunate not to progress past the quarter finals, but by the time England failed to even qualify for the tournament in Germany of 1974 the knives were out for Sir Alf Ramsey. This was a mere foretaste of future media vilification that was to become normal for subsequent England managers.

World Cups and European Championships since have promised much but delivered little. The problems facing the national team fifty years ago are still relevant today. A league structure that is too demanding on the players and fans who still prefer a hard running action game to one based more on possession and strategy.

So whilst we all continue to travel in hope, we can always wallow in that wonderful glow of nostalgia. Bobby Moore and the Jules Rimet trophy still gleaming in the summer sunshine.

Andrew S. Dolloway - May 2016

R. MOORE

R. WILSON

J. CHARLTON

J. ARMFIELD

T. PAINE

G. HURST

I. CALLAGHAN

M. PETERS

J. CONNELLY

N. HUNTER

G. COHEN

A. BALL

R. HUNT

G. BYRNE

R. SPRINGETT

R. CHARLTON

P. BONETTI

G. EASTHAM

J. GREAVES

N. STILES

G. BANKS

R. FLOWERS

Bibliography & Credits

BIBLIOGRAPHY

Finney on Football, Finney T. (1959)

The Golden Age of Football, Jeffs P. (1992)

For Wolves and England, Flowers R. (1961)

Bobby Moore, My Soccer Story, Moore B. (1967)

A Slave to Soccer, Clayton R. (1962)

Captain of England, Wright B. (1951)

World Cup 1962, Saunders D. (1962)

World Cup 1958, Camkin J. (1958)

Winning isn't Everything, Bowler D. (1998)

The Best of Charles Buchan's Football Monthly, Inglis S. (2006)

We have also referred to certain books to clarity dates and statistics
player's details and match reports:
The History of the Fifa World Cup, World Cup Stories, Hunt C. (2006) BBC Publication
England the Complete Post-War Record, Payne M. (1993)

Any extra material from author's own collection.

With special thanks to:
Simon Meakin, Adele Dolloway

Every effort has been made to fulfil requirements with regard to reproducing copyright material.
The publishers will be glad to rectify any omissions at the earliest opportunity.